Preschool
in Three
Cultures
Revisited

Preschool
in Three
Cultures
Revisited

China, Japan,
and the
United States

Joseph Tobin,
Yeh Hsueh,
and
Mayumi Karasawa

The University of Chicago Press
Chicago and London

Joseph Tobin is the Nadine Mathis Basha Professor of early childhood education at Arizona State University and the author or editor of several books.

Yeh Hsueh is associate professor of counseling and educational psychology and research at the University of Memphis.

Mayumi Karasawa is professor of comparative psychology at Tokyo Women's Christian University.

The University of Chicago Press, Chicago 60637
The University of Chicago Press, Ltd., London
© 2009 by The University of Chicago
All rights reserved. Published 2009
Printed in the United States of America

18 17 16 15 14 13 12 11 10   3 4 5

ISBN-13: 978-0-226-80503-0 (cloth)
ISBN-10: 0-226-80503-4 (cloth)

For information on ordering the accompanying DVD for *Preschool in Three Cultures Revisited*, please visit joetobin.net

Library of Congress Cataloging-in-Publication Data

Tobin, Joseph Jay.
  Preschool in three cultures revisited : China, Japan, and the United States / Joseph Tobin, Yeh Hsueh, and Mayumi Karasawa.
      p. cm.
  Includes bibliographical references and index.
  ISBN-13: 978-0-226-80503-0 (cloth : alk. paper)
  ISBN-10: 0-226-80503-4 (cloth : alk. paper)
  1. Nursery schools—Japan—Case studies. 2. Nursery schools—China—Case studies. 3. Nursery schools—United States—Case studies. 4. Educational anthropology. 5. Education, Preschool.
I. Hsueh, Yeh. II. Karasawa, Mayumi. III. Title.
  LB1140.25.J3T63 2009
  372.210951—dc22

                              2008049087

⊚ The paper used in this publication meets the minimum requirements of the American National Standard for Information Sciences—Permanence of Paper for Printed Library Materials, ANSI Z39.48-1992.

We dedicate this book to our mentors.

To Joseph Tobin's mentors, Robert A. LeVine and Doi Takeo;
Yeh Hsueh's mentors, Eleanor Duckworth and Sheldon White;
and Mayumi Karasawa's mentor, Azuma Hiroshi.

Contents

Preface

In the mid-1980s I worked with my colleagues David Wu and Dana Davidson on a research project that in 1989 became the book *Preschool in Three Cultures: Japan, China, and the United States*. The book attracted a broad range of readers, from early childhood educators to parents of preschoolers to anthropologists, sociologists, and psychologists. The reception of the book turned around my then struggling academic career. For several years after the book came out I searched for a way to build on the success of *Preschool in Three Cultures* without repeating myself. *Preschool in Three More Cultures? Primary School in Three Cultures? Preschool in Three Social Classes?* Because none of these project ideas seemed quite right, I eventually decided to leave the *PSin3C* project behind and turn to other lines of research. As the years passed, the old book and accompanying video continued to find an audience, the book becoming a well-known and often used text in the fields of early childhood and comparative education. By the time fifteen years had passed since we conducted the original research, I thought about doing a sequel to bring the book up to date, but I decided against it because I concluded that there would not be enough intellectually or methodologically new in this task.

This all changed one afternoon in 1999. I gave a talk and after it ended, as I was packing up my things, a young man approached me. Yeh Hsueh introduced himself as a recent graduate of the Harvard Graduate School of Education and a fan of *Preschool in Three Cultures*, and he asked me to watch a video he had made. It took only three or four minutes of watching Yeh's tape for me to realize that Chinese preschools had changed so dramatically since we conducted our original study in 1985 that it was time to do a sequel. After the tape ended, as Yeh and I talked about what doing a sequel would entail, it became clear to me that returning to this research would not mean repeating myself methodologically or intellectually because the new study would add a historical dimension that was not a part of the first study. The original study was cross-cultural; the new one would be both cross-cultural and historical, requiring new methods and an engagement with new theories.

Yeh and I ended that conversation that afternoon in the winter of 1999 by shaking hands on an agreement to work together on a sequel to *Preschool in Three Cultures*. For this new study, I put together a new research team. In the original study, there was a lack of balance, as I, an American, was the lead researcher on the Japan research and another American, Dana Davidson, a specialist on early childhood, took the lead on the US research, which meant that we had two American researchers, one Chinese researcher, and no Japanese member of the team. For the new study, Yeh took the place of David Wu, who had recently retired. I invited a Japanese researcher, Mayumi Karasawa, to head up the Japanese side of the study. And I slid over into the slot of the lead US researcher as well as project director.

Yeh Hsueh, Mayumi Karasawa, and I have worked as a team on each step of this project. Yeh, who is from Beijing, is now a professor in the Department of Educational Psychology and Research at the University of Memphis. Mayumi, a comparative psychologist by training, is a professor at Tokyo Women's Christian University. I am an anthropologist by training who has become, thanks to the impact of the first *PSin3C* book, an early childhood education specialist. The three of us traveled together to preschools in Japan, China, and the US to shoot the videotapes and to conduct the first round of focus-group interviews with teachers and directors. We each took the lead in organizing the videotaping and then the interviewing in our home country. In the course of the interviews we took turns asking questions, with the help of interpreters, when needed. Yeh is fluent in Chinese and English and Mayumi in Japanese and English. In our research in Japan I did my best to ask questions and understand the answers using my less-than-fluent Japanese, assisted, when needed, by translation. Yi Che did most of the interpreting in China and Akiko Hayashi in Japan, translating our questions and then providing simultaneous interpretation of our informants' responses, whispering into our ears so as to not unduly interrupt the flow of the conversation. To get insiders' feedback on our emerging interpretations and to fill in gaps in our understanding, we conducted follow-up interviews in person, by e-mail, and by phone right up to the point that the book went to press. We worked collaboratively on analyzing and interpreting the interviews and in developing the core ideas for this book, comparing our insider and outsider perspectives. This book reflects the understandings that emerged from our discussions. To give the book a consistent voice from chapter to chapter, I have taken the lead in the writing.

We were joined in each step of the research by a group of doctoral students. Hong-Ju Jun, Fikriye Kurban, Yi Che, and Akiko Hayashi are talented video-ethnographers and early childhood education specialists who worked on every aspect of the project as my graduate students at Arizona State University and who are in the process of publishing related papers of their own.

In the new project, as in the old one, the method used to study Japanese, Chinese, and American preschools gives preschool directors and teachers the chance to speak directly. In Chapter 1 we describe how we have modified the Preschools in Three Cultures research method of using videotape to stimulate reflections to engage teachers and directors in discussion not only of cultural differences in preschools, but also of processes of continuity and change. In Chapters 2, 3, and 4 we present insiders' and outsiders' explanations of Chinese, Japanese, and American preschools and of how and why they have changed and stayed the same over the past twenty years. Readers familiar with the original study may notice that the order of the chapters has been changed—in this new book China precedes rather than follows Japan, a switch we made to foreground the dramatic changes over the past generation in Chinese education and society that spurred us to do a sequel. As in the first book, the US chapter comes last in the sequence, following the old anthropological adage that ethnography works by first making the exotic familiar and then the familiar exotic. Chapter 5, the conclusion, is a discussion of what our research can contribute to an understanding of the connections between national systems of early childhood education and processes of social change and cultural continuity.

Videos we made of days in preschools in China, Japan, and the US are at the methodological core of this project. Throughout the book we have included images from the old and new videos to add visual support to our written descriptions of continuity and change in each culture's preschools. As in the original Preschool in Three Cultures study, we have produced narrated versions of the six videos, which are available on DVDs (information for ordering can be found on my website—joetobin.net).

Finally, a word on terminology: Daguan You'eryuan typically would be translated into English as "Daguan Kindergarten." We have decided in this book as in the original not to translate you'eryuan or the Japanese equivalent term, yōchien, as "kindergarten" because in most English-speaking countries the word "kindergarten" suggests the first year of primary school rather than a program for children three to six years old. The classrooms serving four-year-old children that are the focus of this study are located in many types of institutions. Four-year-old children attending preschool in China are enrolled in both public and private *you'eryuan*, some of which are boarding programs. Four-year-olds in Japan attend not just *yōchien* but also *hoikuen*, which we translate as "daycare centers." In the US, four-year-olds attend a variety of programs with a variety of names including children's centers, nursery schools, daycare centers, and preschools. There is no simple solution to the problem of translating the names of these early childhood education and care programs across countries, cultures, and languages. Therefore throughout this book we refer to the programs by using the untranslated terms used in each country and, when we are writing about issues across programs, by using the generic term "preschool." A central goal of this book is to get beneath the terms and to provide insiders' understandings of the forms of provision available for four-year-old children in each of the three countries. We refer to the Japanese teachers in this book using the title *sensei* after their names, to the Chinese teachers using the equivalent title *laoshi*, and to the US teachers using their first names because this is most often how they are addressed and referred to by their colleagues and by the children they teach.

This project was made possible by a major grant from the Spencer Foundation. We are particularly grateful to the directors and teachers in all three countries who allowed us to videotape in their preschools and who put so much time and energy into explaining the thinking behind the practices recorded in our videotapes. Our principal partners in this research are the Yoshizawa family and teachers Morita Chisato and Nogami Takaya of Komatsudani Hoikuen in Kyoto; Director Machiyama Yoshio and teacher Kaizawa Mariko of Madoka Yōchien in Tokyo; Director Shi Yonghong, Assistant Director Xie Ping, classroom teachers Zhang Rui, Dong Yanyun, and Yang Jia, and retired directors Wang Xinglan and Wu Qiongzhen of Daguan You'eryuan in Kunming; Director Guo Zongli and teachers Wang Jian and Cheng Jingxiu of Sinanlu You'eryuan in Shanghai; Director Dolores Brockman and teachers Jannie Umeda and Val Moriwaki of St. Timothy's Child Center in Honolulu; and Director Bonnie Lund and teachers Fran Smith and Eva Rangel of Alhambra Preschool in Phoenix. Director Kumagai Ritsuko of Senzan Yōchien in Kyoto, who welcomed my son Sam as a student in her kindergarten twenty-five years ago, provided us with invaluable insight into Japanese early childhood pedagogy for this study as she did for the original study twenty years ago. We were also supported in our research in Japan by Oda Yutaka, Akita Kiyomi, Kadota Riyo, Jimmy Suzuki, Yoshida Hiroshi, and Jeffrey Maret. We are particularly grateful to Professors Cao Nengxiu, Feng Xiaoxia, Hua Aihua, Li Hong, Su Guimin, Zhou Zongkui, and Zhu Jiaxiong for their generous support and for sharing with us their understandings of the early childhood education reform in China. We want to give our heartfelt thanks to the teachers, directors, researchers, and parents in Beijing, Changchun, Chongqing, Kunming, Shanghai, Wuhan, Xi'an, and some smaller cities who commented on our videos from the three cultures and shared with us their perspectives and professional experiences. Chen Sifan coordinated a group of graduate students at the Central China Normal University in transcribing interviews. These students were Chang Baojing, Chen Xiangli, Li Heng, Li Ying, Liu Chaoying, Liu Junjun, Tan Jing, Tan Xueqin, Wang Juan, Xiong Li, Zhang Yangyang, Zhao Dongmei, Zheng Rong, and Zhu Tingting. Wei Guoqing and Maki Obana provided clerical support in Memphis. Anasa Watts and Barbara Sandlin assisted in US data collection. Happy Cheung coordinated and supported the data collection in northeast of China. Mary McMullen, Cary Buzzetti, Rich Johnson, Stephanie Feeney, and Lani Au helped us conduct the research in the US. Mary and Cary gave us insightful feedback on drafts of the manuscript, as did Eyal Ben-Ari of the Hebrew University of Jersusalem and Zhang Jie of East China Normal University. Daniel Walsh and Heidi Ross provided the University of Chicago Press with sage reader reports that served as the scaffolding for our rewriting process. Elizabeth Branch Dyson of the Press encouraged and advised us and guided the manuscript into print. Michael Koplow provided needed copyediting, and Isaac Tobin, who is a designer at the Press as well as my son, designed the cover and the interior layout.

We thank our significant others (Beth Tobin, Katherine Kitzmann, and Shinobu Kitayama) for tolerating our absences while we were away conducting the research and for supporting us in so many ways when we came home.

Joseph Tobin

1.1. Daguan's current and past directors with Tobin, Hsueh, and Karasawa in front of the old Daguan Kindergarten.

1 Introduction

In Japan, the United States, and in urban areas of China, most four-year-old children attend preschool. It has not always been this way. Just a few generations ago in each of these countries formal education began with primary school and most children under age five were cared for, educated, and socialized in settings other than preschools. They were raised in their homes by full-time mothers; taken to the fields by parents who farmed; or supervised by nannies, maiden aunts, grandmothers, or older siblings. Published in 1989, *Preschool in Three Cultures* argued that preschools are relatively new social institutions charged with the task of turning young children into culturally appropriate members of their society. The core conclusion of that book is that preschools in Japan, China, and the US are institutions that both reflect and impart their cultures' core beliefs.

In *Preschools in Three Cultures Revisited* our focus is on what has stayed the same and what has changed over the last twenty years in Chinese, Japanese, and American preschools. In this book we describe how systems of early childhood education in these three countries reflect and pass on cultural values while at the same time responding to changing social pressures and expectations for what young children should learn, do, and be.

In 1984, as part of the original *Preschool in Three Cultures* project, we made a videotape of a day in a classroom for four-year-olds at Daguan You'eryuan, in Kunming, China. (In our 1989 book, given the political climate of the time, we thought it best to replace Daguan's name with a pseudonym, Dong-feng.) In 2002 we returned to Daguan (figure 1.1), where we made a new videotape as well as showing them the old one. As a group of veteran and retired teachers and directors at Daguan watched scenes in our old video that American, Japanese, and Chinese viewers had found problematic (children lined up at a long trough in a bathroom without running water, boarding classrooms, teacher-directed block activities, and patriotic songs), we worried that they might be embarrassed and want to distance themselves from their past. But this is not what happened. The Daguan teachers and directors watched the old video with obvious interest and pleasure, laughingly commenting on how they looked seventeen years ago and pointing out children now grown up and colleagues no longer with them. The discussion after the video focused on how and why Daguan You'eryuan had both changed and stayed the same over the course of a generation. Wang Xinglan, now retired, who had been the director of the *you'eryuan* in 1984, told us, "When I look at these images I realize that of course many things have changed. But I feel proud of how we taught then. In the video I see us all working very hard and doing the best we could with what we had to work with. Those were different times. Then, as now, the staff of Daguan You'eryuan was guided by the same sense of professionalism, hard work, and concern for children."

We start with this vignette of the reactions of staff at Daguan to our old Daguan (Dong-feng) video to emphasize that this book is not just or primarily our version of how and why Daguan and other Chinese, Japanese, and US preschools have changed and stayed the same over the course of the past generation. Instead, in this book we foreground the explanations of insiders, that is, the voices of preschool teachers and directors explaining why they do what they do in their preschools, their reflections on where they have come from professionally, where they see themselves as going, and why.

Preschools, Cultures, Societies, and Eras

Preschools are sites where a variety of domains, interests, and social actors intersect. Preschool is where child rearing meets education; where the world of parents and home first meets the world of teachers and school; and where the labor market's need for working women meets society's need for young children to be well cared for and prepared to be productive in the future. Our goal is to explore the connections in all three countries between what is happening in the early childhood education systems and what is happening in the larger society. In the chapters that follow we identify the forces that Chinese, Japanese, and American informants tell us are pressing on their systems of early childhood education and we describe how early childhood educators in these three nations experience and deal with these pressures. Or to put it more concretely, our task is to find explanations for why a day at Daguan You'eryuan in 2002 has come to look so different from a day there in 1984.

Our focus on understanding change in systems of early childhood education should not blind us to the importance of also understanding and appreciating continuity. Understanding why a day at Komatsudani Day Care Center in Kyoto looks much the same in the new millennium as it did a generation earlier is as compelling a question as understanding why Daguan has changed. Maintaining continuity in a program of early childhood education from one era to the next requires as much effort and creativity as it does to change. If we think of change as being caused by external forces, like the movement of a small boat in a rushing stream, we can see that it takes more energy to stay in place than to move with the flow. Absence of change over time in a preschool can reflect the inertia, stubbornness, or even laziness of the staff. But it can also reflect the courage of teachers and directors to stand up to political pressures to distort their practice in reaction to each educational fad and demand from grandstanding politicians. The challenge for preschools in each country is to strike the right balance between continuity and change. Each nation expects its preschools to change in order to produce children with the kinds of skills and attributes it believes are needed for success in a rapidly changing society. And yet, at the same time, preschools in all three nations are expected to function as sites of cultural continuity that reproduce in a new generation of children traditional ways of seeing, understanding, believing, and interacting. Chinese society demands that its preschools produce children ready to succeed in the twenty-first-century global economy. But they also want these children to be Chinese. The social forces working as pressures on preschools to function as sites of both continuity and change are economic, demographic, political, popular cultural, and intellectual. Factors we discuss in the chapters to come include Japan's continuing population drop and sharp economic downturn from the boom times of the 1980s; China's paradigmatic shift from a planned socialist economy to a strategy of participating aggressively in global capitalism; and the confluence in the US in the early years of the new century of such disparate forces pushing on early childhood education as President Bush's No Child Left Behind Act, new developments in brain research, and the concept of developmentally appropriate practice.

One potential source of change in each country's approach to early childhood education is the importing of ideas from abroad. World system theories of educational borrowing and lending see the world as an increasingly globalized system and chart a growing convergence, over time, in nations' educational ideas and practices (Meyer & Ramirez 2000; Ramirez 2003). Other theorists, in contrast, see the global flow of educational ideas as rising and ebbing over time with shifting political contexts, as policy makers in some eras use the foreign cachet of educational ideas from abroad to justify domestic policy reforms; at other times strip imported ideas of their aura of foreignness to make them more domestically palatable; and at still other times reject and expel foreign ideas as dangerous and unwelcome (Schriewer 2000; 2004; Steiner-Khamsi 2000; 2004). Educational ethnographers tend to contrast the homogenizing force of globalization with the resilience of local educational cultures (Anderson-Levitt 2003).

Because these competing theories make different predictions about continuity and change, they provide us with a compelling research question: Have Chinese, Japanese, and American early childhood education ideas and practices grown more alike since we did our original study in the mid-1980s? With these theories of the power of the global and the local in mind, we asked the early childhood educators we interviewed in China, Japan, and the US to reflect on the influence of foreign ideas on their thinking and practice.

Ethnography and Historiography

In his 1983 book *Time and the Other* Johannes Fabian argues that ethnography as a genre of research lacks a sense of time, as it locates its subjects outside of history, in a timeless ethnographic present. This accusation is somewhat less true today, as ethnographies increasingly are concerned with processes of globalization, cultural adaptation, and hybridization (Marcus 1995). But still, ethnography continues to be better at explaining continuity than change because ethnography, at its core, is the study of culture and culture is most often thought of as that which is passed on from one generation to the next. Moreover, most ethnographies are based on research conducted within a single time frame. Following Fabian's logic, we can fault *Preschool in Three Cultures* for insufficiently historicizing the cultural practices it described. Our new study gives us the chance to address that shortcoming by adding an explicitly historical, diachronic dimension to the original study's synchronic focus on cultural comparison. *Continuity and Change in Preschools in Three Culture* foregrounds the question of historical continuity and change by analyzing preschools in China, Japan, and the US at two points in historical time—circa 1984 and 2004.

The challenge of diachronic ethnography is to add a sense of time to ethnography without placing the other cultures we study on *our* timeline. At its inception, cultural anthropology had a sense of history, as it conceptualized the cultures of the world in terms of their progress toward becoming civilized; anthropologists viewed the cultures they studied as versions of their culture's past. We need to see Chinese, Japanese, and American systems of early childhood education diachronically, as existing in time, without assuming that they are ahead of or behind each other and all moving along the same timeline, as, for example, the timelines of modernization, rationalization, or globalization. We need, that is, a theory and a method that allow us to think simultaneously about space and time, and to place preschools simultaneously in their historical and cultural contexts. As Robin Alexander writes in his study of primary education in five countries: "If making sense . . . is one's principal goal in a study of this kind then culture and history have to be the basic frames within which one's attempts to understand and explain are set . . . No educational policy can be properly understood except by reference to the web of inherited ideas and values, habits and customs, institutions and world views which make one, or one region, or one group, distinct from another" (2000, 5).

Method

The method we used in the new study is an extension of the old one, a method we formally call "video-cued multivocal ethnography" but that others and we most often refer to as "the Preschool in Three Cultures method." In this method we: (1) videotape a day in a preschool in each culture; (2) edit the videotape down to twenty minutes; (3) show this edited tape first to the teacher in whose classroom we filmed; (4) show it to other staff at her preschool; (5) show it to early childhood educators at other preschools around the country; (6) and finally show it to early childhood educators in the other two countries. The result is a video-cued multivocal conversation—early childhood educators in three countries discussing the same set of videos.

This method has multiple origins. We took the original idea of using videotapes as an interviewing cue from the work of anthropologist Linda Connor and the ethnographic filmmakers Tim and Patsy Asch, who videotaped a Balinese shaman during a séance and then later showed her a film of herself in the state of trance and asked her to comment on her actions (Connor, Asch & Asch 1986). Several years after we began the original study we learned that George and Louise Spindler (1987) had made similar use of films in their comparative study of schools in Germany and Wisconsin, as did their students Mariko Fujita and Toshiyuki Sano (1988) in their comparative study of daycare centers in the US and Japan. More recently,

Kathryn Anderson-Levitt (2002) used a video-cued ethnographic method to illuminate dimensions of similarity and difference in approaches to language arts instruction of French and American primary school teachers.

In traditional ethnographic fieldwork, the anthropologist spends the day among cultural insiders participating in and observing daily activities of the culture she is studying and then, in the evening, asking her informants to reflect on and explain those activities. The Preschool in Three Cultures video-cued method collapses and accelerates this process by replacing participant observation with a set of videotapes that provide a focus for the informant interviews. Because it replaces the traditional year of fieldwork with a video-cued interviewing method, some anthropologists would suggest that this study does not meet the strict definition of ethnography. While acknowledging this point, we would add that our work is nevertheless ethnographic in our concern with quotidian aspects of life (ordinary days in preschools in three cultures), our focus on culture as the central explanatory construct, and our privileging of insider explanations and of emic over etic analytic categories and theories (Spindler 2000, xxii).

Another source for this method is the tradition in psychodynamic psychology of using an ambiguous visual stimulus, such as an inkblot or a drawing, as a tool for allowing the investigator to uncover unconscious psychological processes (Henry 1956). Our idea of using ambiguous scenes in videotapes of typical days in preschools as interviewing cues was influenced particularly by the work of Henry A. Murray, the father of projective testing, who argued that people's personality styles and core concerns can be analyzed by asking them to tell stories about drawings selected to get at different psychological issues. In his development of a technique he called the "picture interview," William Caudill adapted Murray's TAT method, turning it from a method for analyzing the psyches of individuals to an ethnographic tool for analyzing cultural beliefs. In one study, Caudill hired an artist to make simple line drawings of scenes of interpersonal intimacy (for example, scenes of children bathing together in a tub, of a woman tending to a sick man, and of a man and woman sitting on a bed) and then showed these drawings to Japanese and American informants and asked them to tell him a story about each picture. Caudill (1962) analyzed these stories told by Japanese and American informants to explicate differences and similarities in the cultural patterning of physical and emotional intimacy in Japan and the United States. Around the same time, George and Louise Spindler developed a similar visually cued interviewing strategy to study Native American culture and personality dynamics using line drawings, a strategy they called the IAI or "instrumental activities inventory" (1965). In our preschool in three cultures method, each scene in our videos is like a moving, noisy version of the drawings used by Caudill and the Spindlers.

We were also influenced in the development of this method by the writings of Mikhail Bakhtin, a Russian literary theorist and social philosopher who introduced the terms "multivocality," "hybridity," and "dialogism." In his 1983 essay, "On Ethnographic Authority," James Clifford cites Bakhtin in his call for the development of "multivocal ethnography." We heeded this call in the original Preschool in Three Cultures study, which, like this new book, is organized as a series of voices commenting on the same scenes. Bakhtin's notion of dialogism also provides theoretical support for our decision to use focus-group rather than individual interviews at most stages of the research. Following Bakhtin, we believe that meanings arise out of dialogical engagement of speakers. Rather than viewing interviewing as a strategy to uncover preexisting positions of research subjects, we view interviews as occasions for the co-construction of meaning by our informants with each other as well as with us.

A final source for the method comes from the Akira Kurosawa film *Rashomon* (based on a short story by Ryūnosuke Akutagawa) in which an encounter between three people on a path in the forest is described differently by each of the participants. The discussions we held with early childhood educators following the viewing of our videotapes show that these audiences often have different understandings not only about what the teachers should do, but also about what transpired in the videotape. Like the participants and eyewitnesses in *Rashomon* who give different accounts of the same crime, our informants reveal something about themselves and their worldviews as they comment on our videotapes.

As each of these influences suggest, in our method the videotapes are not the data; rather, they are cues, stimuli, topics for discussion, interviewing tools. In much of social science research the researcher asks informants verbal questions, questions such as, "What is your philosophy of classroom management?" Preschool teachers tend to find this sort of question difficult to answer because it is too abstract and too much like a final exam question. A better, more concrete question would be "When a child in your class misbehaves, what do you do?" But this question is still ambiguous and abstract: in attempting to answer this question, one teacher may picture children not sitting properly at the lunch table while another teacher may have in mind a sword fight with umbrellas. In our video-cued method, we show teachers a scene in a video in which, for example, a group of girls struggle over a teddy bear, with two of them ending up rolling around on the floor, grabbing and pulling the bear and each other, and we ask, "What would you do in *this* situation?" Each scene in our twenty-minute videos functions as a nonverbal question, a cue to stimulate a response that will provide insight into the beliefs of an informant. In addition to classroom routines, key issues we videotape include: separation (scenes of children and parents saying good-bye in the morning); fighting (including not just the behavior of the fighting children but also the reactions of their class-mates and teachers); misbehavior (for example, a child refusing to follow directions or share); mixed-aged play; and intimacy between teachers and children (for example, a teacher comforting a crying child).

For the new study, in order to allow us to focus on both cross-cultural and historical comparisons, we have modified the method we used in the original study for site selection, shooting, and editing the videotapes, as we explain in the sections that follow. (For reflections on epistemological, ethical, and aesthetic issues of the Preschool in Three Cultures method, see Tobin & Davidson 1991; Tobin 1999; and Tobin & Hsueh 2007).

SITE SELECTION AND THE QUESTION OF TYPICALITY

In the original study we videotaped in one preschool in each country. Clearly, one preschool cannot represent the preschools of a nation. We are careful to avoid making such a claim. In our method, because the videos of preschools function as stimuli for focus-group discussions rather than as data, we make no claim about the representativeness or typicality of the preschools we videotaped, other than to say that they are not atypical, in the sense of being perceived in their communities as odd or extreme. We chose preschools that had good reputations in their communities, but that were not known for being unusual in their curriculum and pedagogy. Each of the preschools in this study is "identifiable" in the sense of being assessed by early childhood educators in each country as being within the range of normal practice (Walsh 2002).

We avoid using the term "representative" to describe our selection of preschools because this term belongs more to the workings of quantitative social science than to the practice of ethnography. We do not think or write in terms of research subjects, representative sampling, and statistical corre-lations but instead in terms of contextualized meanings, cultural patterns, and social discourses. Ethnographers traditionally conduct their fieldwork in one village or urban neighborhood. The typicality of what they find is addressed by comparing their reports with those of ethnographers who have worked in other fieldsites in the same culture.

1.2. An older boy with a younger one at Komatsudani
Hoikuen.

Our study has a more systematic approach to the question of typicality and generalizability than do most ethnographies (Tobin 1992). In our
method, we address the question of typicality by showing the videotape
we shot, for example, at Komatsudani Hoikuen in Kyoto, to teachers and
directors in five other settings in Japan and asking these informants to tell
us in what ways Komatsudani is like and unlike their preschool. When, for
example, a preschool director in Tokyo tells us, "You should have videotaped in Tokyo, not in Kyoto, and in a public program rather than one run
by a Buddhist temple, and in a *yōchien* (nursery school/kindergarten) rather
than in a *hoikuen* (daycare center)," her comments reveal not just variations
in types of Japanese preschools, but also tensions and biases within the
world of Japanese early childhood education, differences, tensions, and
biases we then pursue and attempt to understand in subsequent rounds
of interviewing.

Our methodological orientation is primarily ethnographic, in the sense
that the goal of this new study, as in the original, is to explicate cultural
dimensions of early childhood education within a nation. Some of the
practices seen in our videotapes are not typical, in the sense of statistical
central tendencies among that nation's preschools; but this is not in itself
a problem, as our focus is on the explanations that our informants used to
explain and justify the practices captured in our videotapes, explanations
and justifications that reveal the core beliefs, goals, and concerns about
early childhood education characteristic of each culture. For example, in
our old and new Komatsudani videotapes, we include scenes of older children taking care of babies and toddlers (figure 1.2). Our interviews with
early childhood practitioners and experts across Japan show that while
this practice is not common, none of our Japanese informants found it
particularly surprising, all of them approved of it, and most intuited the

underlying goal of supporting the development of empathy in the older children. These responses suggest that while the practice is not common, the cultural logic is.

Despite our disclaimers and explanations that our videotapes are not data and that we do not claim that our focal preschools are representative of their nation (except in the sense of not being atypical), our method is sometimes faulted for failing to address variation within each nation's preschools. We respond to this charge by emphasizing that our method is at heart ethnographic; that by showing each videotape to hundreds of informants in five or more sites in each country we have a strategy for finding out in what ways the preschools where we videotaped are perceived as typical and atypical of their country; and that our analyses of each culture's approach to early childhood education includes, and indeed emphasizes, discussions of those aspects of early childhood education provision, practice, and philosophy in each country that are most variable and contentious.

The biggest methodological change we have made in our new study is to videotape in two preschools in each country rather than in just one. The reason we made this modification is not to create a representative sample—two preschools per country in countries as large as Japan, China, and the US are hardly more representative than one. Rather, we added a second preschool per country as a strategy to foreground the issue of continuity and change. For this new study, we went back to Daguan You'eryuan in Kunming, Komatsudani Hoikuen in Kyoto, and St. Timothy's Children's Center in Honolulu, where we showed them their old videotapes and made new ones as well. We also videotaped in one new preschool in each country. Our criterion for selecting the new preschools was a program that thinks of itself and is thought of by others as representing a new direction in early childhood education. Our intent in choosing such schools was to create a new set of videotapes that would work to focus discussions with informants on the question of continuity and change. Making a second set of stimulus videotapes and showing all of them to early childhood educators in each country also gives us a more explicit way of getting at the question of typicality and variation in early childhood education practices in all three countries. While two preschools cannot represent the full range of beliefs and practices of a nation's preschools, by asking informants to watch and comment on videotapes of days in two of their nation's preschools, we can more readily focus the discussions on the question of regional, social class, and ideological variation within the nation.

In China, as a contrast with Daguan, which is in Kunming, the provincial capital of Yunnan in the southwest of China, we added as the site for the second focal videotape Sinanlu You'eryuan in Shanghai, China's most economically developed and self-consciously and famously progressive and internationally minded city. Educators in Shanghai played a major role in the development of the recently implemented early education reform in China and Sinanlu is a preschool that is widely seen as exemplifying the principles of the reform. By showing Chinese early childhood educators in various cities in China both the Daguan and Sinanlu videotape, we were able to bring out lively discussions of the direction, pace, logic, regional specificity, and mechanisms of change in Chinese early childhood education. This issue came out most explicitly in discussions at Daguan, Sinanlu, and other Chinese preschools where teachers and directors were asked to answer the question, "Is Daguan Sinanlu's past and Sinanlu Daguan's future?"

In Japan, as a contrast to Komatsudani Hoikuen, we added Madoka Yōchien, in Tokyo. In addition to being a nursery school/kindergarten rather than a daycare center, being private nonsectarian rather than Buddhist, and being in Tokyo rather than in Kyoto, Madoka differs from Komatsudani in having a self-consciously progressive, and even alternative, educational philosophy, a philosophy described in Madoka's pamphlets for parents using such terms as *anākī* (anarchy) and *ajito* (secret space or "hideaway"), terms that describe the philosophy both of the curriculum and of the layout of the preschool, which was influenced by the work of a postmodern architect. And yet Madoka is not alternative or progressive in a way Japanese early childhood educators see as odd or unfamiliar. While it has its own unique philosophy, Madoka is readily identified as belonging to a type of preschool in Japan commonly called *jiyū* (free) or *nobi nobi* ("room to stretch," "easy-going"). The staff of Komatsudani tends to explain the program's practices in terms of maintaining continuity with the past and preserving traditional Japanese values. In contrast, explanations from the teachers and director at Madoka are more often framed in terms of the future. But in the end, as we will see, these two programs, which are unalike in many structural features, end up sharing many core cultural beliefs.

In the US, for a contrast to St. Timothy's Children's Center in Honolulu we added Alhambra Preschool in Phoenix. St. Timothy's is a private, tuition-based preschool located on the grounds of an Episcopal Church serving children of middle- and upper-middle-class parents who drop their children off on their way from the suburbs to downtown, where they work. Alhambra, which at the time of our videotaping was located on the grounds of a middle school, is a public preschool, funded with tax monies and run by a school district for children who are defined as at risk because their families' income qualifies them for free/reduced lunch, because they speak a language other than English at home, or because they have been diagnosed as having a need that qualifies them for special education services. This is a kind of preschool that represents an important new direction in the US, a step toward more universal preschool provision via the expansion of the mandate of public education from kindergarten down to preschool (Fuller 2007). While both St. Timothy's and Alhambra are accredited by the National Association of the Education of Young Children, they have important differences in educational philosophy as well as in the populations they serve, their funding structures, and the organization of their school days.

SHOOTING AND EDITING THE VIDEOS

For the Preschool in Three Cultures method to work, the videotapes have to be artfully constructed (figure 1.3). The videos are shot and edited to present viewers with the sense of the flow of day in a preschool while at the same time engaging interest and provoking reactions. The videos function as a set of interview questions, but they are also narratives, with central characters and dramatic tension. The videos must produce emotional as well as intellectual reactions in viewers to function as effective ethnographic interviewing tools.

Before shooting the video in each preschool we spent a couple of days observing in the classroom, becoming familiar with the routines, and selecting four or five key children on whom to focus our cameras. A preschool classroom has too many characters to fit into one coherent story line. A good teacher appreciates the unique personalities and concerns of each of her students, but a viewer of a twenty-minute video cannot be expected to keep straight, pay attention to, or care about all of the students in a class. In our original Preschool in Three Cultures study, there was one clear star—Hiroki, a naughty four-year-old boy at Komatsudani Hoikuen in Kyoto who interrupted lessons by singing songs from popular cartoons, held a black crayon up to his crotch and announced, to the delight of his classmates, that he had a black penis, and stepped on the hand of Satoshi, leading him to burst out in tears. In the new study, our new Hiroki is Nao, the youngest and least mature of the four-year-olds at Komatsudani, who holds on to her mother's leg at the school gate, refuses to share a stuffed bear, and engages in a prolonged physical and verbal battle with a pair of twins. Another compelling protagonist is Ziyu, a boy at Sinanlu You'eryuan in Shanghai, who in our video we see complaining about a classmate's slight, performing surgery on his teacher during dramatic play, and telling

1.3. Videotaping at Komatsudani.

the class a story that lasts over five minutes and then patiently and without apparent hurt feelings or ill will, listening to his classmates' criticisms of his storytelling. In the US videos, one of the most compelling characters is Ferdie, a bilingual child with learning difficulties who is making great strides in Fran Smith's classroom at Alhambra Preschool in Phoenix (figure 1.4).

In addition to strong characters and dramatic content, the videos in our study have aesthetic appeal. We increased our chances of producing videos with relatively high aesthetic value (relatively high for educational video ethnography, at any rate) by buying the best equipment we could afford and handle and by putting considerable effort into planning shots and doing sound checks on the days before videotaping in each preschool and as we videotaped adjusting the color balance on our cameras each time we moved from inside to outside or back again. In the new study we shot with two cameras, which allowed us to compose sequences with alternating shots from two perspectives, which we could not do in our original videos, shot with one camera. Our efforts to achieve high aesthetic value often, however, came into conflict with other project goals, as for example, that we be as unobtrusive as possible and that we follow the most compelling characters and stories wherever they took us (even if that meant following them into areas of the classroom with low light and poor acoustics).

In our method, the technical quality of the videos should be thought of not as a luxury but rather as a factor, like strong characters, dramatic tensions, and narrative coherence, that works to engage informants and thereby to produce richer data. The absence of aesthetic quality carries the possibility of interfering with the audience's flow of attention. Amateurish shots can interrupt engagement, but so too can slickness. Shots that are out of focus, shaky, or poorly framed are irritating to viewers, but so too are shots that call attention to their artfulness and thus to the video's

1.4. Our stars: Ziyu, Nao, and Ferdie.

constructedness. In the years since we made the videos for our original study, audience expectations for production values have dramatically risen. Eighteen years ago, when we made the videos for our original study, most families did not own videocameras and audiences were forgiving of our amateurish zooms and framing, our trembling shots, and the lack in most scenes of audible children's voices. Now such aesthetic shortcomings are more likely to work against the state of free-flowing engagement that we are after. (The technical and aesthetic differences between our old and new videos are apparent in the juxtaposition of old and new shots we have included in the DVDs that are available as an accompaniment to this book, as well as in figures 2.7 on page 44 and 2.8 on page 49.)

In the editing stage we struggled to decide what shots and scenes to include. In each preschool in this study, we shot with two cameras for one full day, which gave us about ten hours of videotape per school, which we then had to edit down to twenty minutes. Our editing decisions were based on a number of factors. We needed to include scenes that would give a sense of the routine flow of the day (teachers arriving at work, the arrival of the first children, transitions in and out of the classrooms, lessons, lunch, bathroom, free play, and, finally, departure); scenes that would provoke discussion of key issues in early childhood education; and scenes that the teachers in whose classrooms we videotaped were most eager to have us include.

There were times when the school staff and we researchers disagreed about these edits. There are events recorded in our videos that the teacher or director thought were interesting but that we believed would be of little interest or even boring to our audience (that is, to viewers of the videos and readers of this book); events the teacher thought mundane that we believed would be of interest to our audience; and events the teacher was embarrassed by but that we found compelling. In these situations, we gave teachers and directors the right to have scenes cut, but we argued for our perspectives. In the end we found a way to balance the wishes of the teachers in our videos with our research goals and with what we take to be the interests of our audience.

ETHNOGRAPHIC INTERVIEWING

We call our method video-cued *multivocal* ethnography because we collect and then present a series of voices all talking about the same set of videotapes. The voices range from those inside to those much further from the classrooms we videotape. The first level is the voices of the classroom teachers (figure 1.5). As each classroom teacher in this study watched the videotape of a day in her classroom, the three of us, with the help of our research assistants as interpreters, interviewed her, asking her to provide context, reflections, and explanations. The presence of cultural outsiders as interviewers in each setting worked to give the interviews a more ethnographic feel and to push our informants to explain taken-for-granted cultural assumptions. Before each interview we strategized about which of us would ask which questions, with the outsiders to each culture asking

1.5. Interviewing Jannie Umeda at Alhambra.

naïve questions that would seem odd if asked by an insider (for example, Joe Tobin asking a Chinese teacher why her class does calisthenics each morning, Yeh Hsueh asking a Japanese *yōchien* director to explain why the children change from outdoor to indoor shoes and uniforms when they arrive at school, or Mayumi Karasawa asking an American teacher to explain why children's self-esteem is an important developmental goal).

Most of the classroom teachers were interviewed three times. At the end of the week of videotaping in each preschool the three of us sat down with the classroom teacher in front of a small monitor and, fast-forwarding through the ten hours or so of videotape, we asked for clarifications of confusing events, for contextual information that the teacher might not remember months later (e.g., why a child was sad that day), for reflections on her practice, and for advice on scenes she wanted us to cut or include. The second interview with each of the classroom teachers occurred about six months later when we came back to show them a first draft of the twenty-minute video. As in the first interview, the three of us took turns asking questions. This time, with less videotape to watch, we could spend more time asking the teachers to explain the thinking behind the actions captured in our videotapes. We went back a third time to interview the teachers (or, in some cases, we contacted them by telephone or e-mail) as we were writing the first draft of the chapters of this book, to ask them to clarify a point, to expand on an explanation, or to comment on one of our emerging interpretations.

The second level of voices in this study are those of the director and the other teachers at the preschools where we videotaped (figure 1.6). At each of these preschools we arranged screenings for the director and staff. We showed the videotape and then had a discussion, beginning with the ques-

1.6. Interviewing Director Machiyama at Madoka Yochien.

tion, "Does this look like a typical day in your preschool?" before moving on to questions about the thinking that is behind the preschool organization and the teacher actions shown in the video: "Do you do calisthenics every morning? Why?" "What is the thinking behind having older children spend an hour each day with the younger ones?" These interviews, like the ones with the teachers featured in the videos, were conducted by all three of us.

The third level of voices are those of teachers and directors in preschools in other cities in each country commenting on the preschools we videotaped in their country. These are the voices of early childhood educators who are outsiders to the focal preschools but insiders to the culture (figure 1.7). For example, we took the videotape we shot at Alhambra Preschool in Phoenix and showed it to teachers and directors of other preschools in Phoenix; Honolulu; Bloomington, Indiana; Memphis; and New York City. Questions we asked included "Does this look like your preschool?" "Is there anything in this videotape that surprised you?" and "What do you like and what do you not like about the preschool in this video?" In the second part of the session we would ask questions about particular scenes in the video that the focus-group members had not already commented on: "How do you feel about the calendar activity?" "What do you think about the balance of English and Spanish used in this classroom?" We asked follow up questions such as "If you don't think calendar is a good way of teaching about numbers, what is a better way?" "What activities do you do in your classroom to teach children about citizenship?" as well as more general questions such as "What pressures are you feeling to change how you teach?" "What kind of training or support do you get for instituting new

1.7. Focus group with Chinese teachers

curricular ideas?" and "Are you influenced by any early childhood education ideas from abroad?"

The fourth level of voices in the study are those of outsiders, of early
childhood educators commenting on the videotapes of preschools in the
other two countries (figure 1.8). For example, we showed the videotapes
we made in the two preschools in Japan to teachers, directors, and professors of early childhood education in China and the US and asked them
what surprised them in the videos and what they liked best and least. As
these educators comment positively and critically on the videotapes of
typical days in preschools in other countries, they reveal something of
their own core cultural beliefs and concerns. For example, when American
teachers say about the practice of older children at Komatsudani caring
for younger ones, "I think it's a great idea and I agree with the goal, but
we could never do it here because of liability," we learn something about
American beliefs about danger and risk and about some of the constraints
pressing on American preschool teachers. When Chinese teachers criticize Morita-sensei of Komatsudani for not intervening in the girls' fight
over the teddy bear, they provide us with deeper insight into their beliefs
about teachers' educative role in moral development and the function of

1.8. Watching video with Director Kumagai of Senzan Yochien.

preschools in modeling a just society. The fifth level of voices are those of our colleagues, of professors of early childhood education who helped us make sense of what we were seeing and hearing in each country.

Implicit Cultural Practices

In our analyses, we give greatest emphasis not to what teachers in each culture do, but to how they think about what they are doing. Our focus is primarily not on teachers' behaviors, but on their practice or *praxis,* which we define as action plus intention. The videotapes capture behaviors; it is only when we add the explanations of the teachers and directors that we can get at practice. Because the genre of our study is ethnography and our central goal is to identify and explicate cultural approaches to early childhood education, we use the statements we gather from teachers and directors to shed light on both explicit and implicit forms of what Kathryn Anderson-Levitt (2002, 109) refers to as "professional knowledge rooted in national classroom cultures." We are particularly attentive to what we are calling "implicit cultural practices" of teachers, by which we mean practices that though not taught explicitly in schools of education or written down in textbooks reflect an implicit cultural logic. This concept is akin to Jerome Bruner's concept of "folk pedagogy," which he defines as "taken-for-granted practices that emerge from embedded cultural beliefs about how children learn and how teachers should teach" (Bruner 1996, 46); to what Kathryn Anderson-Levitt calls teachers' "knowledge in practice" and "embodied knowledge" (2002, 8); and to what Bruce Fuller refers to, following Geertz (1983) and D'Andrade and Strauss (1995), as "cultural

Japan	Komatsudani 1984 (Kyoto)	Komatsudani 2002	Madoka 2002 (Tokyo)
China	Daguan 1984 (Kunming)	Daguan 2002	Sinan Road 2002 (Shanghai)
US	St. Timothy's 1984 (Honolulu)	St. Timothy's 2002	Alhambra 2002 (Phoenix)

models," which he defines as "a parent's or teacher's tacit understandings of how things should work" (2007, 74).

Our ethnographic orientation at times produces a sense of unease in our informants. We have learned that teachers rarely think of their pedagogical beliefs and practices as cultural. Some of the teachers and directors featured in our old and new studies who have read drafts of our manuscripts have told us that it feels odd to realize that they are informants in an ethnography and to be represented in our text as examples of their culture (Tobin & Davidson 1991). In ethnography, a teacher's ideas about classroom management becomes evidence of a culture belief system, an approach to organizing a lesson is presented as a folk pedagogy. By acknowledging this unease we do not mean to suggest that the teachers and directors who participated in the old and new studies are sorry they did so. To the contrary, most of our informants have told us that any sense of discomfort generated by being a character in an ethnography is more than offset by the opportunity this project provides participants to learn about other cultures' approaches to early childhood education and the gains in self-awareness that accompany the process of explaining oneself to outsiders.

Strategies for Studying Continuity and Change

In this study we analyze processes of continuity and change in each of the three cultures in three ways. The first is by replicating the original study a generation later in the same preschools, once again making videotapes and showing them to our concentric circles of informants, from the classroom teachers, to their counterparts in other regions of their country and abroad. The second is by showing the old videotapes to current and retired staff from each of the three original preschools and asking them to comment on what's changed, what's stayed the same, and why. The third is by videotaping in a second preschool in each culture, one that represents a new direction in each nation's approach to early childhood education, and then conducting focus-group interviews about the video with cultural insiders and outsiders.

This three-pronged approach has the virtue of giving us multiple ways of assessing continuity and change. But it also presents us with the challenge of synthesizing much more information than we had in the original study. The original Preschool in Three Cultures study was based on discussions of three videotapes—one each in Japan, China, and the US. For the new study we have informants reflecting on nine videotapes—the three 1984 tapes, the three tapes we shot when we returned to the old preschools in 2003, and the three tapes we shot in the new preschools in each country. We call this new approach, which focuses on comparisons across time as well as across cultures, "video cued multivocal diachronic ethnography" (or "the new Preschool in Three Cultures method").

To organize these multiple sources of information, each of the three chapters that follow has a similar structure. We begin for each country with a description of the new video we shot in the old preschool. We then turn to a discussion of how and why that preschool has changed and stayed the same over the course of a generation, based mostly on the reflections of current and retired staff members. We next describe the videotape we shot in the new preschool in each country and then present teachers' and directors' reflections on this video. We use differences and similarities between the two videos as a taking-off point for discussion of variation within each country. We conclude each chapter with analyses of the pressures to change and to stay the same that teachers and directors in each location are experiencing and with discussion of how early childhood educators are dealing with these pressures. In the concluding chapter we analyze patterns and processes of continuity and change across the systems of early childhood education in the three countries in our study.

2 China

Return to Daguan

Daguan You'eryuan sits along the bank of the Daguan River in Kunming, the capital city of Yunan province, in southwest China. In the original study, out of concern with the political climate of the time, we called the preschool by a pseudonym, Dong-feng (East Wind). Now neither Daguan's directors nor we see the need to use a pseudonym. It is not only the political climate that has changed. The old Daguan preschool was housed on the grounds of a crumbling estate in a series of rambling, cement-floored, one-story brick buildings that had no running water. In 1998 Daguan moved next door to a newly constructed complex that features a five-story building that is home to twenty classrooms, each with an adjoining nap room; an administration building housing offices, meeting rooms, a large kitchen and staff dining room; and apartment buildings for families of the directors and teachers.

When we returned to Daguan in 2002 after an absence of seventeen years, as the first step to understanding how Daguan had changed and stayed the same over the past generation we arranged a screening of the old Dong-feng video for the current and past directors. We began by showing the old videotape to Director Shi Yonghong and Assistant Director Xie Ping so they could help us identify and locate the teachers and administrators who appeared in the 1985 video. We shared with them our worry that the teachers and directors in the old video might be embarrassed or want to distance themselves from the practices of the past. Director Shi responded, "I don't think they will feel awkward at all because that was us and our life at that time. I am sure that they will feel delighted to see such a complete record of our work in those distant years. The video is precious to us because it preserves our heartfelt memories. Like the teacher's long, long pigtail. Where can you find that these days?"

We were nervous about how the Daguan staff would feel about the old videotape in part because over the years when we have shown the old Daguan videotape at conferences we have been criticized by Chinese viewers for not having chosen a better preschool to represent China. We would respond to this criticism by arguing that: our goal was not to select each nation's best preschools; Daguan at the time we conducted the study was considered to be one of the best preschools in Kunming; among the more than 100,000 preschool programs that existed in China in 1985 (some of which were rural one-room programs, without a trained teacher) Daguan was certainly in the upper half; and too much of the research on Chinese early childhood education by both Chinese and outside scholars had been conducted in elite programs in Beijing and the large coastal cities.

Most Japanese and American viewers of the old videotape also have been critical of Daguan. The features of Daguan circa 1985 that have tended to draw the most ire are the boarding program (at the time about 60% of the children stayed at school from Monday morning through Saturday, with some having a visit home on Wednesday nights); the perceived authoritarianism of the teachers and didacticism of the curriculum (as seen, for example, in scenes where a teacher tells children to eat their lunch silently and of a lesson where the children sitting in rows at desks are told by their teacher to build block structures following a diagram); and the starkness of the facilities (including the drabness of the walls, the absence of toys, and the latrine where boys and girls squat in rows over a trough that lacks running water).

Since its founding in 1951 Daguan has had only three directors. Wang Xinglan, who was Daguan's founding director, was still in charge when we made the first videotape in 1985. The next year she retired and was replaced by Wu Qiongzhen, who was in charge during the physical transformation of the school. She organized the purchase of the land next to the original site, soliciting funds for constructing the new education building, and before retiring in 1998 handing over leadership to Director Shi, who oversaw the move to the new location. Happily, when we returned to Kunming in 2002, both former directors were still alive, living in the staff housing on site, and available to view the 1985 videotape of their school, as were all but two of the eight teachers who are seen in the old video (one teacher had died and another had moved away to care for her aging parents).

As they watched the 1985 videotape, the directors excitedly identified themselves and children, some of whom are now parents of Daguan You'eryuan students. When the videotape ended our first question was, "Does the video match your memory of those days?" The two retired directors and the two current directors, who had been young teachers at the school when we made the original video, responded, unanimously, that this is just how they remember it. When we commented that watching the old videotape makes clear how much Daguan has changed, the former directors disagreed, emphasizing the continuity they perceived between Daguan then and now. Director Wang, now in her eighties, told us that she was especially pleased that the video captured the staff's dedication and collectivist spirit, a spirit, she suggested, characteristic of Daguan in both periods:

> In the old days, our teachers were so diligent and conscientious that they rarely asked for a day off even when they were sick. The whole staff did everything together to make this preschool a great place for children. Together we cleaned, swept the yard, and hauled coal from the retailer in the city all the way to our kitchen and boiler room. I can see that the younger teachers have kept high this spirit of diligence and conscience. That, I would say, has not changed.

Director Wu, who succeeded Director Wang in 1986, added: "Every teacher cared about what happened in the other teachers' classes because our whole preschool was one unit and each of us worked for the good of the whole. There was no division of labor; your job was also mine. We all did everything together, including cleaning the outhouse." Director Shi, who was a young teacher in 1985 when we shot the original Daguan video, emphasized the quality of the care the teachers provided for children: "In particular, we took great care of our children's meals and we did all we could to ensure that their lives were as comfortable as we could make them in those days. The teachers were very caring, patient, and close to children, like parents."

The nostalgic comments of these retired early childhood educators in Kunming resonate with the perspectives of the older residents of Beijing who were interviewed by Judith Farquhar and Qicheng Zhang (2005) in their study of health practices: "Many older Beijingers think of some periods during those first four decades of the history of the PRC as more orderly and more deeply gratifying than the present. . . . Looking back, they can recall a comfortable predictability in the deprivations that everyone suffered together, and they remember a satisfying morality in the everyday life of egalitarian collective labor" (pp. 309–310).

We asked the retired directors whether, in the contemporary period of rapid social and economic change, they worry that Daguan's new teachers

2.1. Old and new Daguan buildings.

are in danger of losing something of the old collective spirit and dedication. Director Wang replied:

> Nowadays, the living conditions in our country are far better than in the old days, when the younger teachers who work here now were just children. They have not experienced the hardship that we experienced. It is our job to remind them constantly of the good traditions and to instill collective pride among the younger teachers so that they will never lose that spirit.

This conversation took place in a classroom that was equipped with a multimedia system controlled via a touch-screen panel that projected onto a large motorized dropdown screen. This room epitomizes the material advances Daguan had undergone in the past twenty years. In addition to the multimedia room, the new Daguan has a gymnasium, a music room, and a block-play room, all housed in a new five-story building. The new classrooms as well as the staff living quarters now have running water and indoor restrooms, in contrast to what we saw on the 1985 video of Daguan where the toilet was an outhouse and teachers had to fetch boiled water for children to drink (figure 2.1).

Director Wu emphasized that this material improvement is mirrored by improvements in the level of training of the staff:

> As we have added new teachers, the average age of our staff has become younger and the level of qualifications higher. The younger teachers have come to us with an associate degree or professional diploma in early childhood education. Over time, we asked our veteran teachers who had only a vocational high school diploma to work to obtain a higher degree or to switch to another job within the preschool.

While they praised the rising level of teacher qualifications, the directors voiced some concern that the young teachers lacked maturity and the resourcefulness and grit that come from living through tough times. Director Wu said, "Some of the young teachers are only eighteen years old, so they need to make an effort to further develop their professional skills and become mature." Director Wang added: "These days, when young teachers are hired, our preschool provides them with comfortable working and living conditions. But we must also teach them our great tradition, and our lifestyle of hard work and plain living. We must pass on to the young teachers the tradition of running the preschool industriously and thriftily."

This is the challenge facing not just Daguan You'eryuan, but also China: how to continue to modernize practices and improve the standard of living while not losing touch with traditional Chinese and socialist virtues including diligence, self-sacrifice, frugality, and communalism.

A Day at Daguan You'eryuan

The second approach we took to assessing continuity and change at Daguan was to make a new video of a typical day, a video we again used as a cue for reflection. The new Daguan video, like the old one, opens with children, ages three through six, arriving with their parents, some on foot and others on bicycles, and passing through the school gate, where they line up to be checked by the school's nurses (figure 2.2). The nurses, with wooden tongue depressors in hand, quickly examine each child following the common Chinese medical practice of look, touch, ask (and, if there is anything to raise concern, examine). Some parents say good-bye to their children at the entrance while others walk their children to their classroom. Amidst the flow of arriving parents and children and departing parents, an assistant director and a senior teacher, brooms in hand, finish sweeping the courtyard and exchange greetings. Two kitchen staff members in white tunics emerge from the kitchen pushing a cart loaded with breakfast for each classroom. While children negotiate the staircase to the third and fourth floors, the kitchen staff uses a food elevator to deliver breakfast to the upper-floor classrooms.

In a classroom on the third floor, Ms. Zhang, one of the two teachers of the Zhongyi ("Middle Class Number 1") of four-year-olds, helps the children get buns and bowls of porridge. As the children quietly eat, Zhang laoshi distributes preserved duck eggs. After most of the children are finished, she reminds them that it is toilet time. The toilets, which are next

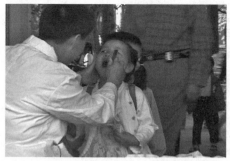

2.2. Nurse check.

door to the classroom, are in a clean bright room covered with white ceramic tiles. As in the toilet scene in the old Daguan video, the children squat over a long trough. The new toilets differ from the old ones in having a wall separating the boys' and girls' sides. Many of the children linger in the bathroom, the girls talking and laughing and the boys engaging in mock martial arts combat.

The formal school day begins with Zhang laoshi leading the class in counting how many children are present. There are thirty-five. The class next troops downstairs to a large multimedia room where Zhang laoshi conducts an art class on *zha ran,* a regional practice of dying cloth in colorful patterns. For this activity, Zhang laoshi has substituted paper for cloth. Holding up a piece of paper she had already dyed, she asks the children, "Isn't it beautiful?" The children respond in one voice: "Beautiful!" After displaying several more examples, she demonstrates how to fold and then dip a piece of rice paper into bowls of dye to produce various patterns and effects. Working at tables, the children make their own textiles of varying color, shape, and size. They then drape their completed products on railings, forming a large display.

Looking at the clock, Zhang laoshi announces that it is time to join the other four-year-old classes on the playground for morning exercise. As music blares from the loudspeakers, the teachers lead the almost two hundred four-year-old children through a series of exercises. This is followed by a dance in which the children are free to select their own partners. Next comes fifteen minutes of free play in the garden and the playground.

The class then walks up to fifth-floor gymnasium featuring balance beams, hanging rings, rolling platforms, and large balls. As the children enthusiastically interact with the equipment, a few conflicts arise and the teachers intervene. One little girl tells Zhang laoshi that another girl took away the ball she was using. The teacher says to the other girl, "You should

2.3. At the lunch table.

let her play with the ball now that you have already had it for a while." Jiejie, a boy who just has his ball snatched away by another boy, looks miserable. A girl asks him what is wrong and comforts him.

Back in their classroom, the children wash their hands and have a drink of water. Each day before lunch a child is selected to tell the class a story. Today's storyteller informs the teacher that his story is about little white rabbits and a big gray wolf. The story is a long, meandering one, which the children find hard to follow. After more than ten minutes of this meandering storytelling, the food buckets arrive. Jiejie, who is on lunch duty today, distributes chopsticks to his classmates. As they did for breakfast, the children line up in front of the teacher, who fills a bowl with rice and stir-fried pork and celery (figure 2.3). While the children are eating quietly, Zhang laoshi fills out a form for the kitchen that records the food consumption of her class. Once finished with lunch, the children drop their bowls and chopsticks in an empty bucket, go to the toilet, and then head to the bedroom adjoining the classroom for nap. As they enter the bedroom, Zhang laoshi touches each child's cheek and forehead. She then urges and helps the children to take off their outer clothes and get under their comforters.

Two hours later the children wake up, make their beds, go to the toilet, and return to the classroom, where teachers comb the girls' hair. The children have a snack of cookies and milk and a period of free play in the classroom. The class then goes downstairs to the music room. Dong laoshi, seated at the piano, leads the children in a song. She then holds up two stuffed monkeys and says, "The two golden monkeys ask you, 'Little friends, do you like me?'" The children reply together, "We do." Dong laoshi continues, providing a voice for the monkey: "Then, little friends, please sit up and I will see if you can learn a great new skill." Selecting a girl to act out the part of one of the monkeys, Dong laoshi then sings a song and demonstrates a stiff-legged dance: "Two golden monkeys take a walk,

2.4. Dong laoshi demonstrates the monkey dance.

taking turns carrying each other on their backs. When they come across a ditch, 'Gudong!' 'Ouch!' They have a big fall" (figure 2.4). The children pair up and pretend to be the two monkeys, dancing to the song and, laughing, falling at the key moment. The monkey song is followed by a song in which children form trains, each child grabbing the waist of the child ahead of them in a line and then chugging around the room.

At the end of the thirty minutes of music, the children return to the classroom. Aware that the children are still very excited, Dong laoshi leads them in a "freeze" game: "Because we are all wooden puppets, we cannot speak and move." At the end of her sentence, the children freeze and try to hold their position as long as possible. The teacher then announces the next activity: "In a moment, I will take you downstairs to play in the block room. What will you build? You can build whatever you like. Let's see which of you builds the best things." The children gleefully jump to their feet and march off down the stairs. The block room on the first floor has big wooden blocks piled against one long wall; two other walls are lined with large containers holding a variety of plastic blocks that snap together. Several boys and girls construct guns and join one of their teachers in a pretend gunfight. A girl uses a block as a mobile phone to chat with a teacher. Children play by themselves or in pairs or in small groups to build a variety of objects and structures. The atmosphere in the room is loud and exuberant.

Back upstairs in their classroom, the children wait for their supper to arrive. When it does, Dong laoshi instructs them: "You should focus on your food. Don't talk. If you talk, you will affect other children. I still can hear someone talking." While the children are eating, Dong laoshi writes in the journal the teachers use to keep each other informed of events of the day. At the same time, outside the entrance gate, hundreds of parents are lined up waiting to pick up their children. At 5:40 p.m., the gate is opened and parents dash across the courtyard and hurry to their children's classrooms

2.5. Opening the gate for the parents.

(figure 2.5). Dong laoshi stands in the classroom doorway greeting the parents and saying good-bye to the children. Jiejie leaves in the company of a young man, his father's employee. About half of the children are waiting not for their parents, but for the teachers of the after-school special interest classes that are held in the older classroom building next door.

Some of the children are enrolled in an after-school dance class, others in a drawing class. The theme for the day in the drawing class is rain. As the children finish their drawings of umbrellas and of people walking amidst big drops of rain, the teacher puts their compositions on the blackboard for display. At 6:30, the main gate is opened again and two hundred or so parents rush in to pick up their children.

Daguan Then and Now

Our return to Daguan to show the staff the video we shot there in the spring of 2002 was delayed by the SARS epidemic that spread through China in 2003. We finally were able to return to Kunming in the fall of 2003. We first showed the video to Zhang Rui and Dong Yanyun, the classroom teachers seen in the video, and to Yang Jia, the class's regular teacher who, for health reasons, was absent most of the week we were shooting. We began our discussion by asking if the fact that Dong laoshi stepped in for Yang laoshi made the day we videotaped atypical. Yang laoshi replied, "I felt that everything was about the same. All the activities went on as scheduled." Dong laoshi added, "I was only with that class for that day, and this group of children was unusually active, with a number of unique characters. It's possible that the children were a bit more high-spirited with me than they would have been if Zhang laoshi had been there." We also showed the new video to Director Shi, Assistant Director Xie Ping, and the other classroom teachers, who all concurred that the video gives an accurate picture of a day at Daguan You'eryuan. In our discussions with Daguan's directors and staff, our primary goal was to hear their insiders' explanations for why Daguan between 1985 and 2002 stayed the same in some ways and changed dramatically in others.

The sections that follow report on what the staff at Daguan had to say about a series of key issues: the phasing out of the boarding program; the business of running a preschool in the new Chinese economy; concerns about contemporary parents; upgrading "hardware" (buildings and materials) and "software" (curriculum and pedagogy); and the toilets. We include a long section on the changes in the toilets at Daguan because it is an interesting story in its own right and also because it is one that can serve as a metaphor for thinking about the relationship in China between changing preschool practices and economic, social, and cultural continuity and change.

BOARDING PROGRAMS AND THE MISSION OF PRESCHOOLS

The classroom we featured in the 1985 video was a boarding class. In the beginning of the video we see a father struggling to drop off his four-year-old daughter, Aimei, on a Monday morning, reassuring her that he will pick her up on Friday. A boarding program for preschoolers was shocking to most Japanese and American viewers of the old Daguan video. But as we explained in the original book, from a Chinese perspective providing boarding classrooms was a service to parents who worked very long hours, often on the night shift and often far from where they lived. It was also a service for children, who otherwise would have spent hours each day on the back of bicycles commuting to and from school in the predawn and dusk. The discourse underlying this practice, which was common in China since the revolution in 1949, was that the primary role of the preschool was to relieve the burden of childcare on working parents so they could concentrate on contributing to the construction of the nation and participate in the ongoing process of socialist revolution. Moreover, putting young children in a boarding class was viewed as a benefit rather than as a hardship for the children. The staff at Daguan took pride in the quality of care and education they provided the children, rejecting the (bourgeois) logic that the best or most normal arrangement is for young children to be cared for primarily by their mothers.

Despite their belief at the time in the value of providing boarding care, in the years we were conducting our original study Daguan was in the process of transitioning from a boarding-only preschool to a preschool with no boarding classes. As Director Wang told us, "We used to run a boarding-only preschool, but in 1983 we started our first day class. The number of day classes quickly increased over the next few years and we completely eliminated the boarding program in September 1987." The Daguan teachers and directors gave us several reasons for the change. By 1983, the one-child family policy, which was initiated in 1979, was in full effect. That meant that by 1987 the great majority of Daguan's students were single children. Tang laoshi, one of the veteran teachers, explained the connection between the drop in the number of children per family and the decline of boarding classes:

> Back then every family had several children and parents worked very hard and they endured a lot of hardship. Parents put their children in our boarding program to reduce the time they needed to spend on housework and caring for children. The single-child policy has made parents' lives easier. When parents began to have only one child, the boarding program became much less needed.

While this drop in births per family led to less demand for boarding programs, it did not lead, as it did in Japan, to an overall drop in preschool enrollment. Even with the shift to one child per family, the increasing numbers of Chinese baby boomers that reached parenting age in the 1980s meant that the overall birthrate remained high and therefore so did the demand on preschool provision. In fact, the demand for early childhood education and care grew precipitously in the 1980s and 1990s as an offshoot of Deng Xiaoping's "four modernizations" movement. The *Guidelines for the Reform and Development of Education in China* issued jointly in 1993 by the Chinese Communist Party and the State Council stated that "in large and medium-sized cities the access of young children to kindergartens should be largely met and in rural areas the proportion of children receiving education in the one-year pre-primary classes should be raised to 70%." As an elite public program in a capital city, Daguan You'eryuan was expected to take a leading role in meeting this call for expanding provision. The most dramatic and immediately effective way for Daguan to increase enrollment was to transition from boarding to day-only classes. Director Shi explained:

> Our growth in enrollment was made possible largely by the elimination of the boarding program. In the boarding program, to cover one class of

twenty-eight four-year-olds, we needed four teachers, who worked on three shifts. We had a quarantine room next to the doctor's office to place sick children under medical care. Children were not sent home when they were ill. Parents didn't have to worry about their children at all. In contrast, now we have only two teachers per class, and we now send sick children home right away without giving the consideration we used to give to parents' availability and the cost to them of medical expenses.

As Daguan made the shift from boarding to day classrooms, the enrollment went from about 200 children in 1983 to about 300 in 1985 to over 400 in 1987. Further increases in enrollment required the expansion of classroom space, which was accomplished when the new buildings were opened in 1998, allowing enrollment to increase to over 600 students. The staff of sixty employees now serves about three times as many students at Daguan as they did during the boarding school era.

The change from boarding to day programs contributed to a shift in Daguan teachers' understanding of themselves and their jobs. Twenty years ago, when young children were under the teachers' care twenty-four hours a day for six days a week, although the teachers valued the curriculum and pedagogy they were providing, they defined themselves primarily as parent surrogates. Signs on the walls of boarding classrooms read, "The *you'eryuan* is my home. My teachers are like my mother," and "Our love for children is as great as a mother's love." Retired Director Wang, who still lives on the Daguan campus and takes a great interest in the school's evolution, told us: "Since the days when you did your original study, the old family model of preschool teaching gradually has been replaced by a professional model, and the education side of preschool teaching has taken precedence over the care function."

Although Daguan You'eryuan no longer has boarding classrooms, boarding classrooms have not disappeared in China. There is a rapid resurgence of boarding programs in some parts of China, particularly in the largest and most economically vibrant cities. These new boarding preschools serve not the children of the working class as they did in the old days, but the children of the new entrepreneurs. Whereas once the boarding schools were needed to allow for the greater good of the ongoing socialist revolution, now they free parents, many of whom are highly educated, for their long work days in the new economy and for their frequent business trips. These boarding schools feature English-language learning, piano lessons, computers, painting, and more. In Beijing, Shanghai, and other larger cities, the majority of these boarding preschools are private, for-profit businesses whose tuitions and fees are beyond the reach of ordinary working parents. A deputy director of the Beijing 21st Century Experimental Kindergarten explained to us that most of their clientele were parents with college or higher degrees and high incomes and that many owned businesses or were government officials.

THE CHANGING BUSINESS OF PRESCHOOL

In the boarding school era most of Daguan You'eryuan's students were children of Yunnan Province government employees. In the 1990s, societal demand for the increased provision of preschool services grew to the point that preschools such as Daguan that originally were mandated to serve only families with special affiliations were pressured to open up to the general public. This shift toward open enrollment resulted not just from government-directed pressure to increase provision but also from the rise of a market economy in which preschools increasingly must compete for tuition-paying clients.

As the business of preschool has become increasingly market driven in China, well-respected programs such as Daguan have increased their enrollment as well as their average class size. Preschools with poor reputations and ratings tend to have lower student/teacher ratios, lower overall enrollments, and low tuition because they have trouble attracting students. Preschools such as Daguan that have excellent reputations and top ratings have relatively high tuition and high student/teacher ratios and enrollments that grow to the capacity of the building. As Director Shi explained:

> If your basic facilities and teacher qualities are not very good, parents will be reluctant to enroll their children in your preschool and you will have a low student/teacher ratio. To keep costs down in this situation, children of different ages have to be mixed in one class. In contrast, preschools with good reputations tend to exceed their enrollment capacity. Some of the best preschools in the city have student/teacher ratios that are even higher than ours. We are licensed by the city to accept 100 more children than we currently enroll. But to maintain balance between quality and reputation and between the teachers' workload and parental demand, we decided to put a limit on enrollment.

The result is that Daguan's classes for four- and five-year-olds have thirty-five students with two teachers.

When we asked how teachers can handle so many children in a class, the administrators at Daguan pointed out that their ratios are typical for China. They also emphasized that their investment in the new building and in state-of-the art equipment has made teachers' work easier. Director Shi told us:

> Since we moved into the new building and left the old courtyard behind in 1998, we have made rapid improvements to our immediate environment. We modernized the classrooms. In each room we installed new furniture and equipment, such as sinks, water coolers, cabinets, televisions, pianos, and books. We equipped the multimedia classroom with advanced computer and audiovisual equipment. The effect has been to increase children's learning opportunities while reducing our teachers' workload, allowing them to spend more time with children.

When we conducted our original study, Daguan's teachers spent many hours of the day not just caring for the around-the-clock needs of boarding children, but also hauling coal to the school from across town and carrying water to the classrooms. The material improvements at Daguan You'eryuan, as in other work sites and home settings across China, have reduced manual labor, allowing for new efficiencies.

It is important to remember that in China as in Japan and other countries in Asia, class size and student/teacher ratios have never been considered key indicators of quality, as they are in North America and Europe (Tobin, Wu & Davidson 1989). Daguan's large (by North American and European standards) class sizes and student/teacher ratios are consistent with the traditions of Chinese early childhood education. These class sizes and ratios are well matched to what has until recently been China's teacher-centered, didactic approach. But as the early childhood educational approach in China becomes more constructivist and the curriculum more child-initiated, ratios as high as twenty children to one adult may come to be perceived as an obstacle to improving quality. Or perhaps the version of constructivist early childhood education that eventually emerges in China will be one that is compatible with high student/teacher ratios, as is the case in Japan.

The ability of Daguan to dramatically expand and upgrade their facilities was fueled by Kunming's rapid pace of economic development over the past twenty years. In the mid-1980s, as the country emerged from the Cultural Revolution, the city of Kunming gradually started to do better economically. During this period Daguan You'eryuan built three apartment buildings on the perimeter of their school grounds to meet the housing needs of their entire staff. A decade later, the city experienced unprecedented economic growth, benefiting from expansion of its flowers, tobacco, tea, mining, and tourism industries and from becoming a key transportation and mercantile hub serving the newly developing economies of neighboring Vietnam, Thailand, and Laos. The construction of Daguan's new five-story educational building was completed in 1998. The pace of economic development in Kunming has accelerated even further since our first revisit in 2002. When we returned to Daguan in 2003 to show the staff the video, we found that the old estate that used to house the preschool had been completely demolished and leveled for new construction. Six months later, when we returned in the summer of 2004 for follow-up interviews, this vacant lot had been turned into a branch of a Shanghai Volkswagen automobile dealership, with a flashy automobile display room sitting where the old school gate and courtyard had been.

The new wealth also has meant that parents in Kunming and elsewhere are increasingly able and willing to invest in their children's education, beginning with preschool. The changing Chinese economy presents opportunities, but also anxiety for parents, who are eager to find ways to give their children the best possible start on the road to being successful in the new capitalist economy. A system of categorization and ranking helps parents choose the best preschool available for their children. Public preschools in China are assigned a rank and a category. In some cities and districts, private schools are similarly evaluated, categorized, and ranked. The ranking is based on the program's physical resources. Many preschools, especially in the countryside, that have very poor conditions, do not qualify for a ranking. The categories reflect teacher quality, based on a combination of their educational background and their teaching competence, as measured by outside inspectors who observe them teach a lesson. Public preschools that are judged to be at the top in both rank and category can charge parents the highest tuition in their city. Although the ranking and categorization system is common to all large cities, the criteria vary greatly from city to city. A rank 1/category 1 program in Kunming might not receive the same scores if it were in Shanghai.

The changing economy has compelled Daguan to market itself competitively. Director Shi explained to us that one key strategy was purchasing an expensive set of specialized gym equipment (figure 2.6). The whole fifth floor of the education building at Daguan is set up as a gym which is equipped with a set of Sensory Integration movement materials and structures developed by A. Jean Ayres, an American occupational therapist. This

2.6. Gym.

investment allowed Daguan to become the first preschool in Kunming to join an organization of preschools run by the Shanghai-based company that manufactured and distributes the gym equipment, a step toward allowing Daguan to compete in the top tier of the Kunming preschool market. Director Shi explained, "We are a large *you'eryuan* in the city, but we have not established a special niche in the *you'eryuan* business. This gym project, once completed, will give Daguan unique visibility." This visibility, in turn, contributes to the vitality of Daguan as a business. It is important to note that although this effort was entrepreneurial, Daguan's involvement in the market economy takes place within a government system. The gym equipment was purchased for Daguan by the provincial government, who also paid for and supervised the renovation of the school. The teachers and directors are government employees. Daguan You'eryuan in the new millennium reflects China's complex, hybrid economy, as it is a program receiving government support and subject to government control that at the same time is increasingly market-driven and entrepreneurial.

CHANGING CHILDREN AND PARENTS

In 1985, when we conducted the fieldwork for our original study, the first single-child cohort was passing through China's preschools, amidst a good deal of public anxiety. Policy makers, psychologists, and educators expressed concern that single children, growing up without siblings, would be socially and emotionally stunted. Much of the blame was placed on the parents and the problem of spoiling, a problem that was called the "4-2-1 syndrome," based on the assumption that four grandparents and two parents would lavish too much attention on one child. Preschools were seen as a solution to this problem, with the task of correcting the tendency of parents and grandparents to spoil single children and with providing children growing up without siblings the experience of living in a group. It took longer for the one-child policy to take hold in provincial areas such as Kunming than it did in Beijing and the large coastal cities. When we conducted the original study in 1985, the majority of children at Daguan still had siblings, but the concern about spoiling was already in the forefront of people's minds. Today, almost all of the children at Daguan are single children (the chief exceptions being twins and children from ethnic minority groups that are exempted from the one-child policy).

The term "spoiling" is still used by educators, but less so than in the 1980s, and it is no longer considered to be a significant threat to China's social and emotional health. The problem of the spoiling of single children turned out to be a bit like a storm that was forecast but never materialized. Many Chinese educators suggest that the new generation of single children as a cohort has turned out to be not just unproblematic, but more capable than their multiple-sibling predecessors. A study by the Shanghai Academy of Social Sciences (cited in Liu 1999) found single children to be active, energetic, willing to try new ideas, lighthearted, willing to demonstrate their ability, not easily persuaded, and eager to implement their own plans. Moreover, they have higher grades than children with siblings. The study reports that single children, as young adults, turn out to be independent, self-confident, and creative. The Shanghai researchers noted that these personality characteristics are congruent with the needs of the emerging market economy. That having been said, the researchers also report that a number of single children in the sample lacked perseverance and the social skills needed to care for others, characteristics that were highly valued in the traditional Chinese agricultural society. With China's rapid urbanization and shift to a market economy, traits that were seen as weaknesses of single children a generation ago are now valued and encouraged by teachers, and spoiling has been dropped down on the list of child-rearing concerns.

The concern placed on the spoiling of single children in the mid-1980s has shifted into a more general concern about the quality of parenting and the rise of a new kind of parental selfishness that complicates the job of preschool teaching. In our interviews with preschool teachers and directors we heard many accusations that parents give their children too much attention, too little attention, the wrong kind of attention, or all three. These accusations can be traced to anxieties and concerns about how the Chinese family and Chinese society are changing in response to the acceleration of economic and social change. For example, the teachers at Daguan explained Jiejie's difficulties in relating to other students and his frequent crying in terms not of spoiling but of parental neglect. His teacher Zhang laoshi told us:

> Jiejie's parents are migrants to the city from the countryside. They are so pre-occupied with their growing business that they don't have enough time to spend with their child. As you can see in the video, Jiejie often gets picked on and bullied by other boys. I have made a special effort to talk about this with his mother but it's difficult because Jiejie's parents are so busy that they usually send an employee to pick him up from school.

Jiejie, according to Zhang laoshi, is suffering from having parents who, having "jumped into the sea" (a contemporary metaphor for starting a business) can spend money on him but not time, making him the country cousin to the Beijing children whose yuppie entrepreneurial parents enroll them in elite boarding preschools so they can work long hours to get rich.

The most ubiquitous form of contemporary parental excess is the pressure being put on preschools by parents to provide more academic preparation. In China's new society the core concern is that one's (only) child must be educated and socialized well in preschool to get a fast start toward becoming economically successful as an adult and not "being left behind at the starting line." This is a heavy mandate for preschools. Ironically, Chinese early childhood educational experts are calling for the curriculum to be more play-oriented and focused on creativity just as many parents are pushing for more academic instruction (Zhu & Zhang 2008, 177). One teacher summarized the dilemma: "What does the preschool focus on: its parents' demands or on what is good for its children?" The teachers and directors at Daguan often feel caught in the middle. Chinese parents' putting pressure on their children to excel academically is hardly a new cultural practice. What is new is that with the expanding provision of preschool this academic pressure has started earlier and is expanding as an ambition for wider portions of society. With China's rapid and ongoing modernization, increased wealth, and expanding access to preschool, more and more working-class and rural parents are viewing education as a route to social mobility for their children and they are looking to their children's preschool teachers to provide a quick start and complaining when they think this is not happening to the degree they feel it should.

Twenty years ago teachers saw their role as supporting and correcting parents and compensating for what they saw as the tendency of parents to spoil their children. Now the parent-teacher relationship has fundamentally changed: parents are becoming customers (a phenomenon familiar to preschool teachers in the US). Teachers at Daguan and elsewhere across China told us that in addition to pressuring them to provide more academic instruction, parents are increasingly aggressive in blaming teachers for any minor injuries—real or imagined—their children receive at school. In our interviews teachers complained about the rise of a new generation of overanxious parents, who instead of giving their children the right kind of attention, displace it into obsessing about their child's health and complaining to the school about the scrapes and bruises that used to be considered marks of a healthy, active childhood. Teachers complain that these days normal conflicts between children lead to parents automatically siding with their own child, accusing other children of wrongdoing, and blaming the teacher for not doing her job properly. When parents come to preschool complaining that their child has suffered a bruise or scratch, they pressure the teachers and directors to take the child to the hospital for a medical examination, to be paid for by the preschool. Most preschools have a policy of asking the teachers to make profuse personal apologies to the parents of a child with a bruise or scratch and to visit the child's home with gifts. It is not uncommon in China for a preschool to hold the teacher financially accountable for any cut on the child's body that requires stitches, with each stitch linked to a significant reduction of the classroom teacher's monthly bonus, even when the directors believe that the teacher was not at fault. Ms. Wu, who was the director of Daguan in the 1980s, commented on the contemporary situation:

> If something goes awry between the parent and the teacher, it may end up in a conflict. Although most of our parents are quite understanding, many of them are as young as our teachers and often get involved in disagreements with our teachers and the teachers then must make a great deal of effort to resolve the conflict. In the past we asked our teachers to act like a mother who treated all children as if they were her own children. Now, we ask them to be extra patient not just with children, but also with their parents.

UPGRADING HARDWARE AND SOFTWARE

In 1985 China was a poor, developing nation, still emerging from the travails of the Cultural Revolution. While proud of the dedication they brought to their work during this difficult period, the veteran teachers at Daguan expressed an appreciation for the improvements China's economic rise has brought to the quality of their personal and professional lives. One of the veteran teachers told us:

> We are happier and more energetic today than we used to be. In the past, our facilities were poor and our teaching methods were limited. We went to work in uniforms of the monotonous color and style that reflected that bygone era. Today, we are creating new teaching methods and working in a better environment, with more materials. The changes we have experienced at school reflect the change of our society.

Many of the veteran teachers spoke of the changes between the two eras using the metaphor of "hardware" and "software." For example, in response to our question, "What is the most significant change in Daguan since 1985?" one veteran teacher replied:

> The hardware. Take TV for example. In 1985, we had only one TV set for the whole preschool of 300 children and 60 staff members. Now we have a TV set in each classroom and in addition, we have an up-to-date multimedia room.

Another teacher replied:

> Yes, but what you've described is only hardware. The software has changed a lot, too. We've worked hard to advance our professional knowledge. Compared to twenty years ago, when we were new to our jobs, we not only have gained experience, but we've also have become more conscious of how and why to design a variety of valuable activities for children.

We suggest that what the teachers at Daguan are calling a change in software constitutes a paradigm shift, one that has taken place, albeit with varying degrees of implementation, in preschools across China. Director Shi described this shift succinctly: "In the old days, we based our teaching on the elementary school model. The 1985 video shows little distinction between a preschool and an elementary school." Assistant Director Xie offered an example:

> Throughout the old video, it is apparent that the teacher teaches and talks all the time. The teacher keeps telling the children what to do, rather than letting them learn something on their own. For example, in the video, the

children sit in their chairs, obediently, with their hands behind them, waiting for the teacher's instruction. Whatever the teacher says, they will do.

Daguan You'eryuan's motto now, as in 1985, is "All we do is for children." In our interviews, we heard the phrase used repeatedly by Daguan's teachers and directors, both old and new, and it is inscribed in meter-high characters on the front of the administration building. But the meaning of this phrase and its implications for practice have changed subtly but significantly in the last twenty years. "All we do is for children" is a quote from Song Qingling, the wife of Sun Yat-sen and the founder, in 1938, of the China Defense League, which later became the China Welfare Institute, an organization that focuses on services for young children. In 1985, "All we do is for children" meant primarily caring for them and training them on behalf of their parents, with an emphasis on *guan*, a Chinese term that combines the English-language meanings of educate, care for, support, control, and love. In the 1980s, *guan* at Daguan mostly took the form of rules, routines, firmness, and teacher-led instruction. The contemporary teachers and directors at Daguan still see themselves as providing *guan* (though they use the term less often these days), but the form their care, love, and instruction now take is more responsive to children's desires and respectful of children's rights.

At the core of the paradigm shift in Chinese early childhood education is a change in the understanding of childhood, learning, and pedagogy. The key terms used to justify this new approach are "respecting children," "active learning," "individualizing instruction," "play-based teaching and learning," and, as a cover term, "humanistic education." These terms are not new to Chinese education. They were introduced by John Dewey, who visited China from 1919 to 1921, and popularized by his Chinese disciples Hu Shi, Tao Xingzhi, and Chen Heqin. After disappearing from discourse and practice during the years of the Cultural Revolution, the progressive agenda started to make a return in the 1980s, first in Nanjing, Beijing, and the large coastal cities, and then reaching provincial cities such as Kunming in the 1990s. In citing the source of their new progressive ideas, teachers and directors we interviewed at Daguan and other preschools rarely mentioned Dewey, instead citing the 1989 "Kindergarten Work Regulations and Procedures," the 2001 *Guidelines for Kindergarten Education*, and the "The Convention on the Rights of Children." The notions of children's rights and of respecting children that were introduced to China in the 1990s give an ethical imperative to the reform movement in early childhood education (Liu & Feng 2005; Zhu & Zhang 2008).

We can see and demonstrate the effects of this reform movement on Daguan most clearly by comparing the 1984 and 2002 versions of block play, toilet routines, and exercise activities. Daguan's staff reflections on these activities provide us with an understanding of the thinking behind the changes of practice.

BLOCK PLAY

Here is how we describe the block play scene in the old Daguan video in our 1989 book:

> The children are told to sit at their desks. Once they are seated, the teachers distribute wooden parquetry blocks to each child. The blocks come in a small box, which also contains pictures of several structures that can be made with them. Ms. Xiang says to the students: "We all know how to build with blocks, right? Just pay attention to the picture of the building and build it. When we play games like this, we must use our minds, right? Once you are done, raise your hand and one of us will come by and check to make sure you've done it correctly. Begin. Do your best. Build according to order." The children begin to work in silence. Those who are working in a non-orderly way are corrected: a child whose box is placed askew on her desk has it placed squarely in the desk's upper right-hand corner by Ms. Xiang. . . . After ten minutes most of the children have completed their structures. The teachers come over to check their work. If a building has been constructed properly (that is, exactly as in the picture), the child is told to take it down piece by piece and then rebuild it. If the teacher spots an error, she tells the child to correct it. After fifteen minutes of building, tearing down, and rebuilding, some of the children grow a bit restive, squirming in their chairs and whispering to their deskmates. Ms. Wang says: "Keep still! There is no need to talk while you are working. Let's work quietly." (Tobin, Wu & Davidson 1989, 77–78)

The blocks children used in this exercise were a version of the Wechsler intelligence test for children. Designed for measuring IQ, the blocks were used at Daguan as an educational tool. The contrast with block play at Daguan circa 2002 is dramatic. While there is still the belief and expectation among teachers that working with blocks is good for developing children's spatial sense and intelligence, the activity is no longer structured or conceptualized as a didactic attempt to raise intelligence. In our 2002 video we hear the teacher tell the children: "In a moment, I will take you downstairs

2.7. Blocks at Daguan, 1985 and 2002.

to play in the block room. What will you build with the blocks? Build whatever you like. Let's see which of you builds the best things." As we described earlier in this chapter, the mood in the block room throughout this period was loud and exuberant with children running, laughing, and screaming and the teachers joining them in their play.

The change in mood and tone between block play at Daguan circa 1985 and 2002 reflects the impact of the paradigm shift towards "play-based teaching and learning," "active learning," and "respecting children," as Dong laoshi's reflections on the activity suggest:

> Each child used to get a small box of blocks, a practice that we can see now limited their creativity and imagination. Children who worked with the small blocks individually missed out on the pleasure of sharing and cooperating with others. Now we have introduced the large blocks, which afford an opportunity for children to play together, providing a much larger space for them to build, exchange, and cooperate [figure 2.7]. This activity is conducive to the development of children's creativity and imagination.

Director Shi explained that the teacher's role in children's play in the new paradigm "is to provide children with guidance, to join them in problem solving, and to share in the joy of their accomplishments."

The two block scenes nearly twenty years apart are a good example of a change both in material conditions and educational philosophy that reflects Daguan's (and China's) dramatic economic rise and social transformation. In 1985 children at Daguan played with blocks sitting at desks in a gray cement room, following the explicit directions of their teachers. In 2002 the children play in a brightly colored room, dedicated to block play, with their teachers following the children's lead.

Many Japanese and US viewers were disturbed by the toilet scene in the original 1985 video of Daguan, in which a class of twenty-eight children were taken to a latrine where the children squatted over a long trough with boys on one side of the room and girls on the other while the teacher stood in the middle, handing out toilet paper and urging the children to not talk and to focus on relieving themselves. Many Chinese educators who viewed the original Daguan video were concerned that the toilet scene would give outsiders the impression that China was a backwards country.

In the new Daguan video, the toilets are inside the building, there is a partition separating the boys and girls, and there is plumbing. But the toilets are still long troughs and the children visit the toilets together as a class. Most of the early childhood educators across China who watched the old and new Daguan videos told us that group visits to the bathroom are still a typical Chinese preschool practice, but one which is gradually disappearing as the new child-centered paradigm takes root. Some Chinese observers noticed that although Daguan You'eryuan still has group toilet visits, the feel of toilet time is much different in the new video than in the old one. For example, Professor Hua Aihua of East China Normal University expressed delight at seeing the boys' mock fighting in the toilet, which she viewed as a sign of progress: "In the past, this kind of free play behavior in the toilets was prohibited, whereas now it requires no teacher intervention." However, she pointed out that Daguan has a long way to go, as she contrasted the situation in Kunming, where it is common for children to go to the toilet in a large group, with that in Shanghai, where "group toilet visits are very rare, if not nonexistent." Other Chinese educators, seeing more continuity between Daguan's old and new toilet routines, criticized Daguan's group visits to the toilet for failing to give children enough autonomy and freedom. For example, an early childhood education specialist in Shanghai commented, "In the video, what makes me uncomfortable is the number of controlled, arranged, and rushed activities. Take going to the toilet, for example. Children flocked in together, squatted down together, and left together. The overall freedom that children could enjoy, including going to the toilet, is rather limited."

The directors and teachers at Daguan defended the group visits to the toilet, disagreeing with the suggestion that this practice is a sign of backwardness and arguing that the scheduled whole-class toilet visits are important for preparing children to make a smooth transition to life in elementary school. As Li laoshi explained, "Around 9 o'clock in the morning children are asked to go to the toilet to reduce the chance that they will need to use the toilet in the middle of the next activity. This is important because this habit will be required in elementary school, where children generally are not allowed to go to the toilet in the middle of a lesson." Wang laoshi agreed with the value of instilling this habit, but she drew a distinction between requiring all the children to go into the toilet and making them squat over the trough. "The teacher should not force children to squat if they don't want to. Two- or three-year-olds usually don't know how to squat because they only use a toilet seat or a chamber pot at home. Now at school we ask them to squat. If they can do it, that's fine. If not, they can just take a tour of the toilets and come right out."

We were curious as to why young Chinese children have trouble adapting to squatting over a trough. Li laoshi explained that, "This takes time for the child to learn. Because some children have difficulty squatting, the teacher will hold their arms to support them. Sometimes a child doesn't like to squat and wants to wait to go to the toilet until she gets home. We offer these children a chamber pot as a transition." Li laoshi, a veteran teacher, explained that this difficulty with squatting began only recently:

> In the 1980s and on into the early 1990s we never had a big problem with children knowing how to squat over a trough. But things have changed with the availability of toilet seats at home. Almost every home has one today, so the children come to preschool needing to adapt to the school's toilet facilities.

Toilets are changing in China from troughs to toilet seats, but gradually, with sit-down toilets first appearing in hotels serving foreigners, then in private residences in apartment buildings, then in "five-star" public toilets, and then in sleeping cars on trains. Because China's modernization is uneven, the ratio of troughs to sit-down toilets varies dramatically by setting and region. Sit-down toilets are rarely found in the countryside. In a provincial city such as Kunming they are available in hotels and new homes but still uncommon in schools. They are a topic of controversy among urban residents in most of China, the majority of whom still prefer the traditional squat toilet, especially in public places. However, they are increasingly common in Beijing and they have become the norm in homes in Shanghai.

The question of whether to replace troughs with sit-down toilets is a difficult one for preschool directors because while the sit-down toilet represents modernization and development, it also is associated in many people's minds with disease. A survey conducted in 2005 in Beijing by the Institute of Psychology of the Chinese Academy of Sciences showed that the great majority of Beijing residents considered toilet seats in public bathrooms as undesirable because they are disease spreading and hard to sanitize. This concern with hygiene, which favors the continuation of squatting toilets in preschools and other public settings, must be balanced with the responsibility preschools feel to prepare children for the lives they will lead in the future. Some teachers told us that because troughs are the most common form of public and school toilets in China, it is the responsibility of the preschool to teach them how to use it. Li laoshi of Daguan commented: "If they don't learn how to use it, how can they use the public restrooms on the street, which all have the same design as ours?" On the other hand, early childhood educators also feel a responsibility to prepare their students for the life that awaits them in the years to come, a life that they assume will increasingly feature Western customs, including sit-down toilets in both home and public settings. As the director of a *you'eryuan* in Shanghai explained, "Nowadays, most residents in Shanghai live in new apartment buildings in which the toilet seat is a piece of standard equipment. Children grow up using it. Because of this, we had to remodel our school toilets to bridge the gap between children's lives at preschool and at home."

The change under way in the toilet routines of Chinese preschools also can be understood as a shift towards more privacy and less communalism. Some Chinese early childhood educators criticized the Daguan toilets for not providing adequate privacy. For example, a preschool teacher in Hubei Province pointed out the difference between the toilets at Daguan and at her preschool: "We have dividers between toilets. Each child has her own space when in the stall. The divider gives children a sense of security, and a sense of privacy so they can respect each other in the toilet."

Along with the rise in concern with toilet privacy comes an increased tendency to separate boys from girls. Director Shi told us the history of Daguan's decision to separate the girls and boys: "We became aware of the issue of sex difference in the late 1980s and began to separate boys from girls in their toilet visits, with girls going first and then boys. In the 1990s when the new building was being designed we asked the architects for a wall dividing the toilet facility into two halves. At that time, we thought only in terms of separating the boys and girls." We can see evidence of the connection in Chinese educators' minds between the questions of privacy and gender segregation in Director Shi's use of the word "only" in the phrase "we thought *only* in terms of separating the boys and girls." We suggest that her use of "only" here implies that the separation of the sexes is a stage on the path that leads to eventually providing individual privacy in toilet stalls. This suggests that a dimension of bourgeois sexuality and gender is the introduction of earlier and earlier sexual modesty, a modesty that implies its opposite—sexual interest and curiosity.

Body modesty is associated with modernization, but also with a loss of the communalism and collectivism that characterized Chinese social relations in the past. In *siheyuan*, the traditional courtyard residences that until recently were common in Beijing and other Chinese cities, most homes had no toilet of any kind and residents used a public latrine. These toilets could accommodate five to ten people at a time, squatting next to each other, without dividers. People who lived along the same *hutong* (lane) who otherwise would not know each other met and socialized in these public toilets. Visited throughout the day by people of all ages and from all walks of life, these public toilets were sites for lively conversations about current events and for swapping jokes, stories, and rumors. This was a place where people made friends, where adults teased children, and where young people helped seniors squat down and stand up.

This kind of communal life as epitomized by the pubic toilets is gradually disappearing as high-rise apartment buildings replace the traditional Chinese urban residential geography of courtyards and lanes in cities across China. A controversial but popular play, *Public Toilet*, opened in 2004. This play centers on a public toilet in an old Beijing neighborhood. The characters' relationships interweave and unfold over a period of three decades from the early 1970s, when Nixon first visited China, into the late 1990s. In the first scene, set in the in the 1970s, the public toilet is a simple brick and cement building, not unlike Daguan's outhouse-style toilet as seen in our original video. People engaged in lively interactions with one another as they used the toilet with no regard for privacy. In the second scene, set in the 1980s, the old brick latrine has been covered with white tiles, the toilets divided by boards, and the public toilet has become a pay-per-use facility. In the third scene, set in the late 1990s, the old structure has been torn down and rebuilt as a Western-style toilet facility with a "5 star rating." Patrons sit alone on toilet seats in stalls behind locked doors. The public toilet is no longer a communal site. The play ends with the characters quoting a saying found in an ancient Roman bathhouse: "People that go to the toilet in a group have great solidarity." They then add a line that reflects modern life in Beijing: "People who go to the toilet privately are a civilized people."

At Daguan, the toilets are becoming gradually more private, but there is

2.8. Toilet at Daguan, 1985 and 2002.

still a feeling of community. The boys and girls have been segregated, but on both sides of the dividing wall there is lively talk, laughter, and games. With no teachers present, toilet time becomes free-play time for the children (figure 2.8). When we asked the Daguan teachers if they considered the children's liveliness in the toilet area to be a problem Dong laoshi replied, "No. Children have a chance to express themselves and show their personal characteristics. It is very positive." Zhang laoshi added:

> This video clip has truly captured the behavior of the children, and their lovely, unadulterated childish moments. The children seem to enjoy interacting with one another while visiting the toilet, just as adults do when they have some leisure time. In the 1980s, our thinking was old and stale. We emphasized order and tidiness. And children were not as lively as they are today. In the old days, when the teacher asked children to squat and be quiet, they would do it. Now, it is impossible to ask children not to talk while doing anything.

Then as now the trough and the practice of having whole-class visits to the toilet reflect culture and social values. Many people in China still prefer squatting to sitting in public toilets on hygienic grounds. For us, the more significant cultural practice in Daguan's toilet routine is not the squatting but the communalism. Privacy, in the toilet as well as in other contexts, is rapidly gaining strength as a value in China. With growing privacy comes a loss of the communalism of the traditional Chinese public toilet, where the shared experience of bodily processes worked to create connections between people from different backgrounds and circumstances. The Chinese public toilet long functioned, like the marketplace and the carnival as described by Mikhail Bakhtin (1941/1984) in *Rabelais and His World*, as a site where the individuality that divides people is replaced, if only temporarily, by a sense of fusion. Squatting together to eliminate and talk is an experience that is enjoyable for young children, as it once was as well for adults. But growing up in a modern, bourgeois society means losing touch with such pleasures.

As recently as 1996, "the long trough" was stated in government policy documents as the most desirable form of toilets for preschools. When Daguan built their new building in 1998, they put in long troughs with flush plumbing and a divider separating the girls and boys, which at the time seemed to them to be state-of-the art. But things change quickly in China. When we returned to Daguan in 2004, Director Shi told us that they were planning to remodel the toilets:

> We began to reexamine this issue in 2003, soon after you shot the new video in our preschool and showed us our old video. It was after viewing and discussing the videos of Daguan You'eryuan from both the old and the recent study that we felt the need to change and to remodel the toilets for children. China's open-door policy led in the 1990s in Kunming to the construction of new hotels that introduced the custom of toilet seats and urinals. But until your visit it did not occur to us that these facilities could be combined with our determination to make children's lives easier in preschool. Compared to the old toilets in the Dong-feng video, the current toilet setup is a great improvement. It is adjacent to the classroom, has running water, and it's fully tiled. But now we must redesign the toilets from the children's points of view, from their needs, and from a humanistic perspective. After reading the original book and watching the videos you made, past and present, we became resolved to change because our current toilet design does not embody our understanding of how to respect children, protect their privacy, and provide a sense of sex difference, in short, of how to provide a more humanistic education.

These comments of Director Shi made us uneasy. Although we were fully aware that participating in our research would give all of the preschools in the study opportunities to learn about each other and about themselves and to reflect on processes of change, we did not expect our research to influence Daguan in such a direct way. We are not entirely comfortable with the thought that we led the staff at Daguan to rethink their toilets. But we are not so grandiose as to believe that our influence has been all that profound or decisive. The changes Daguan is considering making to its toilets are going on across preschools in China. We would argue that at most our study may have accelerated the rate of change, but not given the impetus or the direction to a process that is national and that seems to be inexorable. That having been said, we speculate that the next versions of toilets Daguan and other Chinese preschools will build will not look like those found in preschools in the US but will instead be hybrid structures that mix Western and Japanese models with what one Chinese teacher described to us as "the unique cultural characteristics of the Chinese toilet."

What is clear to us is that the traditional Chinese practice of the toilet serving as a common ground for communal life is giving way to an understanding of the toilet as a site of privacy and separation from society. Ms. Yang Qing, a Beijing municipal district preschool researcher who earned a master's degree in early childhood education in Japan, told us that it would be a pity to see the long trough disappear from preschools. She recalled the time a few years back when she led a group of Japanese preschool directors on a visit to Beijing preschools. One Japanese director was very excited to see the long trough in a preschool toilet. He asked a colleague to take a picture of himself squatting over it. He told Ms. Yang that the picture would document a disappearing cultural artifact and in this way help to preserve a cultural memory. He told her that although in contemporary Japan men and women sometimes can still mingle in a bath at a hot springs resort, toilet visits have became an entirely private matter. The Chinese public toilet seems to be going the way of the Japanese and Chinese public baths. China's striving to jump into late modernity and to participate successfully in global capitalism is accompanied by a process of bourgeoisification that is manifested in changing notions of self, privacy, space, property, propriety, and the body. The disappearance of the non-partitioned public toilet, in preschools and other settings, is both a cause and an effect of this process.

EXERCISE

Every morning at Daguan, as at almost every preschool in China, children gather in the courtyard for *guangbo ticao* (literally, "broadcast physical exercise," or group calisthenics). As shown in our video, the children exercise accompanied by music and instructions coming from a loudspeaker. The children, standing in long lines, face their teachers, who model the movements (figure 2.9). The entering group of three-year-old children is taught a simpler version of these exercises at the beginning of each school year.

When we asked about the purpose of the group exercise, Dong laoshi explained that, "This is an important daily event that induces a sense of pride in being part of the group. We adults, too, do this kind of group exercise every day." Indeed, group exercise activities are a characteristic sight

2.9. Zhong laoshi leads exercise.

in parks and other public spaces across China. In their 2005 study on "biopolitical Beijing," Farquhar and Zhang locate calisthenics within the larger category of *yangsheng*, which they translate as "the arts of life cultivation." Other forms of *yangsheng* include *taiji*, *qigong* ("breath work"), dance, playing music, calligraphy, writing poetry, and flying kites. As Farquhar and Zhang write:

> Some common *yangsheng* images from modern China have circulated in the global media from the 1970s to the present: there have been lots of pictures of Chinese urbanites exercising in the early morning light of parks and other public places; in the late Maoist period of the 1970s, there were group calisthenics accompanied by patriotic music and loud instructions blaring from scratchy loud-speakers; in the reform period, there were pictures of *taiji* and *qigong* practitioners moving gracefully under the trees in parks. (306)

The group calisthenics conducted every morning in the courtyard of Daguan and every other preschool in China is just one manifestation of this ubiquitous cultural practice. Farquhar and Zhang argue that calisthenics and other forms of *yangsheng* reflect a view of the body as collective and as improved by discipline. Drawing on and at the same time arguing with the implicit Eurocentrism of Foucault's writings on how disciplinary power works to produce docile (that is, compliant) bodies, Farquhar and Zhang argue that in China participating in group exercises following instructions from a loudspeaker does not carry the feeling of knuckling under to authoritarian control it carries in the United States because Chinese conceptions of the nation lack the binary opposition of "the government" and "the people" that lies at the core of American notions of individualism and democracy. In their discussion of "taking comfort in conformity," Farquhar and Zhange write:

Yangsheng practices are one of the joys of dwelling in the mainstream. For many settled urbanites in China, the chief pleasures in life have to do with conformity, obedience, regularity, the predictable comforts of home, the intimate joys and challenges of family and neighborhood, and even the patriotic glow arising from the practice of good citizenship. . . . This notion of the mainstream (*zhuliu*, or in Beijing slang, *sui daliu*), often used in conversation and the media, makes no deep divide between the state and the people, or between individual and society. In relation to both a Chinese cultural tradition of sociality and to the recent history of state penetration of everyday life in the PRC, this should not be surprising. . . . In China, "government" and "people" are not generally experienced as two different modes of being. (2005, 6)

Following this logic, to participate in group exercise, as to visit the toilet or block room as a group, is not to be governed by above or to have one's individual desires ignored, but instead to participate in the pleasure of merging one's desires with the desires of the group and the satisfaction of being a member in good standing of the body politic.

Wondering if there is a necessary tension between the collectivist values that underlie group exercise and the focus on individualism and choice that underlies the new early childhood education paradigm, we asked the teachers at Daguan if they thought group exercise and other whole-group activities would eventually disappear. The teachers responded that they were sure group exercises would continue. As Dong laoshi commented, "Yes, we are promoting individuality, but at the same time we still believe that a sense of collectivism needs to be instilled in children. So group activities, including group exercise, will continue."

CAUGHT BETWEEN PARADIGMS

Some of the teachers and directors from other preschools who viewed the Daguan video expressed envy, pointing out that the presence of the gym, the block room, and the music room is evidence that Daguan has been exceptionally well provided for by the Yunnan provincial government. But these expressions of envy sometimes were mixed with critique. A director of a *you'eryuan* in Hubei commented that the block play scene in the Daguan video shows that "Daguan's hardware development is ahead of the software," a situation that she described as not uncommon for preschools in contemporary China during an era of such rapid change. A teacher in Hubei commented, "Daguan's facilities are by all means advanced, consistent with our current understanding of what a preschool should have. We believe that excellent hardware like theirs is indispensable. But that is not the sole factor for determining whether it is an advanced preschool. The key factor is the change of educational ideas."

Many Chinese early childhood educators who watched the new Daguan video praised the teachers for joining in the block play. But some suggested that the teachers did not understand how best to facilitate children's play. As one teacher in Shanghai suggested, "Rather than playing with the children, like a child, the teacher should scaffold the children's play, introducing greater complexity to the activity."

These comments suggest that at the time we were conducting our fieldwork in China (2002–2005), Daguan, like many Chinese preschools, and indeed like Chinese society as a whole, was in the midst of a paradigm change. As we were conducting the research, we had the feeling that we were catching Daguan, to borrow a concept from Piaget, in a moment of *decalage*, a moment of growth and change in which competency varies across domains and in which the old equilibrium has become destabilized but a new equilibrium has not yet been established. Or, to employ another metaphor, it is as if in our new research we encountered early childhood education at Daguan, and in China in general, in its adolescence, having just enjoyed a physical growth spurt (which Chinese tend to describe as the acquisition of new hardware) with which it was still struggling to catch up cognitively and emotionally (in terms of software). As Director Shi explained to us, "We know where we would like to go, but we are struggling to figure out how to get there."

Or to introduce yet another metaphor, it is as if Chinese early childhood educators see themselves as in the midst of a journey of reform. They know where they have been and they have a clear sense of where they are headed, but they also know that it will take effort to get there and that there are obstacles to negotiate and wrong turns to avoid along the way. On this road, Daguan is ahead of some Chinese preschools but behind others. To better locate Daguan in the larger context of change in early childhood educational change in China, we turn now to a second preschool, one that is in a more economically advanced and globalized city and one that is considered among the more progressive preschools in the country.

A Day at Sinanlu You'eryuan

Sinanlu You'eryuan is located in the heart of Shanghai near the bustling business district of Nanjing Road and Huaihai Road. It is one of seventeen

2.10. Director Guo and nurse greet arriving children and parents.

public preschools operated by the Luwan District of Shanghai. Sinanlu had two campuses in 2002; a third was added in 2007. We shot our video on the south campus, which is surrounded by a *xiaoqu*, a residential community that the city developed over a decade ago. The south campus serves 150 children three to five years of age in six classes. Most live nearby, but about one-fifth of the children come from outside the *xiaoqu*.

At 8 o'clock on a Wednesday morning in the spring of 2002, Cheng Jingxiu and Wang Jian, the two teachers of the four-year-old class, discuss plans for the day and begin to prepare the room for the children's arrival. Jin-*ayi* (Aunt Jin), the *baoyuyuan* (caregiver) who assists the two teachers, mops the floor, wipes the tables, and cleans the windows. At 8:30, children and their parents who come to school walking or by bicycle, motorcycle, car, and bus start to arrive. After passing through the medical checkpoint (figure 2.10), and waving good-bye to their parents, children hop and skip to the classroom. Teachers and children exchange morning greetings. Some children go to the dining area adjoining the classrooms to have breakfast, which is an optional meal at Sinanlu You'eryuan. A few minutes before 9 a.m., the school bus arrives, bringing children from outside the *xiaoqu*. As children enter the classroom they sign in by placing their name cards on a tray bearing an image, drawn by a child, of their teacher. Sitting on the floor, Zouzou organizes red and yellow plastic chips on a grid. Cheng laoshi joins him in finding a new way to arrange the chips in an untried pattern.

At 9:30 a.m., Wang laoshi turns on the music to indicate that it is cleanup time. The children quickly put away what they have been playing with and gather as a group in front of Cheng laoshi. Several children volunteer to demonstrate what they have learned or made during the free play. Zouzou shows the color patterns he arranged on the grid. Cheng laoshi comments, approvingly, to the class that Zouzou's newest arrangement is the fifth type of pattern created since the class began this pattern activity. Zouzou uses red and blue markers to record his pattern on a piece of paper for the class's future reference. The children then break into two groups, each group following a teacher to outdoor play, one group going to the playground area in the back of the school with Wang laoshi and the other group following Cheng laoshi up the staircase to the rooftop playground. The preschool building is three stories tall, surrounded and dwarfed by residential high rises. The rooftop playground is shielded on all sides by a high wall. The children play ball, skip rope, play hopscotch, and practice balancing on large blocks. Cheng laoshi approaches two boys, Ziyu and Yi, who are squabbling.

> CHENG LAOSHI: Ziyu, he really wants to play with you. How come you don't want to play with him?
> ZIYU: He kept snatching my basketball and he laughed at me when I fell down.
> YI: I didn't laugh at him. When did I laugh at him?
> CHENG LAOSHI (TO ZIYU): He didn't. He didn't laugh at you when you fell down.
> ZIYU: But my head remembers him laughing.
> CHENG LAOSHI: Then you can forget about it now, can't you? After you forget about it, things will feel all right. If you haven't yet forgotten, just wait a little while. (Turning to Yi) Can you play with me for a while? Let's see if you can steal the ball from me while I am dribbling it.

A minute or so later, Cheng laoshi asks Yi to invite Ziyu to dribble the ball with him. The two boys then start to play and talk, their disagreement, apparently, forgotten.

The children return to the classroom hot and sweaty from their exertion. Each picks up a warm wet towel and hands it to their teacher, who wipes the children's backs under their shirts. The children then gather in a half circle on the floor in front of Cheng laoshi, who tells them it's time to work on their gardening activity. A few weeks earlier the children brought from home seeds of various vegetables that they then planted in jars and small pots. Some of these seeds have sprouted and some have not. Those without seedlings to transplant stay inside with Cheng laoshi to sew seeds in jars. Those whose seeds have sprouted follow Wang laoshi outside to plant them in the small garden in the back of the school building, an area the children call "the big field." The doorman, who is also the preschool's gardener, joins the children in helping to pull up garlic shoots and scal-

2.11. Ziyu records what he planted.

lions. Some children wash this produce in a basin while others transplant their seedlings into the ground. Children's hands and feet soon are covered with dirt and mud. Taoran, who usually plays alone and shuns group activities, shows enthusiasm in pulling up the scallions and washing them. Back inside the classroom the children write or draw on recording sheets posted on the wall what they have done in the garden. Ziyu, not knowing how to write the characters for okra, looks at an example on the wall and copies it (figure 2.11).

It is time now for morning exercise. Holding hands in pairs, the children march out of the gate into the large garden across the street, in the residential housing complex. In front of a gathering group of grandparents and babysitters with infants from the neighborhood, the children go through a set of calisthenics and some dances to musical accompaniment from a portable CD player music and then head back to the classroom.

Back inside their classroom, the children gather in front of Cheng laoshi to talk about their gardening experiences. Ziyu reports that he washed scallions with Ziruo. Other children talk about their transplanting. Cheng laoshi makes special mention of Taoran, and asks the class to applaud him for his exceptional effort.

It is time to get ready for lunch. The children go to use the toilet, which has one long trough divided with partitions that provide three semiprivate personal spaces for squatting. On the boy's side there is also a urinal. Next door to the classroom in the dining room Jin-ayi, the caregiver, has set the tables. Wang laoshi and Jin-ayi serve buns and sautéed shrimp and cabbage soup to the children, who are seated at tables. Children who have finished eating put their bowls and plates in a bucket and pick up a wet towel from another bucket to wipe their face (figure 2.12).

After fifteen minutes of outside play, the children return to the classroom, where they again gather on the floor in a semicircle. With Ziyu

2.12. Girl eating lunch.

standing next to her, Wang laoshi asks the whole group, "What story is Ziyu going to tell us?" (figure 2.13). "Gudong," the children respond, in unison. Ziyu steadies himself and announces:

> I am going to tell you a story called "Gudong." One day an owl heard a strange noise in the pond, "Gudong," that scared him. He went to tell others. Those who went to investigate thought that there was a monster in the pond. In the end, a lion went to the pond to check only to discover that a ripe papaya falling from a nearby tree was the source of the noise. Everyone was relieved.

Ziyu finishes the story with a short bow and a "Thank you, everyone" and takes a seat on the floor with his classmates. The children start discussing the story they have heard. Wang laoshi draws the group's attention to one child's comment:

WANG LAOSHI: Yunqi said that his story was the same as that in the recording we heard before.
SEVERAL CHILDREN: No. It was not the same.
WANG LAOSHI: What was the owl doing in the story?
SEVERAL CHILDREN: It was capturing mice.
WANG LAOSHI: Ziyu used a word that sounded very nice. Did you notice? He mentioned that it turned out to be what kind of papaya that fell into the pond?
SEVERAL CHILDREN, TOGETHER: A *wooden* papaya.
WANG LAOSHI: What kind of wooden papaya?
ZIYU: I didn't say "wooden."
WANG LAOSHI: Not "wooden." What was it?
ZIYU: Ripe.
WANG LAOSHI: Right, he said there was a *ripe* papaya.

2.13. 1. Ziyu begins his story.

2. The story continues.

3. Counting the votes.

4. Asking for criticisms.

5. Receiving critique.

6. The Story Telling King.

Wang laoshi then asks the group: "Can we name him Story Telling King?" Voices call out in response, some saying "Yes," others "No."

WANG LAOSHI: Well, I would like to ask those little friends who say "Yes" to raise their hands. We will see how many of you say "Yes." How many agree that he will be named the Story Telling King? (Turning to Ziyu) Why don't you count the votes?

(Ziyu counts the hands and reports that there are eighteen children who have agreed).

WANG LAOSHI: Eighteen! Isn't that a big number of votes?

With eighteen of twenty-four children voting "Yes," Ziyu, having won the honor of being named Story Telling King, writes his name on the red Story Telling King poster, which already has many children's names on it.

WANG LAOSHI: Good. He can be Story Telling King today. But a number of little friends did not raise their hands for him. Let's hear what they have to say, Okay?
ONE BOY: In his sentences, some words were clear and some were not clear.
ANOTHER BOY: I have trouble hearing him.
WANG LAOSHI: Ziyu can be King of Story Tellers. (Turning to Ziyu) But next time when you tell another story, you need to be louder and clearer. Now, it is your turn to invite a storyteller for tomorrow.
ZIYU: I want to invite Yunqi to tell a story tomorrow.
WANG LAOSHI: Yunqi, would you have a story to tell? Yes? (The girl nods her head).

Cheng laoshi leads the children to the bedroom that this group shares with a younger group, who are already in bed asleep. The older children quietly remove their outer clothes, climb into bed, and tuck themselves under their comforters. The children nap for about two hours, a period when the teachers sit together to prepare teaching materials. Meanwhile, in the kitchen, a cook is pouring the broad beans the children picked in the morning into a soup.

At 2:30 p.m., the children return to their classroom. The teachers comb the girls' hair and help children who need assistance pull on their shirts and sweaters. Children are fascinated with snails they captured in the morning during the gardening activity. Wang laoshi moves from one child to the other, asking questions about the snails. When a boy holds up his hand to show a snail, she suggests, "If you put the snail on the back of your hand, will it fall off? Give it a try." To another child, she asks, "Why do you think that snail leaves a shiny line on your hand?"

At the snack time that follows Jin-ayi serves the children portions of broad bean soup. As the children finish the soup they head back to the classroom, where they move furniture around and take toys and props off of the shelves to construct areas they set up as a supermarket, a kitchen, a school, a

2.14. Wang laoshi at the beauty parlor.

McDonald's, a beauty parlor and a hospital. Wang laoshi first sits down in the beauty parlor to get her hair done (figure 2.14). She then moves over to the hospital, putting on a facial expression of intense suffering and holding her belly. Ziyu, wearing a surgical cap, mask, and stethoscope, and holding a plastic scalpel, asks whether she has a fever and proceeds to take her temperature.

WANG LAOSHI: What is my temperature?
DR. ZIYU: Eighty degrees [Celsius; equivalent to 176°F].
WANG LAOSHI: Eighty degrees? That is really high! This fever is burning me to death! I can't stand it any more. The pain is killing me.

The doctors and nurses all agree that she needs an operation. As Wang laoshi lies down on the rug in a corner of the hospital, the children, holding thermometers, stethoscopes, and oxygen masks, surround her. When the surgery is completed, Wang laoshi sits up:

WANG LAOSHI: Is everything all right?
ZIYU (STILL HOLDING THE SCALPEL): You will feel better in an hour.
WANG LAOSHI: What happened inside me?
ZIYU: There were worms.
WANG LAOSHI: Really?
ZIYU: Indeed.
WANG LAOSHI: Did you take them out?
ZIYU: Yes. We took them all out.
WANG LAOSHI: How many worms were there?
ZIYU: One hundred.

Hearing this response, Wang laoshi falls back in a faint.
Meanwhile across the room, two boys wearing police caps and carrying

2.15. The police take a call.

toy guns are suddenly called to the supermarket by Yunqi, who tells them that there has been a civil dispute (figure 2.15). The policemen put their guns under the belt and go to investigate.

At the McDonald's, Wang laoshi comes to get a meal. She orders a hamburger, french fries, and a pineapple pie and asks, "How much is it?" "One yuan," replies the boy behind the counter. "One yuan? I don't have any money with me. What can I do?" The boy suggests that she bring money next time. Wang laoshi sits down at a table to eat her meal with other customers. Bao runs over to inform her that Ziruo is crying in the beauty parlor. Wang laoshi replies: "Really? Why is she crying?" and then returns to her eating and chatting.

In the beauty parlor, a policeman has come to investigate why Ziruo is crying. Bao explains that Ziruo wanted to use the comb, but Zouzou, the self-designated hairdresser, would not give it to her and their verbal disagreement then became a physical struggle between the two beauticians. As the second policeman arrives on the scene, Ziruo complains to them: "I want to be a hairdresser, but he refuses to let me have the comb." The first policeman tells Zouzou: "Now, give her the comb!" The hairstylist refuses: "Why? Doing hair is my job." The policeman replies: "We will arrest you if you do not give her the comb." Zouzou offers the comb to Ziruo who, wiping back tears, accepts it, and the business in the beauty parlor returns to normal. The policemen, job accomplished, compare guns (figure 2.16).

After cleanup time, the whole class gathers in a semicircle on the floor. Cheng laoshi starts the discussion by asking, "How did we play today?"

ZIRUO: I wanted to be the hairdresser once, but Zouzou didn't let me and he pulled on my hand and hurt me.

2.16. 1. Bao reports the dispute.

2. The police arrive.

3. Zirou makes her complaint.

4. Zhouzho defends himself.

5. Back to work.

6. Comparing guns.

CHENG LAOSHI: So, there was a conflict in the beauty parlor. Did you ask him why he didn't want to give you the comb?

ZIRUO: He said that I shouldn't comb.

CHENG LAOSHI (TO ZOUZOU): Why didn't you let her have the comb?

ZOUZOU: I said only one other person could comb, not her.

ONE OF THE POLICEMEN: I spoke with him but still he didn't give the comb to her.

CHENG LAOSHI: I see, the police came to investigate the case.

ZOUZOU: Later, I did give the comb to her.

CHENG LAOSHI: So you did, didn't you? Why?

THE SECOND POLICEMAN: He was afraid of being arrested.

CHENG LAOSHI: He was afraid of being arrested? You decided to arrest him just because he did not give her the comb?

A group discussion continues, reporting other conflicts. One child mentions that the manager of the supermarket stole money from the hospital. One of the policemen comments, "He did not steal the money. I took the money from him." Another child reports, "When I went grocery shopping, I saw the manager returning the money." "So the money was returned? There was a mistake after all," Cheng laoshi, summarizes, ending the conversation. It is now 4:30, and parents and grandparents are waiting outside the classroom door. Children put away their mats and run out to be picked up. Many walk home; many others who live in the surrounding neighborhood linger in the residential garden and play in groups, and still others board the shuttle bus that heads off into the busy streets of Shanghai.

From Direct Instruction to Child-Initiated Activities

In 2001 the national Ministry of Education published *Guidelines for Kindergarten Education — Trial Version*. A cycle of curricular reform of early childhood education had begun years earlier but the publication of the *Guidelines* marked the official launch of the new educational paradigm as national policy. In 2000 the city of Shanghai released its own new guidelines for early childhood education, a document that while consistent with the national guidelines goes further in its calls for a new direction and in its greater specificity about how to implement change. The emphasis we see in the Sinanlu video on child-initiated activities and the de-emphasis on direct instruction reflects the direction laid out in both the national and Shanghai reform documents. The key terms of this new direction, as summarized in a review by Liu Yan and Feng Xiaoxia, are "respecting children," "active learning," "teaching for individual learning needs," "play-based teaching and learning," and "teaching and learning through daily life" (2005, 93–94). This new direction can be seen clearly in the reflections of Chinese educators on two scenes in the Sinanlu video: storytelling and sociodramatic play.

Cheng laoshi explained to us the origins of the Story Telling King activity: "At first, children just wanted to listen to a story that the teacher would tell. Later, a couple of children who were interested in telling stories asked if they could come to the front to tell a story. We encouraged them to give it a try. Soon, many children began to prepare their own stories and asked for turns." Wang laoshi continued: "After the first semester, when so many children wanted to tell a story in front of the group, they got into a discussion among themselves about how to organize the event. They reached agreement that whoever was the story person of the day could choose the story person for the next day. There was a suggestion that the choice should be made by the teachers, but most of the children disagreed."

Familiar with sharing time activities in the US and Japan and believing that preschoolers tend to be egocentric in their talking and listening, we were impressed that these four-year-olds could tell a complete story in front of the group, listen patiently to critiques, and offer meaningful comments on other children's stories. The teachers emphasized that these abilities emerged bit by bit as the Story Telling King activity evolved. Cheng laoshi explained:

> We couldn't have done this when the children were younger than four years old, when their language development did not allow them to tell a complete story, nor could they listen carefully to a story for information. The important thing at the beginning was for them to have the courage to get up in front of the group to tell a story. We encouraged them not to be afraid.

Director Guo emphasized to us that the Story Telling King activity is a good example of how a traditional preschool activity such as storytelling can be transformed from being teacher-directed to child-initiated:

> Storytelling is a time-honored preschool activity. In the past, teachers told or read stories and the children just listened. When we decided to change this to let children be the storytellers, we struggled with how to get children to listen. Each child believes his own story is interesting but most children aren't interested in other children's stories. At first, the teachers tried to encourage listening by asking the storytellers questions. But they were asking too many questions and doing too much of the talking. Eventually, the children became the ones who asked the questions of each other.

Chinese early childhood educators who watched the Sinanlu video generally praised the Story Telling King activity. Professor Zhu Jiaxiong of East China Normal University emphasized the virtues of the activity's curriculum integration:

> Traditionally, preschool teachers would design subject-based educational activities for learning mathematics, literacy, drawing, social events, or nature, one at a time. How would you categorize the Story Telling King as a learning activity? This spontaneous activity integrates many important social and academic skills, such as interacting within the group, making rules, voting, practicing democracy, listening, thinking reflectively, learning mathematics, and improving language skills.

Many Chinese educators were impressed with how this activity promoted democratic principles. As one teacher commented: "The socialization of peer interaction here comes through listening to each other's stories. The teacher respects the children's perspectives and practices democracy. At the same time, the children can learn to make rules, observe the workings of a majority vote, relate their own opinions to the group decision, and argue for fairness." The activity was also praised for embodying the reform's key principle of "respect for children." As a director of a *you'eryuan* in Kunming observed, "When the teacher asks, 'What is your reason for not granting him the title of Story Telling King?' she not only shows respect for children, but also fosters children's thinking."

The feature of the Story Telling King activity that produced the most discussion among early childhood educators in the US and Japan was not the focus on democratic values, curriculum integration, or child initiation—it was the encouragement of criticism. In US early childhood education, critiquing a peer's storytelling is generally not considered appropriate (Katz 1993; Newkirk 1992; Tobin 1995). In Japan, children are encouraged by their teachers to be self-critical, but generally not to critique one another. Many Japanese viewers said the Story Telling King activity, while impressive, made them a bit uncomfortable because the focus on critiquing a classmate's performance felt a little harsh. The director of a Kyoto preschool commented, "I think you could have seen this sort of thing a long time ago in Japan, but we've changed. They emphasize the mind over the heart, but we, at least in my preschool, focus on supporting the development of the heart (*kokoro*). Their feedback focuses on negative things, whereas we would emphasize the positive. I don't think it is good for children." Several Japanese informants drew a distinction between the

Japanese primary school practice of *hanseikai* (small group self-reflection meetings) and the critiques in the Story Telling King activity. A Japanese professor of education explained, "In this Chinese video we see children criticizing a classmate, under the direction of the teacher. In Japanese *hanseikai*, a small group of children, ideally with little or no direction from their teacher, criticize not a classmate but themselves and they reflect on the shortcomings of their collective rather than individual efforts."

Concern about the fragility of young children's self-esteem was cited by most of our US informants as the main reason they were surprised and, in some cases, disturbed by the critique portion of the Story Telling King activity at Sinanlu, as in this discussion among preschool teachers in Phoenix:

PAM: I find it a little strange to put children in a situation where they are openly critical of other children. That's not something we would do here.

BARB: When some of them did vote no, they had good reasons. I liked that. You can say "No," but you also have to say why you said "No."

HSUEH: Can you see encouraging more critical feedback in your classrooms?

BARB: Sure.

PAM: No.

JILL: Maybe in a small group.

COREY: We're more fearful of damaging children's self-esteem.

BECKY: I'm not sure how I feel about putting individual children "on the spot" as in the Story Telling King. What does it do to a child's self esteem to be told by his peers, in front of everyone, that he is not a good storyteller?

BARB: What would it do to my self-esteem! I'm forty-five years old and I would start crying if my storytelling got voted down. But maybe that's because I didn't have the chance these Chinese kids do to give and get critical feedback while they're young. If we don't give our kids a chance to learn this when they are young, no wonder we can't handle criticism as adults.

When we asked the teachers at Sinanlu if they were concerned about the potential of the Story Telling King activity to produce hurt feelings, Wang laoshi replied: "If the teacher tells them what they did is not good enough some children may feel hurt. However, if the criticism comes from their peers, the children seem to find it easier to take it, and aren't nearly as likely to feel hurt." Cheng laoshi added: "Children's critical remarks generally reflect a typically child's way of thinking, while the critical evaluations of adults tend to reflect an adult point of view."

The Story Telling King activity suggests that even though Sinanlu and other Chinese preschools have been drawing heavily in recent years on ideas from abroad, the new approaches to early childhood education that are emerging at Sinanlu and other progressive Chinese preschools retain a characteristically Chinese inflection. The Story Telling King activity is a perfect example of the emerging hybridity of Chinese educational practice (Zhu & Zhang 2008, 176), as it combines progressive beliefs in child-initiated curricula, a Deweyian notion of the democratic classroom, self-expression, and content-area integration with Chinese traditions of verbal performance and mastery and a belief that is both traditional and Chinese socialist in the pedagogical value of constructive criticism.

Straightforward criticism has long been a common feature of Chinese daily life, not only in the first thirty years of the People's Republic, when the Cultural Revolution and other social movements required people to be self-critical as well as critical of others, but also in the pre-revolutionary periods, when Confucianism encouraged criticism as a means towards cultivating learning and promoting social values. As a familiar component of Chinese everyday life in families, neighborhoods, schools, business dealings and social life, criticizing others does not carry as harsh a feel in China as it does in the US, Japan, and many other cultures. Constructive feedback from both experts and peers can be found in Chinese education not just in the early childhood classroom, but also in the preparation and ongoing professional development of teachers (see, for example, Paine & Fang 2007). Lynn Paine's description of a veteran teacher and a group of seminar students giving feedback to a student teacher on a trial lesson is strikingly similar to the Story Telling King activity:

> In deference to his expertise, the group automatically waited for the veteran teacher to lead with his evaluation. His comments pertained to the technical aspects of her performance — her audio-visual materials (a poster) needed correction, her timing required work, and she needed to change her body movements. Once he was through, the student teacher's classmates joined in, criticizing problems and suggesting alternative strategies. It was very much the mood of a postperformance critique of an athletic or musical event. The student teacher voiced her concerns about presenting the material and the session eventually became an open discussion centered around improving the next performance. (1990, 61)

Our fieldwork across China offered us opportunities to observe teachers engaged in such reciprocal critique and discussions in groups, which they call *qiecuo* (learning from each other by exchanging ideas). The Story Telling King activity differs from the teacher preparation session described by Paine only in emphasizing peer over expert (teacher) critical feedback. In both activities we find a belief not just in the value of constructively giving and humbly accepting critical feedback but also in the value of oral performance, "virtuosity" (Paine 1990), and of learning as a process of "self-perfection" (Li 2003, 147). Both the critical feedback and the pursuit of virtuosity seen in this activity are examples of what we are calling culturally implicit practices and of what Jerome Bruner (1990; 1996) calls "folk pedagogy," in that although these practices are not encouraged or even mentioned in the new curriculum guidelines, they are common features of contemporary Chinese early childhood educational practice that survive from one social upheaval and pedagogical paradigm shift to the next and which Chinese teachers feel no need to explain, justify, or reflect on until they are prompted to do by outsiders.

SOCIODRAMATIC PLAY

According to teachers Cheng and Wang, the genesis of the sociodramatic play activity we videotaped in their classroom was similar to the history of the Story Telling King, as both were emergent co-constructions of the children and the teachers. As Cheng laoshi explained:

> All the social settings you see in the room during sociodramatic play were of the children's own invention. They began by playing family, with mommy, daddy, baby, and cooking for the family. Eventually, some children, in their roles as parents, wanted to take their babies to see a doctor, to shop for groceries, or to get a haircut. So children began to set up new social organizations. They brought from home shampoo bottles, lotion containers, McDonalds packages, and other real life objects to use in their play.

When we asked the teachers to explain more about their role in the development of the dramatic play from playing house to creating a whole mini-society, the two teachers reflected:

> CHENG LAOSHI: When the children ran into problems in the new settings they created they would turn to us for solutions. We listened carefully

to understand their concerns and we found that the issues the children brought up could be woven back into their play to enrich the complexity. So we decided to join the children in their play, and in the process we found ways to introduce new problems for them to work out.

WANG LAOSHI: At the moment we become playmates with the children, we stop being teachers. When they invite us to their "home" or "store," we are just guests or customers. As guests or as customers, we act like children would in the play, and do not provide adult guidance.

CHENG LAOSHI: Imagine if after the policemen had facilitated the dispute in the beauty salon, we teachers stepped in anyway, as teachers. The effect would be unhelpful and the social play less satisfactory.

The key here is the Sinanlu You'eryuan teachers' artful and unobtrusive scaffolding of child-initiated activities. We can usefully contrast this approach with the strategic non-intervention in interactions among children we found at Komatsudani Hoikuen in Japan both in 1985 and again in our new study. Most Chinese educators who watched our old and new Komatsudani videos were critical of the Japanese teachers' non-intervention in children's disputes, some seeing this (non)action by the teachers not just as a dereliction of duty but even as a precursor to what they see as Japan's aggressive national character. And yet, while critical of the Japanese teachers, many of the Chinese educators we interviewed in the new study said that they value the concept of teachers giving children latitude to work out their own solutions to problems, both cognitive and social. Most Chinese educators favor not so much a Japanese-style non-intervention as teacher scaffolding. We see examples of such scaffolding in Cheng laoshi's mediation of the dispute between the two boys on the roof during morning recess and in Wang laoshi's role-playing of a customer at McDonalds, where she introduces a new problem by telling the counter staff that she has no money to pay for her food. The teachers decide when their not getting involved can work to raise the level of complexity (as it did in the beauty salon situation, where their non-intervention created the opportunity for the beauticians and the police to work things out and the whole class later to debrief) versus in the hospital and McDonalds' situations where, by playing the roles of patients and customers and limiting their interventions to actions and statements children could plausibly offer (but didn't), the teachers raised the level of the interactions' social, emotional, and cognitive complexity. The Sinanlu teachers' approach here is consistent with John Dewey's call in *The School and Society* "To make each one of our schools an embryonic community life, active with types of occupations that reflect

2.17. Cheng laoshi asks the children to listen to
Zirou's account of the beauty parlor dispute as Bao,
Zhouzhou, and the policemen listen intently.

the life of the larger society" (Dewey 1889/1956, 29). Although only a few
of the Chinese teachers we interviewed about the Sinanlu video referred
explicitly to Dewey, many praised the sociodramatic play activity for giving the children the opportunity to develop an understanding of what it
means to live in society.

Many viewers of the Sinanlu video in the US and Japan as well as in
China were also impressed with the way Cheng laoshi led the children just
before they went home in a whole-class debriefing of the day and particularly of the sociodramatic play (figure 2.17). Cheng laoshi invited children
to report on what had happened and she also asked probing questions to
push them to reflect about the dispute in the beauty salon, the "misunder-
standing" about the money taken from the hospital, and more generally
on the role of the police in society. Having been impressed with this debriefing session, we were surprised to learn when we returned to Sinanlu
eighteen months after shooting the video that the classroom teachers were
now critical of this large-group activity:

CHENG LAOSHI: Over a year ago when you were here, we often had large-
group discussions of this sort. We now believe it is neither necessary nor
useful to hold a discussion like this after the children have already found
a solution to their problem.

WANG LAOSHI: The purpose of having a large-group discussion was to ensure that children would learn from their experiences and know what to
do next time. But as this situation in the beauty parlor only involved a few
children, other children might not be interested in the discussion.

CHENG LAOSHI: We regret that in those days we had too many large group
activities. They were not meaningful for children's personal learning.

WANG LAOSHI: Now that we see children more as individuals than as a group, we tend to think that only those who were involved in the incident might really want to have a discussion with the teacher. Of course, we keep weighing the value of having or not having such large-group activities.

CHENG LAOSHI: During this period of reform, we often feel ambivalent about many things we used to do for seemingly good reasons. It is particularly hard to decide if and when a large-group activity is appropriate. How should a teacher raise questions with children? How can a teacher accommodate children's own interests rather than pushing her own?

The teachers' reflections here are interesting on several levels: as an example of the value, as discussed earlier, placed on self-criticism of practice and on an iterative process of critique, reflection, and change; of the direction of change during this period focusing on continuously reducing the directive role of the teacher in favor of the self-initiated actions of children; and of a growing disdain for whole-class as opposed to small-group and individualized activities.

Group activities are a topic of heated debate among contemporary Chinese early childhood educators. The new national early childhood education guidelines encourage teachers to reduce large-group activities and create opportunities for more individualized instruction. As a preschool director told us, "Although large group activities are necessary, the high frequency of such activities affects the development of children's autonomy and self-expression." On the other hand, many Chinese early childhood educators, believing that the goal of reform should not be to mimic the preschool structures of the West, but instead to develop a "modern system with Chinese characteristics," argue that a large-group size is both appropriate and necessary in contemporary China. As a director of a *you'eryuan* in Chongqing explained to us,

In reexamining our long-time tradition of large-group activities, we are aware of the two sides of the coin. We are making every effort to cut down large-group activities. Whenever children can do something individually and whenever we can replace group activities with individual activities, we will not pass up that opportunity. On the other side, many of our teachers will inevitably find themselves having to take care of more than thirty children, a number that can be forty to fifty in rural areas, so large-group activities are sometimes necessary. Also, interacting with the same-age and mixed-age peers is a valuable experience for children. The Story Telling King is one good example; the group physical exercise is another.

Some Japanese and US teachers were bothered by the commercialism they saw in the inclusion of a McDonald's restaurant in the children's constructed community and of the McDonald's signage and french fry and drink containers the children used in their play. But teachers Cheng and Wang disagreed, telling us that they view the McDonald's paraphernalia and pretend play in McDonald's and other commercial settings as an opportunity for their students to engage with the reality of the rapidly changing world in which they live. The children's McDonald's, like their bank, hospital, and beauty parlor and their ever-ready-to-assist police force help to prepare children for joining the workforce (and consumer ranks) of their postindustrialized, commercialized society. Children use commercial setting and artifacts as tools to make sense of their changing world. When Wang laoshi said to the McDonald's worker "I don't have money with me—what can I do?" she used the McDonald's setting to pose a question that goes right to the heart of capitalism. The sociodramatic play in this way functions as a curricular exercise in the realities and ethics of capitalism, with the child's answer to this question becoming a rehearsal of the repertoire of skills, perspectives, and beliefs needed to function as a citizen in Shanghai's (and China's) new economy and new society.

Gun Play and Patriotism

Most American early childhood educators who watched the block play scene in the Daguan video and the sociodramatic play scene at Sinanlu commented on the pretend gunplay (figure 2.18). Many expressed surprise and, in some instances, criticism that the children at Daguan were not discouraged from making guns out of their blocks, that a teacher in the video engages in a mock gunfight with a group of children, and that the props available for the sociodramatic play at Sinanlu included toy guns. When we returned to Daguan to interview the teachers, we shared with them this American reaction to the video and asked them how they would explain to Americans why they do not prohibit pretend guns and gunplay. The teachers, puzzled by the question, responded that it had never occurred to them to ban pretend guns from the classroom, and they asked us to explain why teachers in the United States are so bothered by children engaging in dramatic play with toy guns. We explained that many American early childhood educators believe that there is a connection between children's play with toy guns and school shootings, as at Columbine, and more generally with gun-related violence in society; that they are concerned that pretend

2.18. Playing with block guns.

play with weapons and mock fighting can be scary to some children; that children who live in homes with firearms may mistake a real gun for a toy gun with potentially disastrous results; and that they want to discourage the notion that problems should be solved with weapons and violence. The teachers at Daguan and Sinanlu expressed surprise at these explanations and laughed at the irony that in the US real guns are readily available and toy guns are banned, while the opposite is the case in China. Yang laoshi responded: "Toy guns have never been an issue for us. We have them simply because our children enjoy playing with them. They are children's playthings and children who play with them do so because they are children. I also see a connection between their playing with guns and the general respect for soldiers in our country. These children see battle scenes on television that they then want to imitate. In general, we consider this play a positive thing." Dong laoshi added: "Our children admire the People's Liberation Army soldiers and police. Even some girls like to play with guns, and they ask their parents to get them pants that have a pocket that can hold a toy gun. No one worries about any violent behavior resulting from this play." Several teachers and the director at a *you'eryuan* in Chongqing who watched the Daguan video argued that allowing children to use toy guns in their dramatic play is a way of providing patriotic education, with the director commenting, "This kind of play encourages children to emulate those who defend and protect our country."

Communism and the Contemporary Early Childhood Education Curriculum

In our 1985 Daguan video there are several scenes of teachers leading children in singing, dancing, and playing games related to the People's

Liberation Army and patriotic slogans were displayed on posters on the classroom walls. When we made our new video at Daguan in 2002, we saw no such displays and we heard no singing of patriotic songs or telling of stories about revolutionary heroes. Furthermore, in our interviews with the teachers and directors, we heard no direct mentions of Marxism or of the thoughts of Mao Zedong. When we pointed out this observation to the teachers, they assured us that patriotic activities are still important to them. They told us that we did not see such activities during our visit because they are not taught every day, but they are still present in many lessons. At the same time, Dong laoshi told us, "We don't try to teach young children what is beyond their comprehension. For example, the picture of Chairman Mao is still a popular image, known as Grandpa Mao, that our children recognize; but Mao Zedong's thought is beyond them. In the past we promoted heroes in our teaching, like learning from Comrade Lei Feng; but we no longer give this kind of lesson high priority."

A professor of early childhood education told us that Daguan's approach to patriotism is typical, and that in today's China, "For three-year-olds, patriotic education means to sing the national anthem, to love our family members, and to love people around us. For five-year-olds, patriotic education means to love our hometown, and our country. Children are not interested in stories about revolutionary heroes." Yang laoshi pointed out that the recent preschool curriculum reform left little time or space for the direct teaching of patriotism and that the official teaching materials for preschool include only a few explicitly patriotic stories and lessons. The Daguan teachers emphasized that socialism and communism are left out of the daily education of preschool children because these topics are too abstract. When we asked the same question to the classroom teachers at Sinanlu, they paused for a moment before Wang laoshi replied, "If we are to do any patriotic education, we must concretize everything for the children." Cheng laoshi gave an example of this concretizing: "Patriotism? We don't use this word. But we do teach children that we are Chinese; we have Chinese traditional holidays like the Spring Festival, which we prioritize over Christmas."

The emphasis on concreteness over abstractness and on the practical over the ideological that the teachers at both Daguan and Sinanlu use to explain and justify their not including the thoughts of Chairman Mao, stories of heroes of the revolution, or direct discussion of socialism and communism in their curriculum mirrors the decline of explicit discussions of communism in the larger contemporary Chinese social and political discourse. The Chinese Communist Party itself has encouraged such a turning away from a focus on ideology and politics with the economic pragmatism introduced by Deng Xiaoping in the 1980s and the more recent emphases articulated by President Hu Jintao on "building a harmonious society" and on "scientific principles of development."

Given the shift of the Chinese Communist Party in recent years toward pragmatism and away from ideology it is not surprising that the preschool teachers and directors we interviewed found our questions about Mao and communism difficult to answer, not we think because our informants were afraid or embarrassed to tell us their true feelings but because for most of our informants the question no longer feels relevant or compelling. A graduate student in early childhood education in Shanghai explained the problem with our line of questioning by saying, "You and other Western scholars try to use ideological concepts such as 'communism' and 'socialism' in your analyses of Chinese educational and social change. But in our everyday lives, we Chinese people have less and less of a tendency nowadays to look at things and interpret them from an ideological or political perspective. Even Chinese Communist Party members and government officials nowadays try to shy away from talking about ideological issues."

A few of our informants were critical of this pragmatic turn of the Chinese Communist Party as, for example, a professor who answered our question about the effect of China's engagement with global capitalism on Chinese education and society by saying:

> The Chinese Communist Party claims that China is still in the initial stage of socialism. But in reality, it is in a primitive stage of capital accumulation. In this stage, many essential aspects of the Chinese society are totally capitalist. The Communist Party you see today has undergone a fundamental change. Many members of the Party today are outright capitalists.

However, not everyone we interviewed expressed disinterest in ideology or cynicism about the emerging version of Chinese socialism that is adapted to participation in the global market economy. In our last interview with Director Guo of Sinanlu You'eryuan in 2007 we got up the nerve to ask her directly about her political beliefs (figure 2.19):

TOBIN: Are you a member of the Communist Party?
DIRECTOR GUO: Yes!
TOBIN: You grew up under communism.
DIRECTOR GUO: I was born in the early 1950s, so I have seen a lot of changes and lived through very difficult and turbulent times. Like the rest of my generation, the education we received emphasized communist ideals.

2.19. Interview with Director Guo and other directors.

TOBIN: Does this influence your work as the director of the kindergarten?

DIRECTOR GUO: Yes. In addition to being the Director of Sinanlu You'eryuan, I am also the secretary of our school's local party branch. So part of my work I do as a school administrator and part as the branch secretary, such as working closely with the Chinese Communist Youth League and with the teachers' union, organizing their political studies, motivating them, and passing down government policies.

TOBIN: Can you explain the role of the Communist Party in a society that looks to an outsider like me to have become so capitalist?

DIRECTOR GUO: The policy of the government, which represents the goals of the Party, is to work to promote a higher quality of life for the people. In each historical period we have had different emphases. Now we are talking about becoming an advanced society, with an advanced productive force. This means that not only education inevitably has to change, but also our political and social system. In recent years, as we are becoming more open to the outside world and new ideas, we are changing in the direction of more respect for individuals. But while coming to value individuality more highly, we Chinese prefer to follow the Doctrine of the Mean: neither too free nor too controlled. We made a wrong turn during the Cultural Revolution, which badly damaged our society, impacting three generations. Now we must respect human beings. I always had excellent teachers who valued harmony, patience, politeness, and compromising with others. They taught us that the more you lose, the more you gain and that short-term interests should not interfere with a view to the future. These are very valuable ideas, ideas that have made China a stable society and have held us together as a huge nation over thousands of years.

Director Guo showed no hesitation in identifying herself as a cadre of the communist party. But her current understanding of Chinese communism as a form of social organization that includes Confucian, Taoist, and Buddhist virtues in addition to Western thoughts is a long way from the communism of her youth and from the communism we found at Daguan in 1984.

Typicality

We asked informants in seven Chinese cities who watched the videos to comment on Daguan and Sinanlu's typicality, which in our interviewing we most often translated into Chinese as *dianxing*. Because *dianxing* carries both the meaning of "common" and "exemplary," some of our informants took our question to mean not if the preschools in our videos are typical, but whether they are exemplary, a notion steeped in Confucian thinking about the value of exemplars (Munro 1975). The majority of Chinese teachers and directors' told us that they found Daguan to be typical of the majority of urban preschools that are struggling to implement the spirit of the new reforms and that they found Sinanlu to be exemplary, a program that is ahead of most in China in having already figured out how to put the new paradigm into practice. For example, when we asked about the typicality of Daguan and Sinanlu, a teacher in Wuhan replied, "Sinanlu's approach is to enlighten children by inspiring them. This is the kind of preschool that both families and society are seeking today. We are striving to move closer to what Sinanlu is doing. But the real typical preschool is Daguan, where they still force-feed children in large groups and most activities are prescribed and fixed by a plan." The director of a *you'eryuan* in Xi'an found Daguan to be typical in having old software that lags behind its new hardware: "Although Daguan's facility is new, its practice does not represent new ideas. In our country, there is nothing more common than continuing to teach preschoolers using out-of-date ideas. Changing teachers' beliefs about teaching is a very sticky problem because beliefs are part of our being. As the old saying goes, 'Dynasties change more easily than one's personality.'"

Assessments of Daguan by educators and researchers from Beijing and Shanghai tended to be particularly critical. For example, the director of a Beijing preschool found the sensory integration exercise "merely an expensive form of free play, lacking a clear purpose and organizing effort" and the block activity "not well thought out for the educational benefit of children." A Shanghai director said of the Daguan video: "The children appeared chatty, lively, active, and free; and the physical environment was well furnished, but the teachers' understandings of teaching continued to follow the traditional practice. Daguan represents a transitional phase in curriculum reform. The easy changes come first; the difficult changes come more slowly."

In cities other than Beijing and Shanghai the teachers and directors we interviewed generally evaluated Daguan more positively. Several Chinese educators who watched the Daguan video cautioned that care should be taken in making criticism, because, as one teacher argued:

> We tend to compare our strengths to their shortcomings, and we are comparing ourselves today with them in a video that is several years old. Regional difference and local resources also must be taken into account. Daguan may have changed their approach over the past couple of years so much that you wouldn't recognize it if you went back to make another video. The new *Guidelines*, blended with notions from Japan, the US, and other developed countries, have stimulated our rethinking about our traditional approach. Now, every few months we see great change in preschools all across China.

Teachers and directors in Beijing, which has a competitive relationship to Shanghai, its rival as the leading edge of China's (post)modernization, tended to praise Sinanlu You'eryuan for being similar to leading programs in Beijing in its progressiveness. For example a preschool education researcher from Beijing remarked: "The Sinanlu teachers truly respect the children. There is communication on an equal footing between teachers and children. The teachers are interested in the children's thoughts and they empathize with the children. This is exactly what we have been doing in our preschool education reform." Her colleague praised Sinanlu and emphasized that reform should be thought of as a never-ending process: "Sinanlu embodies the spirit advocated in the new *Guidelines for Kindergarten Education*. Some Beijing preschools may have exceeded Sinanlu in realizing this spirit. But we should not point to one model and ask others to emulate it. And it is even more wrongheaded to suggest that there is an ultimate goal to attain. Reform should be thought of a movement that pushes us all to keep moving forward."

Teachers and directors from programs outside Shanghai and Beijing most often described Sinanlu as being ahead of them on the road toward achieving the educational reform agenda. For example, a teacher in Wuhan praised Sinanlu for having incorporated progressive ideas from other countries:

> Sinanlu conforms closely to our image of preschools in developed countries such the US and Japan. For example, you can see how well the teachers have organized the science education activities, with the children all recording their thoughts in their lab books. Looking at many *you'eryuan* in the north, we have talked a lot about these ideas, but rarely taken them into practice. I do admire this kindergarten.

The director of a *you'eryuan* in Wuhan told us that Sinanlu is far ahead of his program, and he emphasized the hurdles to be overcome by preschools in "inland regions" of the country:

> The Sinanlu teachers' approach is not a case of blindly copying from abroad; instead, they have assimilated ideas from foreign countries and turned them into indigenous innovations. Teachers in the inland regions have much less exposure to new ideas than Shanghai teachers do and often are resistant to innovations developed in other cities in China and abroad. It will take a long time to change our ideas and beliefs, and an even longer time to implement new ideas.

Other teachers and directors, although agreeing that Sinanlu embodies the new reforms, were not so sure that this is the direction they want to go. A teacher in Wuhan told us: "Sinanlu does not represent most preschools in China. It is the preschools that are regimented, with teacher-prescribed large-group lessons that are representative. The Sinanlu children are not learning the things they are supposed to master at this age." Ms. Li, another teacher added, "It is good to give real-life-like experiences to children; but it is necessary to show children what they must learn. They should have group instruction."

Part of the problem with determining the typicality of any single pre-school in China is that there are so many: In 2005, there were 124,400 public preschools, with an enrollment of almost 22,000,000 children and 68,800 privately run preschools, with an enrollment of nearly 7,000,000. Another problem is that there are a variety of forms of provision, each of which has its own characteristics. There are preschools that are "enterprise-affiliated," meaning that they are connected to and in some cases run by factories, businesses, labor organizations, universities, and the military. Within the category of public, there are preschools that belong to provinces, cities, and communities. And the public/private divide is ambiguous, as there are preschools that are state-owned, but privately run. Within the public preschools, the ranking/categorizing system divides programs into three ranks and three categories. And then there are preschools such as Sinanlu that are designated as model programs.

For these reasons, our study of continuity and change in Chinese preschools can claim to tell a national story not in the sense of reporting on the full range and quality of provision in a country as large and diverse as China but in the more narrow sense of reporting on the contemporary national discourse and about reactions of educators in seven cities across China to the national governmental efforts to reform understandings of what constitutes quality in early childhood education. While there are big differences in provision and quality across China, our research suggests that in urban areas as far-flung and unalike as Shanghai, Kunming, Beijing, Changchun, Wuhan, Chongqing, and Xi'an, there is a considerable degree of agreement about the direction of change.

The Missing Rural Story

A significant limitation of our study is the missing voices of teachers and directors working in rural preschools. This is a serious gap because there is evidence to suggest that the most extreme variation to be found in Chinese schools is not between regions but between urban and rural programs. Recent studies on childhood in rural China document the disparities between the cities and the country in social, human, and cultural resources and the quality of education experienced by school-age children (Hannum 2003; Hannum & Wang 2006; Adams 2006; Postiglione 2006). The disparity may be even more pronounced for pre-primary education, which in China is non-compulsory and therefore more dependent on local conditions and community resources. The little scholarship that has been done on early childhood education in rural China suggests that in comparison with urban programs, rural preschools are lagging behind not only in provision but also in quality (Tang 2005; Zhou & Xie 2004; Zhu & Zhang 2008, 179–180).

Factors that keep rural preschools behind their counterparts in large cities include not just rural poverty and poor health (Yu & Hannum 2006), but also an uneven distribution of the limited financial resources available (in poorer areas, compulsory education takes precedence over early childhood education and local education officers sometimes use the tuition fees collected by a preschool to support a higher level of schooling); a lack of parent support (many rural parents spend much of the year as migrant workers in cities, leaving their pre-school-age children at home in the countryside); a shortage of qualified teachers (few rural preschool teachers have received professional training in child development or early childhood education, and many are retired or have been let go as unqualified by local primary schools); limited access of teachers to training and to exposure to new ideas (Zhu & Zhang 2008, 181); and a brain drain that draws away the best trained and most capable potential teachers (Sargent & Hannum 2005; Yu 2005).

Although rural preschools in China are severely under-resourced, the centralization and verticality of the Chinese early childhood education system means that even in remote areas, many preschool teachers are aware of the early childhood education reforms and generally sympathetic to the reform goals, even if they lack access to the kinds of professional development they would need to understand and implement the new practices (Che 2007).

The Ongoing Reform of Early Childhood Education and Its Discontents

The degree of agreement we found in our interviews across seven cities in China about the general direction, sensibility, and timeliness of the early childhood education reforms is a reflection of the power of top-down planning in China, of the sense of shared national purpose, and of the impact of the 2001 *Guidelines for Kindergarten Education*. The teachers, directors, and experts we interviewed hold varying views and beliefs about what needs to be done to adapt the reforms to local conditions and about the direction the reform movement should go in the future; but there is widespread agreement that early childhood education needs to change to meet the demands of China's changing economic and social conditions and that the direction of this change should be toward less direct instruction and more learning through play; less single-subject lessons and more thematic, integrated activities; and a curriculum that is less teacher driven and more children initiated.

That having been said, it is important to view the *Guidelines* neither as a new idea that appeared out of the blue nor as a final product but instead as one step in an ongoing reform process of early childhood education in China that has been underway for over twenty years. This process is complex, collaborative, and dialectic, with multiple stakeholders discussing, debating, reworking, and negotiating. From setting to setting and one year to the next, reform ideas are comprehended as well as misunderstood; implemented as well as resisted. The result is an iterative process playing out across a country that, although centrally governed, is also huge and disjointed. In China, new ideas and approaches, including those advocated in the *Guidelines for Kindergarten Education,* are conceptualized, drafted, and published in the largest cities by the central government but they take effect in disparate local settings, where they are given new meanings and adjusted to local conditions. Great disparities in the resources and staff sophistication needed to implement the new reform ideas are found not only in areas of the country that are physically remote, but also even in Beijing and Shanghai in preschool programs that have poorly educated staff and that are struggling financially.

Professor Feng Xiaoxia of Beijing Normal University, who from 1997 on led the state-commissioned project to draft the guidelines, provided some background: "The ideas written in the guidelines were the result of a nationwide effort that had been ongoing since the publication in 1989 of *Kindergarten Work Regulations and Procedures.* The 1989 document was not specifically about curriculum, so the central task in drafting the 2001 guidelines was to add curriculum standards." Professor Feng emphasized that the *Guidelines* was developed through a collaborative process as the document went through several drafts that were circulated among administrators, researchers, university professors, and education bureaus at the provincial and city levels; these readers gave feedback and suggestions for what to add and what to cut. The feedback was then synthesized and the document rewritten by the Basic Education Department of the Ministry of Education. The *Guidelines* should be understood as a step in an ongoing process, not as a final product, as indicated by the words "trial version," which appeared on the title page when the *Guidelines* first was published and have never been removed.

Professor Hua of East China Normal University explained to us that the *Guidelines* borrowed liberally from ideas from abroad, without making the debt to foreign sources explicit:

Let's be clear: the basic idea of preschool education reform is meant to assimilate international experiences. While in the drafting stage, ideas from different parts of the world were widely discussed such as the Project Approach, Reggio, Developmentally Appropriate Practice, Vygotsky's Zone of Proximal Development, and Multiple Intelligences. There is no question that this modification bears the traces of having assimilated these ideas as well as many key ideas from Japan. However, none of these theories and ideas was explicitly named in the 2001 version of the *Guidelines*. Instead, all of these were integrated under the concepts of "respecting children" and "children's life-long learning."

Professor Hua's description here is consistent with analyses of educational change in various national settings by Jürgen Schriewer (2000; 2004) and Gita Steiner-Khamsi (2000; 2004), whose analyses of international educational borrowing suggest that in some situations ideas imported from abroad are strategically stripped of their foreignness to make them more palatable domestically while at other times the foreignness of imported ideas is accentuated to give them added cultural and political capital. The drafting of the 2001 *Guidelines* is a case of the former.

In the late 1990s, as the national government and a group of China's early childhood education experts were at work on the *Guidelines*, a parallel process was under way at local levels of government to adapt reform ideas to their local conditions. The national government required that all local governments issue their own guidelines for their region, city, or district. Shanghai issued its guidelines in 2000, six months in advance of the release of the national version. Shanghai was well positioned to get out in front on the reform for a variety of reasons: Shanghai has a tradition of investing heavily in early childhood education; Shanghai has a well-developed educational research and curriculum development infrastructure; and the Shanghai city government had recently developed a comprehensive reform of basic (preschool through primary) education that anticipated many of the key features of the national reform. In 2002, Shanghai released another version of its guidelines, which combined ideas from the earlier Shanghai document and the national *Guidelines*.

In contrast, government bureaus of education in less wealthy cities and in remote and impoverished areas of the country were unable to respond to this central government demand to produce their own early childhood education guidelines or to the expectation that they immediately modify their preschool teaching according to the reform directives. Consequently, there were many complaints from poor and outlying areas, with some communities demanding more time to implement the changes and others demanding help to speed implementation. Professor Hua explained:

"If a teacher in a rural preschool has seventy children in her class, how can you ask her to pay attention to each individual child and to respect their individual needs? It is understandable that practitioners in many parts of China cried out 'It's so difficult to implement the guidelines!'" Professor Hua emphasized that the reform is being held back by a shortage of qualified trainers, especially in the countryside:

> The success of the reform depends on teachers' understandings of how and why to teach children in the ways the *Guidelines* suggest. But many of the supervisors whose job is to facilitate teachers' efforts to change are themselves muddle-headed about what the changes mean. The integrated curriculum requires skills and perspectives that teachers did not acquire in their professional training in school. Teachers are paralyzed, so to speak, and at a loss for what to do. Eventually they resist the reform.

Liu and Feng (2005) reach a similar conclusion:

> The top-down approach has been one of the main features of the kindergarten educational reform since 1989. This approach has led to a division between those involved in initiating the reforms and those expected to carry them out. This latter group was composed of practitioners who lacked motivation to make these changes, due, in part, to the absence of consultation. In other words, the need to implement the reforms was imposed on the practitioners, whose participation in making the reforms led to the abandonment of their own familiar ideas and skills. This, in turn, was probably followed by a loss of confidence experienced by the practitioners in their capacity to teach. (2005, 98)

Parents are also an important piece of the equation. Teachers and directors feel pressured on one side by the Ministry of Education to make their curriculum more child-initiated and play-based and on the other by parents who want more direct instruction and preparation for the examinations that lie ahead. Parents with middle-class aspirations for their children look to preschools to provide cultural capital, in the form of after-school "special interest classes" in drawing, dancing, English, math, and piano. As Professor Feng of Beijing Normal University told us, many preschools are eager to cash in:

> The Beijing government prohibits "special interest classes" in kindergartens. The Ministry of Education asked all the kindergartens in China not to col-

lect fees for such classes. However, the ministry's demand doesn't have much power. Go visit any kindergarten and you're likely to find special interest classes, with fees attached. The ministry also said that kindergartens should not be using textbooks, but textbooks are everywhere! The big publishers keep printing more and more textbooks for kindergartens.

As these comments suggest, the profit motive is impacting the reforms in many ways. Professor Hua told us that the reform movement has created a thriving market for experts who can help kindergartens implement the *Guidelines*:

Professional development opportunities for teachers abound. These lectures are arranged with the goal, of course, of attracting a large number of participants, to produce a profit. With financial gains in mind, the organizers invite experts from universities to give lectures. These classes expose teachers to different voices and analyses of well-known scholars about the reform. But the value of these classes is limited. Do these professional development classes help teachers change and improve their practice? Not really. Speakers in these classes address general issues, but not the teachers' daily concerns or specific needs.

Su Guimin of Southwest University in Chongqing, echoed this concern, which has deep resonance in China, that professors and heads of ministries of education are out of touch with the problems faced by workers, in this case by teachers:

The experts' presentations rarely help teachers. When I visit kindergartens in small towns and rural areas, a comment I often hear from teachers about the reform is "We understand what you are saying; but can you show us how to *do* it?" There is no coherent, adequate plan for teachers' professional development, leaving most preschools unable to bring their staff up to speed. The *Guidelines* are vague and they do not make enough allowance for local conditions. Also, teachers in most areas of China are faced with heavy pressures to survive in their local market economy; the *Guidelines* run up against parents' demands for didactic instruction, special interest classes, and early preparation for success in schools and on examinations.

In our interviews with preschool teachers and directors in the US we often heard complaints about how No Child Left Behind and other top-down government initiatives undermine their professionalism and intrude into their classrooms. We hear a different kind of complaint in Professor Su's criticisms, less of the suggestion that the government should not have attempted to lead a reform of the nation's preschools than a complaint that the government should have done its job better. His criticisms are not so much a renunciation of top-down reform, of borrowing ideas from "more advanced countries," or of making the curriculum more child-centered as they are a criticism of the government for not giving clearer guidance on how these desirable ends can be achieved, not being more realistic about the challenges faced by preschools across the country, and not being more accommodating of local conditions. In Su's frustration and impatience we hear a voicing of concerns characteristic of China's contemporary moment; and in his lofty expectations of the government we hear a characteristic Chinese cultural logic, a logic that can be traced back to 1949, when the Chinese Communist Party unified the country and ended a century of having been invaded and occupied by foreign countries and divided by warlords. The existence and ongoing development of China's socialist society was seen then and continues to be widely seen today to depend on the government's vision and efficacy. In both the *Guidelines* and the criticisms of the *Guidelines* we see a widely shared if implicit Chinese cultural belief in the role of the government to improve the lives of the people.

The Future of Chinese Early Childhood Education

Our study that claims to be a comparison of Chinese early childhood education at two points in time in fact is a look at several points — at 1984, when we shot the video and 1985 when we conducted the interviews for the original *Preschool in Three Cultures* study; at 2002, when we shot our new videos at Daguan and Sinanlu (the year after the *Guidelines* had been released); at 2003–5, when we conducted the bulk of the interviews for the new study (when there was an emerging sense of the difficulty of putting the guidelines into practice); and at 2006–7, when we did follow-up interviews with experts to clarify points in our China chapter draft (and calls were being issued for a reform of the reform).

Back in 2002, after a year spent shooting and editing videos of Daguan and Sinanlu, we thought we had our story line set: In the late 1980s China had decided to enter the global economy. The new economy required a new kind of citizen. A new approach to early childhood education was a key strategy for producing this new kind of citizen. Following this logic,

Chinese early childhood education was rapidly and inexorably becoming more constructivist, play-oriented, and child-initiated, borrowing progressive ideas freely from Western countries. Sinanlu represented the leading edge of this reform; Daguan was a school struggling to catch up. From this point of view, Daguan was Sinanlu's past, Sinanlu Daguan's (and China's) future. This narrative was not just our meta-level interpretation of our interviews—it was one we heard expressed explicitly and often in the early years of the decade from informants across China.

As we complete this book six years after shooting the Daguan and Sinanlu videos, we have come to see the story of early childhood education that is unfolding in China as more complex. We now see our understanding of Sinanlu as Daguan's future not necessarily as wrong, but as just one of several ways of understanding what is going on now and what is likely to transpire in the future. The idea that Sinanlu is Daguan's future is based on the notion that China is moving now and will continue to move in a linear direction, towards more Western- and Japanese-influenced, child-centered approaches to early childhood education. This is indeed one plausible future. It will take several more years before the 2001 *Guidelines*, which unambiguously articulated this direction, reach peripheral areas and before they have a chance to be implemented fully, not only in preschools in peripheral cities such as Kunming. In this sense, the 2001 *Guidelines* are like a tidal wave of reform that is still just reaching distant shores. Even if and when the Ministry of Education makes the kinds of changes to the 2001 *Guidelines* that Professors Hua and Su and others are calling for, it will take time for these changes to reach the periphery. In this sense, Chinese preschools will continue to "modernize" according to the direction set in the 2001 *Guidelines* for some years to come.

However, the idea that Sinanlu is Daguan's future fails to take into account the power of local meanings and contexts and the resilience of traditional Chinese culture. Daguan is trying, in some ways, to become more like Sinanlu, and Daguan's directors told us that they see Sinanlu as a model and an inspiration. However, this does not mean that they think it possible or desirable that they will ever become just like Sinanlu. After watching our video of a day at Sinanlu You'eryuan, we asked Director Shi, "Have you attempted to implement this kind of curriculum at Daguan?" Director Shi replied:

> We have actively explored the new ideas and introduced them to our teachers. Some teachers have started to try out these ideas. But this is not yet the

case for the majority, in large part because we administrators have been hesitant to make any radical change. We are afraid that only a few teachers would be able to thrive, but many others would be at loss for what to do. For this reason we do not want to plunge into a radical change. The *Guidelines* encourage us to follow children's interests and to tap their potentials. But if you let children take the lead, what then is the role of the teacher? We have been thinking about this issue for several years. Furthermore, our country is known for its emphasis on traditions such as patriotism and morality. If all we do is to follow children's interests, I don't think we will be able to impart these traditional values; the guidance of teachers is necessary for such education to occur. Unless we figure out ways to solve these problems, we do not want to try out one approach today and then try out another tomorrow, running around searching for what works. Instead, we prefer to build on our established foundation and to follow traditional pedagogy. Kunming is not Shanghai and it never will be. Nor should Daguan become Sinanlu.

At Yunnan Normal University in Kunming, two early childhood educators we interviewed emphasized the vitality of the growing Neo-Confucian and neo-classical movements in Chinese education and society:

PROFESSOR LI: I don't think the new guidelines represent our future. The *Guidelines* are too Westernized. Westernized education prioritizes individuality, democracy, and equality. This educational ideal is in direct conflict with our Confucian culture. A tree transplanted from the West into Confucian soil will have difficulty taking root. The Confucian tradition fits with Chinese parents' experiences growing up and with their wishes for their children's education. The Shanghai model could be adopted only if people's mindsets were to change completely. An intense debate is going on in China about cultural beliefs. We hear official voices supporting Western ideas. But among ordinary people there is a widespread desire to restore the traditional education approach, that is, to restore Confucian culture. Many parents are enrolling their children in traditional schools where the teachers follow traditional pedagogical procedures and rules of learning and children read the classics. The name of the movement is "classic studies." This is a phenomenon that can be seen across China, like bamboo shoots pushing out of the dirt after a spring rain.

PROFESSOR CAO: We've learned a lot from the West but we try to combine the ideas from the West with the local situation in China. In the Chinese phrase, we call this *"bentuhua"* (nativization). These days we are giving preference to things that have been "ben-tu-ized" (localized). I recall a saying from a famous Japanese educator: "First globalize, then localize."

Our interviews with Director Shi, Professors Li and Cao, and other Chinese educators have led us to become aware of a second story line, one in which the 2001 *Guidelines* are seen, retrospectively, as the high-water mark of the reform effort begun in the 1980s. Reactions and resistance to the 2001 *Guidelines* have recently led to a change of mood and direction, with an emerging consensus around the need to make more concessions for local conditions and more effort to re-connect the reforms with Chinese pedagogical, philosophical, and ideological traditions. Reform in China of early childhood education, as of society as a whole, is a contentious, dialectic, ongoing process. Complaints from practitioners about both the means and ends of the 2001 *Guidelines* are viewed by Professor Hua and other veteran observers of early childhood education reform in China not only or primarily as foot dragging but as appropriate feedback that needs to be taken into account as the *Guidelines* are reworked and the form of the reform reconceptualized and restructured. Some leaders of the early childhood reform movement recently have joined practitioners in expressing concerns about the dangers of going too far and in calling for the creation of a system of early childhood education that instead of being a copy of the West is a hybrid of the best of each approach. This second story line would suggest that a teacher-directed curriculum was China's past, a child-centered approach the present, and a hybrid form the future. Or, to restate this story line using Raymond William's concept of residual, dominant, and emergent social forms (1973), we can suggest that a play-oriented, child-centered approach is dominant; a didactic, content-masterly approach is residual; and a hybrid form, combining the two, is emerging.

Professor Zhu, of East China Normal University, could be said to embody this conceptualizion of early education reform in China. Trained first in Soviet-influenced Chinese early childhood educational approaches in the 1970s and 1980s, Professor Zhu had the opportunity in the late 1980s to study in the US, earning a master's degree in early childhood education at the University of Massachusetts, Amherst, where he was introduced to a variety of progressive approaches. In the late 1990s Professor Zhu became well known in China for his writings and presentations on Reggio Emilia, the Project Approach, and other ideas from Europe and North America. Professor Zhu was active in promoting the directions of the curriculum reform when we first interviewed him in 2002, arguing that the applications of the new approaches, even at Sinanlu, had not gone far enough in realizing the goals of progressivism. But in the past few years, Professor Zhu, while still pushing the reform agenda, has been giving more emphasis to the importance of indigenizing ideas from the West and preserving Chinese values and wisdom. As he emphasized to us in a 2007 interview:

> Twenty years ago we started to change the curriculum. As the Chinese curriculum tried to make its values more like those of Western culture, old textbooks were replaced and classic stories that had more morals and traditional values disappeared. In contemporary schoolbooks we find mostly stories that emphasize the Western values of independence, individuality, and autonomy. Concern about the loss of Chinese values led the government last year to issue a document saying that the curriculum should have more Chinese content. When we are exposed to a new way of thinking we should not swallow it all at once without tasting it first. Chinese culture has a long history and many merits worth preserving. Our educational reform has undergone a long journey. We have learned a lot from the West. But we have many good things in our own culture, too, and our preschool education should reflect those merits. Educational approaches have a cultural character: American education has its American cultural values; Japanese has its Japanese values; we have our values. Because we have different values and different cultural backgrounds, we have different types of early childhood education. We need to learn from and complement each other.

Professor Zhu's comments here support an idealistic, optimistic story line, one in which rational planning and the give and take of ideas lead to the emergence of a hybrid system of early childhood education combining the best features of foreign and Chinese approaches (Zhu & Zhang 2008, 175–176). But a third story line comes to mind, one that also features hybridity but is less optimistic, as it suggests not the inclusion of the best features of both worlds but the intrusion of some of the worst elements of Western capitalism into China's chaotic post-socialist society. The hallmarks of this third story line are the commercialization and privatization of China's preschools.

One alarming trend is the selling off of public *you'eryuan* to private companies or individuals, a practice that began in 2000 in the city of Shenzhen (the first "special economic zone" in China) and other coastal cities, and then spread to inland cities. Recently, in response to teachers' complaints of a cut in salaries and the loss of benefits following privatization of their preschools, the central government intervened, at least temporarily blocking the sales. Concern about the effects of privatization has spread among teachers throughout the country. It is not only salaries and benefits that change. As Professor Hua explained to us, "Once a public preschool has been sold, the government's policies no longer have to be followed. These preschools can take up or ignore the *Guidelines*, as they wish."

Indeed, it could be argued that the rationale driving privatization is not only for local governments to cut costs and make a quick profit but also to free programs from national control and in this way to allow them to be more responsive to the demands of the market, which means to the preferences of parents. Even preschools, such as Daguan and Sinanlu that remain (at least for now) firmly within the public sector, are feeling increased pressure to market themselves competitively. A special feature of China's current hybrid form of state socialism and commercialism is that the tuitions preschools can charge are determined in part by the ratings on "hardware" and "software" they receive from government inspectors. By constructing a new school building and upgrading the training of its teachers, Daguan was able to position itself to charge higher tuition. In today's China, a higher tuition, counterintuitively and counter to the traditional laws of pricing in capitalist systems, generally attracts more rather than fewer customers. And these higher-paying customers expect to have a larger say in the curriculum. Educators complain that these parents are often more swayed by fancy equipment than by sound pedagogy; anxious about the examinations that lie ahead for their children, they often prefer didactic instruction to the more abstract benefits of a constructivist approach. As the director of a preschool in Wuhan explained, "The bottom line for us is that a private program like ours must meet parents' demands. A parent will ask us how many characters her child has learned, how many English words her child has memorized, and how many songs her child can sing. Our goal is to have children master knowledge, and to reach that goal we take a different approach from public *you'eryuan* by having teacher-prescribed outcomes for the lessons."

The "open-door policy" for economic reform begun in the early 1980s has come to the world of Chinese early education, leading to a burgeoning industry of joint ventures, foreign investment, and homegrown entrepreneurs. Taiwanese and other foreign chains have entered the market, providing preschools promoting bilingual (Chinese and English) instruction, twenty-four-hour care (the return of the boarding school), and technology-aided curricula. Many new Chinese companies have emerged to jump into the space created by privatization and to compete with foreign ventures. As the number of public preschools has shrunk a bit in the last ten years, the number of private preschools has mushroomed. An example perhaps of what is to come is the Beijing 21st Century Experimental Kindergarten. This corporate-run kindergarten, which features boarding programs, bilingual Chinese and English education, and infant care and has its own research division, boasts that with the near-completion of the construction of sixty classrooms, it is poised to be the world's biggest preschool, with a capacity of almost 2,000 children.

There are also private early childhood education programs and afterschool tutoring programs springing up that feature not English lessons, computers, and Westernized pedagogy but instead Confucianism and classic Chinese children's texts such as the 700-year-old "Three Character Classic," which young children are taught to memorize and which begins:

Men at their birth
Are naturally good.
Their natures are much the same,
But their habits become widely different.
If foolishly there is no teaching,
Their nature will deteriorate.
The right way in teaching,
Is to attach the utmost importance to thoroughness.

Daguan is still a public program of the Yunnan government, but Director Shi is worrying about and preparing for the eventuality of either going private or having to compete directly with private schools. Meanwhile, Sinanlu, though still securely in the fold of Shanghai's Luwan District, is nevertheless increasingly aware of the need to position itself in the market, not just locally, but regionally, nationally, and even internationally. In 2007 we were invited guests at an international conference hosted by the Luwan District Bureau of Education in conjunction with the fiftieth birthday of Sinanlu You'eryuan. For the event, which was timed to coincide with the opening of a new set of school buildings, Sinanlu published a small book that contains a new mission statement that states:

We will create Siyou [a new nickname for Sinanlu You'eryuan, made up of a character that means "thinking of" and a character that means "excellence"] as a brand name that embodies our aspiration of "constantly pursuing the best" quality early education and service and, in this way, exerting an impact on Shanghai and on the nation. Our brand name will come to stand for the finest *you'eryuan* in Luwan District and guide many more *you'eryuan* as they pursue their own brand names, marching into modernization, creating "The Finest Education," and building up "Modern Schools."

We find in this mission statement a fascinating hybridity of the idioms of Chinese socialism and the twenty-first-century free market, with notions of model schools, the power of exemplars deeply embedded in Confucianism, and a confident forward march into modernization mixing with notions of branding and positioning oneself in the marketplace. Who can predict where such an emerging hybrid form will head?

3 Japan

Return to Komatsudani

The question we are most often asked about the original Preschool in Three Cultures study is, "What happened to Hiroki?" In the original study, four-year-old Hiroki, a boy in the Peach Class at Komatsudani Hoikuen in Kyoto, emerged as the star not just of the Japan section of the video and book, but of the project as a whole. For example, in her 1990 review of *Preschool in Three Cultures*, Merry White writes:

> The most interesting case in the book is that of the Japanese boy, Hiroki, a relentlessly recalcitrant child, who persisted in antisocial and even hurtful behavior. . . . The serendipity of the discovery of "handling Hiroki" as a focal cross-cultural issue is central to [the study's] methodology . . . The "Hiroki problem" acted as a perfect Rorschach for assumptions about control, the teacher's role, age- and gender-appropriate behavior, and even class size. (1135–1136)

The relentlessly recalcitrant behavior White refers to include shots in the 1984 video of Hiroki interrupting lessons, stepping on the hand of one boy and slugging another, and throwing flash cards off the balcony. The response of Hiroki's teacher, Fukui-sensei, to each of these indiscretions was to refrain from intervention because, she explained, her intervention would give Hiroki and his classmates the impression that the control of their behavior was the responsibility of the teacher rather than of themselves and it would deprive them of a valuable learning opportunity to develop their own solutions to social problems. When a girl points out to Fukui-sensei that Hiroki is misbehaving, she replies, "If it's bothering you, you do something about it." Instructors in the US who have used *Preschool in Three Cultures* as a text in their classes have reported to us that for American viewers of the video and readers of the book, Fukui-sensei's reluctance to intervene in Hiroki's mischief coupled with the explanations of Fukui-sensei and other Japanese educators of the thinking behind this practice proved to be the most compelling example in the study of the salience of cross-cultural difference.

When we returned to Komatsudani in 2002 we met with the preschool's recently retired director, Yoshizawa Hidenori. When we inquired about Hiroki, Director Yoshizawa gently chided us: "Why are you always so interested in Hiroki? Each time you have visited over the years, he is the only child you ask about. He wasn't the only child in that class or necessarily the most interesting." When we explained that readers of the book are curious about how Hiroki turned out, Director Yoshizawa told us: "I haven't seen him recently, but I hear that he's doing fine. He has a job and he's married." On previous return visits to Komatsudani, when we asked what happened to Hiroki, we found out that he was a star of his neighborhood baseball team during his elementary and junior high years and had graduated from a trade high school in Kyoto. What did we expect to hear? That a boy who was naughty as a four-year-old in preschool would end up in prison?

Hiroki seems to have done well in the time that passed between our first and second studies. How about Komatsudani? Director Yoshizawa told us that he had recently retired as the head priest of the temple and principal of the preschool. In 1998, Director Yoshizawa's eldest son married the daughter of the director of another Buddhist preschool in the Kyoto area. The daughter-in-law, Yoshizawa Norie, who had seven years experience teaching in her father's preschool before moving to Komatsudani, served as assistant director under her father-in-law's tutelage for two years before assuming the directorship in 2001. When we asked Director Yoshizawa what else had changed, he told us about the new classroom buildings that the school moved into in 1999, the addition of bus service and a kitchen that prepares hot lunches, and the struggles to keep up enrollment in an era of falling birthrates; but the program, he told us, is much the same, both in practice and philosophy.

A Day at Komatsudani Hoikuen

Komatsudani Hoikuen (daycare center) is on the grounds of the three-hundred-year-old Buddhist temple in Kyoto (figure 3.1). Twelve infants, fourteen toddlers, and twenty-two three-year-olds occupy the first floor of the new building. Upstairs is home to the classrooms for the seventeen four-year-olds and twenty-five five-year-olds. Adjoining the back of the

3.1. Komatsudani Temple.

new building is a kitchen and dining room where meals are prepared and the older children have lunch.

The teachers on the earliest shift arrive a few minutes before 7 a.m. and the first children soon after. A teacher stands in the doorway of the *genkan* (covered entranceway) to greet children and parents. Parents of the older children generally say their good-byes in the *genkan*, while parents of infants and toddlers leave their shoes in the doorway and step up into the inner hall to carry their children to their classrooms. On this day five-year-old Yusuke, the first of the older children to arrive, drops off his backpack in his classroom upstairs and then goes to the baby room to fetch one-year-old Masaki, whom he plays with near the entrance and then carries out to the playground.

At 8:00, the brightly colored Komatsudani Hoikuen bus, driven by Yoshizawa Hiroshi (the younger son of the old director and brother-in-law of the new director) arrives at the gate, depositing a load of eighteen children and a teacher before setting off again for a second run. Morita-sensei, the teacher of the Fuji (Wisteria) class for children four and five years old, arrives at school this day at 8:30 a.m. As she crosses the playground, she stops and bows in prayer in front of the main building of the temple. She then enters the daycare building, where she puts away her hat and backpack, before returning to the playground. By 8:30, about half of the program's ninety students have arrived when Nao-chan, the youngest child in the Fuji class, enters the playground with her mother and three-month-old sister. While her mother chats with other mothers on the playground, Nao runs upstairs to put away her knapsack and then returns to the playground, where she stays close to her mother, who encourages her to play with her friends. Ten minutes later, when Nao's mother announces that it is time for her to return home, Nao holds on to her mother's leg, plead-

3.2. Nao parts from her mother.

ing with her to stay longer. After a few minutes of watching this scene from nearby, Morita-sensei approaches, saying "Nao-chan, it's time to say good-bye." Nao shakes her head, whimpers, and continues to cling to her mother's hand." Nao's classmate, Maki, comes over to watch the interaction and offer encouragement to Nao (figure 3.2). Nao eventually lets go of her mother's hand as Morita-sensei lifts the little girl into her arms. Nao, Morita-sensei, and Maki stay by the gate for a few seconds waving goodbye. The teacher and the two girls then turn and walk back towards the playground, and Maki, taking hold of Nao's hand, invites her to play in the sandbox. Nao, now smiling, accepts Maki's offer, and the two girls run off to the sandbox, where they join other girls in their class.

At 9:15, a musical chime from the loudspeaker announces that it is time to put away the bikes, balls, and sand toys, and line up to go inside (figure 3.3). Morita-sensei's Fuji class of four-year-olds shares a large, partially divided room with Nogami-sensei's Sakura (Cherry Blossom) class of five-year-olds. During the free play period that begins the day inside, the children from the Fuji and Sakura classes go back and forth between the adjoining rooms. As soon as she enters the Fuji classroom, Nao runs to the box of stuffed animals and dolls and grabs her favorite teddy bear. After a few minutes, she puts the bear down and joins some other girls in play. As the children play with dolls, put together puzzles, read books, and chat, Morita-sensei gets materials together for the day. A skirmish breaks out between Nao and the twins, Reiko and Seiko, over the teddy bear. Reiko admonishes Nao for trying to grab the bear from them. Nao, with tears in her eyes, whines, "Reiko-chan and Seiko-chan are stupid." Seiko replies, "Well, it's your own fault. You put the bear down. That's why we took it."

Morita-sensei announces that free play is over, and that it is time to get into their small groups. The children take their assigned seats at the four

3.3. The Tampopo class lines up.

tables. Morita-sensei sits down at the piano and leads the children in the morning song,

> *Sensei, ohayō.*
> *Minna-san, ohayō,*
> *Genki ni asobimashō.*
> *ohayō, ohayō.*

> (Teacher, good morning.
> Everyone, good morning.
> Let's play happily.
> Good morning, good morning.)

Morita-sensei asks the children "How many children have come to school today? Is anyone missing?" The children look around, and decide no one is absent. "Right," says Morita-sensei, "Everyone is healthy. No one is absent today, so that means there are seventeen of you here."

Morita-sensei launches into a song, the children immediately joining her: "The fish jumps out of water and attaches itself to . . . your underpants! Just kidding!" The children howl with laughter. "Shall we make underpants today? No. We're going to make fish today."

Morita-sensei then holds up a stack of brightly colored origami paper and says, "I wonder, what color fish should I make? Who wants to use blue? Raise your hands. Okay, now who wants yellow? Here you go. Hold on, I'll bring it over to you." Once each of the children has a sheet of square paper, Morita-sensei folds her paper in half, saying, "First we make a triangle. That's right. Our fish are now triangles. And then fold in both sides, right, like that, just like when you make a tulip. Then fold the two end points in, like this. And one more fold, like this. Got it? Good. No? Here, I'll help you."

Once the children have folded their papers into the shape of a fish, Morita-sensei says, "It seems so sad without a mouth or eyes. What should we do? I'll take a marker, and draw an eye on my fish, like this." When the children finish folding and drawing their fish, they bring them over to Morita-sensei, who writes their names on the back and attaches a metal clip, which the children will use later to catch the fish with magnets on the end of fishing poles.

Morita-sensei next announces that it is time for swimming. Children change into their suits in the classroom. After some brief calisthenics, the children go outside and climb into the above-the-ground pool that is set up for a month each summer. Morita-sensei and the director, Yoshizawa Norie, take turns squirting the children with a hose and the children respond by splashing the adults. After fifteen minutes, the children step out of the pool, remove their swimwear, and then naked and dripping wet, they line up near the entrance to the school where Yoshizawa Hiroshi (the bus driver and school aide) dries each child off with a towel before they head inside.

Back in the classroom, there is a second extended period of free play. Eventually, another argument breaks out among the girls (figure 3.4). Nao, Yoko, and the twins Reiko and Seiko are pulling and tugging on the teddy bear as Maki attempts to mediate. With help from Yoko and Seiko, Reiko eventually comes away with the bear. Nao tries to grabs it away from Reiko, and twin sister Seiko intervenes, pulling on the back of Nao's dress. The three girls fall to the floor into a pile of twisting, pushing and pulling bodies. From across the room, we hear Morita-sensei call out "*Kora kora, kora kora*" (which has a meaning somewhere between "Hey!" and "Stop"), but she doesn't come over to break up the fight. Eventually, Reiko emerges from the pile with the bear, which she puts under her dress (making her appear pregnant) and then crawls under the table, where it will be harder for Nao to get at her. Reiko tells Nao, "Stop it. It's not yours, it's Reiko's." Maki suggests that Reiko should give the bear to Nao. Reiko pokes her head out from under the table and Nao says to her, "Give it to me." Seiko, Reiko, and Maki discuss what to do. Reiko says to Seiko, "You should scold her!" Seiko admonishes Nao, "That's bad! You can't just grab the bear away like that!" Nao responds, "But I had it first." Seiko replies, "But then you put it down, so your turn was over." Nao is led away to the other side of the room by Reiko, who says to her, "You can't do that. Do you understand? Promise?" Linking little fingers with Nao, the two girls swing their arms back and forth as they sing, "Keep this promise, or swallow a thousand

3.4. Fight. 1. Nao attempts to grab the bear from Seiko.

2. Yoko joins the struggle.

3. The girls wrestle for control of the bear.

4. "Give it to me."

5. "You can't just grab the bear."

6. The girls admonish Nao.

7. "Keep this promise or swallow a 1000 needles."

8. Seiko comforts Nao.

needles." Reiko then puts her arm around Nao's shoulders and says to Nao, "Understand? Good." Morita-sensei, who throughout this altercation has been walking back and forth near the fighting girls, ignoring their altercation as she cleans up the morning fishing materials, then announces that it is time to clean up for lunch. Reiko, her arm around Nao, rubs her back and leads her to the line of children forming in the doorway. Morita-sensei comes to the front of the line and tells them they can go, and the children hurry down the stairs, and out the side door, to the dining room.

Entering the wood-paneled dining room, each child picks up a tray of food from the counter and takes a seat with three or four classmates at one of the low tables. Once all of the children in the Fuji class are seated with their trays in front of them, Morita-sensei leads the children in saying the lunch blessing—"*Itadakimasu*" ("Thank you for this food we're about to receive")—and the children dig in with chopsticks, forks, and spoons. The children of Nogami-sensei's Sakura class enter the room a minute later, grab their trays, say the blessing, and start eating. Nogami-sensei sits on the floor in a corner of the dining room and plugs in an electric hair dryer. One by one, children come and sit on his lap while he blow-dries their hair.

After fifteen minutes or so, the fastest eaters clear their trays and scatter around the edges of the dining room, where they sit and talk and play with toys that have been laid out in baskets. Morita-sensei sits at one of the tables with three of the girls, who eat slowly, talking as they eat. Morita-sensei alternates between writing in the children's daily contact books, chatting with the girls, eating her own lunch, encouraging the girls to eat, and occasionally loading up Nao's spoon with food. Eventually, after encouragement from Morita-sensei to have one more bite, the girls clear their places, stop off at the bathroom, and then join their classmates back in the classroom.

In the classroom, some of the children change into pajamas; others strip down to a T-shirt and underpants. They then walk down the hall to the multipurpose room, which serves as a nap space for the older children in the hot summer months (the older children don't take naps the rest of the year). Nogami-sensei, who has nap duty this day, distributes futons to the children, who spread their futons out on the floor, and then come over to sit in front of Nogami-sensei as he reads a story aloud. Once the story is over, Nogami-sensei tells the children to lie down on their futons. He then turns down the lights and says, "Please be quiet and go to sleep."

An hour later, Nogami-sensei turns up the lights and plays a video of a Disney cartoon on the large TV. As the children wake up, they fold and stack their futons, go to the bathroom, and then return to the nap room to watch the video. When the video ends, the children return to their classrooms, where they put on their clothes and get ready for a snack.

The four children in Nogami-sensei's class of five-year-olds who are this day's *tōban* (monitors) put on aprons and head downstairs to assist in the baby and toddler rooms. Five-year-old Kenichi takes two-year-old Taro to the bathroom. Positioning Taro in front of the urinal, Kenichi commands, "Pee, please." Noticing that Taro is oblivious to the position of his dangling pajama top, Kenichi reaches over and pulls up the top, keeping it clear of the stream of urine. "Is it coming out?" asks Kenichi, and a few seconds later, "Nothing left in your pee-pee?" Reaching up and pushing the button on top of the urinal, Kenichi says, "Now I'm going to flush." Noticing that the roar of the flush is both exciting and a bit scary to young Taro, Kenichi puts on a look of exaggerated surprise, opening his mouth wide and cupping his face in his hands. Taro, laughing, points at Kenichi's face. Kenichi, turning toward the camera, rolls his eyes in a gesture of mock irritation, suggesting amusement, affection, and intimate knowledge of the pleasures and concerns of two-year-olds (figure 3.8).

In the toddler's classroom, Yasuko helps a two-year-old out of her soiled undershirt and into a new one. In the hallway outside the infant room, Hiro and Yusuke encourage one-year-old Masaki, who has spent the day crawling, to stand up and walk (figure 3.5). With the older boys' encouragement, Masaki stands and takes three or four halting steps, before dropping back down to the floor and crawling away. Next comes snack time. In the toddler room, two older children lead the younger ones in the blessing: "Everyone, let's put our hands together and say '*Itadakimasu.*'" Next door in the baby room, Yusuke sits at the low table next to Masaki and feeds him his snack. When Yusuke pushes the spoon a bit too far into Masaki's mouth, Masaki quietly protests by pulling back his head and turning his eyes imploringly towards his teacher, sitting next to him. Kawai-sensei acknowledges Masaki's concern with a nod meant to reassure Masaki and to remind Yusuke not to push too hard on the spoon (figure 3.6).

Meanwhile, upstairs, the children of the Fuji and Sakura classes who are not on monitor duty have said the blessing and are having a snack of cake and milk. After the snack, there is another round of free play. Children move easily back and forth between the two classrooms. Morita-sensei combs Reiko's hair. Nogami-sensei, an avid supporter of the Japanese national team in that summer's World Cup (cohosted by Japan), sits on the floor with a set of marking pens. Children approach him one at a time and put their heads in his lap so he can draw on their cheeks the flag of their favorite soccer-playing country (figure 3.7).

3.5. Helping baby walk.

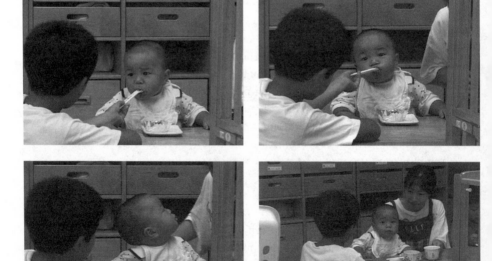

3.6. Feeding baby.

3.7. Nogami-sensei paints a flag on a girl's face.

Maki and Yuki engage in a mock karate battle. Yuki accidentally punches her in the chest and immediately bows towards her and apologizes, "*Gomen*" ("Sorry"). Morita-sensei announces it is clean up time. Children scurry around the room, putting away toys, organizing their backpacks, and lining up the chairs along the far wall. The children then circle around Morita-sensei at the piano. "What shall we sing today? Do-re-mi? Okay." Morita-sensei pounds out the familiar first chords of "Doe, a Deer" and the children sing:

Do, donattsuu no Do
Re, remon no Re
Mi, minna no M

(Do, the Do in "donut"
Le, the Le in "lemon"
Mi, the Mi in "*minna*" [everybody]. . .)

This is followed by the good-bye song: "Teacher, good-bye, See you again tomorrow. Everyone, good-bye. . ." The children then stand in a circle and bowing first to Morita-sensei and then to each other, they chant, "*Sensei, sayonara. Minna-san, sayonara.*" The children grab their backpacks and line up at the door. Morita-sensei then dismisses class, saying good-bye to each of the children as they file past her out the classroom doorway. The children exit the building, put on their shoes, and head for the playground where they park their backpacks alongside one of the temple buildings and then grab a ball, tricycle, or sand toy. The playground is soon filled with all of the older children in the school and many of the toddlers and babies, who have come outside with their teachers or under the care of one of the older children. Two older girls argue over a shovel, settling their dispute by doing *janken* (paper, rock, scissors). At 4:30, there is an announcement that the first bus is ready to depart. Twenty of the children and a teacher board. About half the children play outside on the playground, the other half moving inside to the largest of the toddler classrooms, to engage with the infants and toddlers. During the next hour, parents arrive on bicycles and on foot, most spending five or ten minutes chatting with other parents and teachers before departing for home. Nao's mother, carrying her three-month-old baby, chats with other mothers while Nao hovers nearby. At five o'clock, the second bus loads up and departs, as do Morita-sensei and Nao and her mother and sister. The remaining older children and teachers move inside. By five-thirty, there are about a dozen children left, and three teachers. Parents enter the room one by one to pick up their children. The last child departs just before six.

Interpreting Komatsudani

Six months after shooting we returned to Komatsudani to show a draft of the edited video to teachers Morita-sensei and Nogami-sensei and old and new directors Yoshizawa Hidenori and his daughter-in-law, Yoshizawa Norie. We began by asking the teachers if the day in their classrooms, as captured in our video, seemed typical. Both agreed that it was, although Morita-sensei felt that the presence of our cameras made her a bit self-conscious and tentative at points and some of the children more rambunctious than they tend to be on normal days. Both teachers said they enjoyed getting the chance to watch the children interacting on video, but Morita-sensei found it uncomfortable to watch and listen to herself.

We were particularly eager to hear the teachers' explanations of those practices shown in the video that we anticipated early childhood educators in the United States and China would find surprising and disturbing: namely the non-intervention of teachers in children's fights; the care of younger children by older ones; and displays of physical intimacy between male staff members and young children.

NON-INTERVENTION IN FIGHTS

In our new Komatsudani video, as in the old one, we once again are presented with scenes of fighting and of teacher non-intervention. But this time the fighting children are a group of girls rather than a pair of boys, which some viewers of our video find even more disturbing, perhaps because physical fights seem more natural for boys than for girls or perhaps because the aggression seems to come from a group rather than from an individual, which more strongly raises the specter of bullying (*ijime*), which is considered a serious problem in Japanese classrooms.

Indeed, one take on the fight for the teddy bear is that this is a group of older girls ganging up on the youngest one. But we suggest that a more accurate and useful way to think about what is going on here is to view the teddy bear struggles as a group of older girls engaging and socializing their least mature classmate. We suggest that this second point of view is more accurate and useful because this is how Morita-sensei and the other staff members at Komatsudani view it and also because it is consistent with a traditionally Japanese theory of child socialization, familiar as a cultural script to Japanese teachers, which would suggest that Nao's behavior here, though babyish and seemingly counterproductive, is in fact pro-social, as is the older girls' aggressive responses. Watching the videotape with us six months after it was made, Morita-sensei emphasized that Nao's fighting and crying were her ways of engaging with the other girls by letting them know her feelings:

TOBIN: Do the girls often fight?

MORITA-SENSEI: Yes, and as a result, Nao is often crying.

KARASAWA: What kind of child is she?

MORITA-SENSEI: She is strong. All the children have strong personalities, so in this kind of situation they all want to make their case and put forward their opinion. Compared with the other children, Nao is not very good at speaking. She cries when she can't express what she wants to say verbally. But as you saw in the videotape, even while she was crying, Nao tried to pull the teddy bear back. She has a strong core. People think of crying as a sign of weakness or immaturity, but her crying is not like that. Crying is not a sign that she is weak.

KARASAWA: Is she younger than the others?

MORITA-SENSEI: Yes. Her birthday is in February, which makes her the youngest in the class. And she was the last child in the class to enter Komatsudani. Most of the other children in my class have been here since they were one or two years old. So, it can be said that at that moment in the video, she was a new child. If you saw her right now, you'd see she has changed a lot.

The Japanese psychoanalyst Takeo Doi would see in Nao's behavior a form of *amae* (a dependency wish), an appeal for attention and inclusion that is presented awkwardly, but in a form that the older girls understand and respond to (Doi 1967). By fighting with and correcting Nao the older girls choose to include rather than ignore or ostracize her, which they could do by letting her have the bear, which means more to her than to them. Morita-sensei told us that the scenes we caught on video of the girls fighting over the bear go on, intermittently, every day. Sometimes the older girls provoke Nao, by one of them beating her to the favorite bear at the beginning of a free play period or snatching the bear the second she puts it down; more often Nao is the initiator of the struggle. In either case, the staff at Komatsudani conceptualizes the actions as the initiation of a game rather than as the first assault in a fight, with a victim and aggressors. Thus, the question here is not "Who started the fight?" but "Who initiated the social interaction?" Whoever initiates, once the game is on, the older girls' contribution is to block Nao's selfish desire to keep the bear to herself, to correct her behavior, and then to comfort her. The older girls sometimes provoke Nao, but they rarely leave her frustrated (as would be the situation if this were a case of bullying). Nao is repeatedly scolded by the girls, but also frequently consoled. Indeed, it could be argued that the purpose of the scolding is to provide an opportunity for the consoling and the purpose of Nao's misbehavior to provide an opportunity to be scolded, and thereby eventually consoled. The girls are physically aggressive, but also physically affectionate.

Many of the Japanese teachers and directors who approved of Morita-sensei's non-intervention approach expressed appreciation for the value of young children being given the opportunity to be *kodomo-rashii* (childlike). Compared to their Chinese and American counterparts, Japanese early childhood educators tend to give a higher value to and to have a higher tolerance for the child-like, physically expressed behaviors of children. To many Japanese viewers of this scene, in these physical tussles the girls are not so much out of control as they are acting like four-year-old children, children who are not so much misbehaving as behaving pro-socially, but in an immature, *kodomo-rashii* way. Just as Kenichi's pee lesson is a five-year-old's rather than an adult's version of pedagogy, the older girls' interactions with Nao are how four-year-olds deal with a classmate's selfishness and babyishness: their approach is less abstract, more physical, more cathartic, and less logocentric than when adults try to teach immature four-year-olds the importance of sharing. The girls' pattern of interaction is intensely pro-social, in contrast to the break in the social flow and the sense of a being a community of peers that often occurs when an adult teacher intrudes into a children's play space. As many of our Japanese informants tell us, the main reason children in contemporary Japan need preschool is to have opportunities to experience a level of social complexity lacking at home. Adult intervention interferes with this complexity. Contemporary Japanese children at home get adult instruction on how to behave properly. The philosophy and practice followed at Komatsudani and many other Japanese preschools is that children do not need more of this adult intervention when they come to preschool.

Some Japanese viewers of the Komatsudani video were critical of Morita-sensei's non-intervention in the girls' disputes. We can place the criticisms into four categories. First, some saw value in the practice of teachers giving children opportunities to work out their disputes, but say that in this situation they would have intervened more quickly and more aggressively than Morita-sensei did. For example, a *yōchien* teacher in Tokyo commented, "It's good to let children argue and even fight a little, but I think in this case the teacher let the fighting go too far. I would have come over and told the girls to stop fighting."

A second category of criticism is a Japanese version of neo-Vygotskian constructivism, a viewpoint that emphasizes the teacher's role in scaffolding children's cognitive and social development in situations including their fighting. We heard this perspective, for example, from a director of a public *yōchien* who said, "I try to help my teachers see how in situations such as these the teacher can step in not to stop the children's interaction but to ask some questions that can support the children in finding new strategies for dealing with their disagreements."

In the third category are criticisms from teachers and directors at Christian preschools who see non-intervention in children's fights as a traditional Japanese practice that they see as a flaw of Japanese society. This was a theme addressed in the original *Preschool in Three Cultures*, which included comments from directors and teachers at Christian *yōchien* and *hoikuen* who criticized Fukui-sensei's failure in their eyes to stop Hiroki from bullying his classmates. A teacher at a Christian *yōchien* in Osaka said, "It is cruel to let children hurt each other in fights without trying to do something to stop it," and the head teacher of a Hiroshima Christian *hoikuen* called the non-intervention by teachers in Hiroki's fighting "an example of what's wrong with Japanese education and with Japanese society. This is the kind of approach that leads to fascism and blind following of leaders. There is no place in this kind of school for the soul and for individual self-expression" (Tobin, Wu & Davidson 1989, 51).

The fourth category of criticism is that this approach promotes bullying, as Masakazu Mitsamura, who is conducting research on *ijime*, or bullying, explained to us:

> Around the time you were doing your original research, *ijime* was becoming a national concern. On February 1, 1986, a bullied eighth-grade student committed suicide. This heartbreaking case became a high-profile news story that shocked the Japanese society. *Ijime* is considered mostly a lower secondary school problem, but these days concern about the antecedents of *ijime* behavior makes even preschool teachers worry about bullying in their classrooms. What we see happening in this scene in your video in my opinion might contribute to the development of *ijime* behavior later. I worry less about the children directly involved in the fight than about the effect on the bystanders, who are watching and developing bad habits of following the lead of the dominant figures in the classroom and becoming passive bullies.

Many Chinese and American viewers see Morita-sensei's non-intervention as a failure or a lack; a failure to protect the children from harming each other and a lack of awareness of what is going on in her classroom, of concern for the children's well being, and of attention to their social development. We see a difference between these outsiders' critiques and the critiques of Japanese insiders. While the majority of Japanese educators who were critical of Morita-sensei's handling of the girls' fight faulted her for not intervening as quickly, artfully, or aggressively as they believe she should have, most of her Chinese and American critics ascribed her failure as one of not inaction but of inattention, based on the assumption that if she had been aware of the girls' fight, she would have done something. But our video-cued interviews with Morita-sensei demonstrate that she was keenly aware of what was going on in her classroom on that and other days. We suggest that her appearance of indifference to the girls' fighting was a performance intended to encourage the girls to relate to each other and solve their own problems rather than to turn to her. Knowing the girls well enough to anticipate when and where a situation has the potential to become dangerous or to spin out of control, Morita-sensei can give them time and space to work issues out on their own, rather than adopting the strategy favored by preschool teachers in the US and (at least until recently) in China of preemptive intervention to head off disputes before they have a chance to develop. In those cases where the children's fighting becomes dangerous, as it did on the day we videotaped when the girls were scuffling too close to the sharp corner of the piano, Morita-sensei, monitoring even when she appears not to be, does intervene. In the fight over the bear, at the point when the physical aggression seems about to escalate, Morita-sensei calls out to the children, "Hey" ("*Kora kora*"), to cue them to lower the intensity a bit. As she explained to us: "If I think a fight, such as this one in the video, is unlikely to result in anybody getting hurt, I stay back and wait and observe. I want the children to learn to be strong enough to handle such small quarrels. I want them to have the power to endure. If it's not dangerous, I welcome their fighting."

The word Morita-sensei used here for staying back and observing is *mimamoru*, which is a combination of two verbs that mean literally "to look" and "to guard, protect, or watch over." We see a similar strategy of *mimamoru* at work in the baby room during snack time, where the infant/ toddler room teacher, Kawai-sensei watches as Yusuke, feeding one-year-old Masaki, pushes the spoon in a bit too far and Masaki looks over to his teacher for help. Kawai-sensei intervenes as lightly as possible, moving in a just a bit closer, a gesture that both gives baby Masaki encouragement and cues Yusuke to attend more carefully to what he is doing. With these tactics, she manages to monitor and subtly scaffold the boys' interaction without breaking the flow or making either lose confidence in himself or the other. These Japanese teachers are able to resist the temptation to intervene preemptively, as they balance the risk that a situation might deteriorate without their intervention with their appreciation of the value of the social experiences that would be lost if they were to act before it becomes absolutely necessary. This stands in sharp contrast to how most contemporary Chinese and American teachers calculate risk, as we see in the Chinese and US chapters.

Morita-sensei reads in the girls' fights signs of a gradual process of social development, both for Nao and for the other girls. Over time, the older girls are getting better at dealing with Nao without getting too frustrated; Nao is getting better at controlling her temper and willfulness and interacting in ways other than fighting over toys; and Nao and the older girls gradually are becoming a peer group. This is a primary function of the preschool in contemporary Japanese society, a function that would be compromised by too aggressive or frequent teacher intervention.

CARING FOR YOUNGER CHILDREN

Our 1985 Komatsudani video shows four- and five-year-old girls carrying toddlers down a short flight of steps and out to the playground. In 1986, when we told Assistant Director Higashino that Americans who viewed the videos found this practice alarming, she assured us that the older children are careful with the babies and that staff members are always nearby when older children play with younger ones. She emphasized that this activity is especially valuable for the older children, most of whom do not have younger siblings, because it gives them "a chance they might not otherwise have to develop empathy (*omoiyari*) and to learn how to know and anticipate the needs of another (*ki ga tsuku*)" (Tobin, Wu & Davidson 1989, 35).

In 1985, older children playing with and caring for babies was a practice the administrators and teachers supported, but did not orchestrate. In 2000 the teachers and administrators at Komatsudani decided to institutionalize mixed-age interactions by having the older children take turns as helpers (*tōban*) in the infant and toddler rooms. A system was introduced in which each day four children from the five-year-old class would spend half an hour downstairs, helping out the zero- to two-year-olds during afternoon snack time.

This move was an evolution in Komatsudani's program, as Nogami-sensei, teacher of the five-year-old class, explained:

NOGAMI: In this new system the older children don't just play with the younger ones; they learn to care for them. They help the little ones change clothes, eat, play, and even to use the bathroom.

TOBIN: Isn't it sometimes dangerous? Like when Yusuke was pushing the spoon into Masaki's mouth?

NOGAMI: We keep a close eye on the children. They're careful. And the little ones are good at letting the older ones know when they don't like how things are being done for them.

This is an interesting case of institutional change and what, to borrow a term from Max Weber, we can describe as "routinization," as a once spontaneous practice recognized as fulfilling an important function became institutionalized.

There are several things to point out about the development of this practice. One is that it would have been less likely to develop in a preschool that has more rapid turnover of staff and a less consistent vision. The current director, Yoshizawa Norie, herself grew up and learned to teach in a temple *hoikuen* in the Kyoto area. After marrying into the Yoshizawa family and joining the staff of Komatsudani, she apprenticed as director for two years under the tutelage of her father-in-law, Yoshizawa Hidenori.

Nogami-sensei, who was a student teacher at Komatsudani in 1984 when we shot the original video and in 2002 was in his eighteenth year on staff, had the chance to observe the younger and older children's spontaneous behavior over a long stretch of time and to use what he learned from his experience to initiate a curricular innovation. It is unlikely he could have been successful in launching this innovation were it not for the rapport he enjoys with the teachers in the infant and toddler rooms—over the years he has taught in each of the rooms at Komatsudani, working with each of the other teachers.

Komatsudani's contemporary approach to mixed-aged interactions is not found in most other Japanese preschools. However, the logic behind the practice was widely endorsed by Japanese early childhood education experts and by the teachers and directors of other Japanese preschools who have watched our new video. The technical term for mixed-aged interaction in Japanese preschools is *tate-wari kyōiku* (vertical, or mixed-age, education) (cf. Ben-Ari 1996, 61, 81n). Because *yōchien* have no children under the age of three, they cannot provide the opportunities *hoikuen* can for older children to interact with infants and toddlers. But many *yōchien* staff members who have watched our Komatsudani video told us that they encourage spontaneous interactions between older and younger children and that they have instituted systematic interactions between older and younger classes (as for example, having them collaborate on projects or assigning older children as "older siblings" to younger ones). *Hoikuen* directors report that their older children often interact spontaneously with their babies and toddlers and that while they had not considered initiating a *tōban* system for mixed-aged interaction prior to seeing our video, it is something they might now consider.

When we stopped by Komatsudani to make a courtesy call in the summer of 2007, we learned that the institutionalized *tōban* form of mixed-age interaction was on temporary hold. Nogami-sensei, recently promoted to being the head teacher of the school, told us that they decided to wait a bit further into the new school year (which begins in April in Japan), perhaps in July, to re-start the routine of having older children care for the younger ones. Nogami-sensei added that even when the formal *tōban* system is in place, no children are required to participate and even when it is not in place, older children spontaneously care for younger ones.

One of the key findings of the original study was that preschools are inherently conservative in that they are relatively new social institutions charged with making sure young children are taught traditional cultural values. Preschools are asked to compensate for experiences of social and emotional complexity children in earlier eras enjoyed in their families and communities but which are disappearing under contemporary social conditions. One of the traditional values that is perceived to be at risk among contemporary Japanese young people is *omoiyari*, the ability and willingness to understand and respond to the feelings and needs of others. Komatsudani's innovative practice of having the older children take turns serving as child minders can be seen as bringing the history of childcare full circle. In *Children of Different Worlds* (1988) Bea Whiting and Carolyn Edwards explain that until the last one hundred years or so, while their parents worked, most children in most of the world's cultures were cared for most of the day by other (older) children. This is still the case in subsistence agricultural societies in many parts of the world. In industrialized societies older children minding younger ones is becoming a lost art, a vanishing experience, and a forgotten form of knowledge. The innovative child-minding program at Komatsudani can be thought of as a rediscovery of an important form of cultural logic lost in most modern societies.

We see the wisdom of this old logic most clearly in the scene in our video where a five-year-old boy gives a lesson in using the urinal to a two-year-old. Nogami-sensei emphasized to us, as did Assistant Director Higashino eighteen years ago, the value that mixed-age interactions hold for the older children, as a chance to learn empathy. There are some tasks of childcare and socialization that five- and six-year-old children can handle not just competently, but better than can adults. This, we would suggest, is the case in the urinal lesson, where we see a child of five instructing a toddler in a manner that would be difficult for an adult to do. The understanding and empathy displayed by the older boy in the pee lesson are extraordinary (figure 3.8). When Kenichi asks Taro, "Did it all come out?," he is perfectly cued in to the younger boy's mind set. When Kenichi pantomimes excitement at the sound of the flush, he is empathizing with the toddler's interest, fear, and excitement at this new experience. The sound of the flush can no longer be exciting, surprising, or scary to five-year-old Kenichi, who we must therefore assume is performing rather than feeling interest, surprise, or fear at the sound of the flush in order to help Taro, for whom flushing is still relatively new, become comfortable with the experience. The slight smile on Kenichi's face communicates his pleasure in the shared experience—after all, one of the great pleasures of teaching, like parenting, is the opportunity to re-experience moments of learning and mastery from our own childhood. The pleasure in the sound of the flush (and more generally in mastering urination) is one lost to most adults, but still present to this five-year-old boy, which makes him the ideal pee instructor.

3.8. Pee lesson.

In societies such as China and Japan, where the majority of younger children have no older siblings, and such as the United States, where the age segregation of children keeps younger and older children apart for most of the day, opportunities for older and younger children to interact are rare. In the absence of opportunities for younger children to be taught to urinate by older children, the task falls on adult women to teach boys to use a urinal, a task they generally take on more awkwardly and with less relish than does Kenichi—you have to have a keen knowledge of and interest in a subject to teach it well.

We can see in the evolution of Komatsudani's custom of having older children take turns being caretakers for the little ones a cycling back to a kind of childhood and a mode of child socialization that was characteristic of most human communities until very recently. We suspect that many adult viewers of the pee lesson scene find it uncanny, which Sigmund Freud defined as simultaneously strange and familiar, like visiting a place for the first time, but having a strong feeling of having been there before. The pee lesson seems strange only when looked at through a contemporary filter in which we assume separation of younger and older children and, in the US case, in which fears of sexual abuse in childcare settings intrude on the scene's innocence. But on a deeper level, this scene is familiar, a memory from both our own childhoods and from our collective cultural memory.

The third category of events seen in our Komatsudani video that caused alarm in some US viewers is the physical intimacy between male staff members and children. In our video, we see both Nogami-sensei and Yoshizawa Hiroshi interacting physically and affectionately with children. The bearded male teacher with children lying with their heads in his lap as he paints flags on their cheeks and the bare-chested, muscular bus driver drying the naked children as they come out of the pool (figure 3.9) were lightening rods for American reactions. Because these reactions have much to tell us about moral panics in American society and little to tell us about Japan, we will put off discussion of American reactions to the teacher-child physical intimacy in the Komatsudani video to the US chapter that follows. But the absence of concern in Japan about physical intimacy between adult male caretakers and young children is a topic worth discussing in its own right for what it can help us appreciate about gender, intimacy, and the body in Japanese early childhood education and, more generally, in Japanese society and culture.

The scenes in our Komatsudani video of male and female staff members physically caring for young children along with the scenes of staff accepting, even expecting, children to get dirty, to interact physically, and to enjoy and take an interest in bodily functions suggests a greater ease with the body than we see in our Chinese and American videos. Because they serve infants and toddlers as well as children three- to six-years old, *hoikuen* are more physical and embodied sites than are *yōchien*. Routines for feeding, changing, dressing, disciplining, and soothing infants and toddlers require a level of intimacy and touch that is unnecessary when working with older children. And yet at Madoka Yōchien as well as at Komatsudani Hoikuen we observed a high level of comfort in and acceptance of touch, dirt, and bodies and an appreciation for the physicality of three- and four-year-old children and of the importance of emphasizing physical activity in the preschool curriculum. As Daniel Walsh writes, a core cultural belief of Japanese educators is that "children are physical beings, and their physical development and expression critical to their well being" (2004, p. 104).

Japanese preschool teachers do not often hug and kiss the older children (as we see teachers doing in our US videos) not because they are not

3.9. Driver dries girl.

emotionally or physically affectionate but because Japan is not a culture that gives great emphasis to hugging and kissing. Instead, teachers in Japanese preschool are more often physically affectionate with children in the context of caring for their physical needs, as we see in the examples of Yoshizawa Hiroshi drying the children with a towel as they come out of the pool, Nogami-sensei blow-drying girls' hair in the cafeteria, and Fukui-sensei brushing children's hair at the end of the day. There is more physical intimacy among the children than among teachers and children. At Komatsudani and Madoka, unlike at the American preschools in this study, we rarely heard teachers telling children to sit farther apart or to keep their hands to themselves. The comfort with touch and with the body characteristic of Japanese preschools is the kind of pleasure in the body described by Mikhail Bakhtin in *Rabelais and His World* (1941/1984), a pleasure to be found not in the body of the individual, but in the collective body of the people, in bodies in contact in large gatherings, and in the gleeful acknowledgment of the fact that everyone has a body and these bodies have orifices.

The pleasure Japanese take in the porous, collective body is expressed clearly in Taro Gomi's best-selling children's book, *Minna Unchi* (1977), translated into English in 1993 as *Everyone Poops*. This same matter-of-fact acceptance of children's scatological interests and pleasures can be seen as well in the displays of animal scat that are routine in Japanese zoos and in the jokes about feces and farts that are common in cartoons for young children in Japan. In Japanese interactions with young children there is a general openness and lack of embarrassment about the body, with talk about bodily functions being just one example. This acceptance of the body is a focus of Eyal Ben-Ari's 1997 book, *Body Projects in Japanese Childcare: Culture, Organization, and Emotions in a Preschool*. In addition to being comfortable with the body, Japanese early childhood educators emphasize physical expression, in the form of movement and even rough play. As Daniel Walsh observes, "Japanese preschools are, compared to contemporary American preschools, raucous places, filled with loud rambunctious kids who run, wrestle, hit, roughhouse, and climb on and over everything" (2004, 3).

At Komatsudani in both our original and new studies we found this ease with the body and a commitment to giving children opportunities to engage in messy or even risky physical play. In the first study, we described a day when Director Yoshizawa took the children and teachers to an empty, muddy lot to do their morning exercises with the expectation and hope that the children would end up playing in the puddles and mud. We see it as well in the original video in Hiroki's penis jokes, which his teacher, Fukui-sensei, does not admonish and in the new video, in the urinal scene and in Morita-sensei's introduction to the origami lesson, where she jokes with the children that they will be making paper underpants. At Madoka Yōchien, as discussed later in this chapter, we see a similar acceptance of the body and its functions in the encouragement during outdoor play of the children to play in the water and mud and in Kaizawa-sensei's song about sparrows, which includes a reference to the smell of bird poop.

This comfort with the body and its functions has been noted by several generations of anthropologists of Japan. This ease was described, for example, by John Embree in *Suye Mura* (1939), his ethnography of a Japanese farm village. Based on a year he and his wife Ella spent living among the villagers, Embree's book documents the raucous sexual jokes shared by farmers, female as well as male. Forty years later, in his ethnography *Japan: A View from the Bath*, Scott Clark (1994) found a similar comfort in the communal body, as enjoyed by groups of families, friends, and strangers bathing together at hot springs and public baths, a pleasure described in Japan with the neologism, "skinship."

There is reason to view this traditional acceptance of the body as at risk in contemporary Japan. Clark describes parents taking their children to the public bath once a year in a sort of recuperative project to give them at least occasional experiences of a kind of physical closeness and pleasure in the communal body children once enjoyed daily. John Embree's widow, Ella Wiswell, who had participated with him in the original study of a Japanese farm community in the 1930s, returned to the village of Suye almost fifty years later. Writing in collaboration with Robert Smith, in *The Women of Suye Mura* (Smith & Wiswell 1982) Wiswell describes the changes she found, changes associated with modernization. Her guide, a young woman from the village educated in the city, was much prissier and more proper and less comfortable with the body than were the young village women Wiswell had come to know fifty years before. Wiswell and Smith suggest that this change is a by-product of cultural change and urbanization, as villages become caught up in the morés and values of modern urban society, losing their rural matter-of-factness and acceptance of bodies and sexuality. This shift, which we found as well in China, can be conceived of as a form of *embourgeoisement*, the spread of middle-class Western styles, values, and notions of the self to other classes and cultural contexts.

Preschools, along with the *sento* (public baths) and *onsen* (hot springs) and certain festivals where men in loincloths squish in together to carry heavy shrines are sites in contemporary Japan that retain a sense of pre-bourgeoise embodiment and provide a context for the public (in the sense of communal and non-private) enjoyment of the body. This is a theme we have already established in the previous sections and one we return to in the sections that follow: Japanese preschools are looked to as sites for recuperation of cultural values and practices that are at risk of being lost or that are already lost and need to be recovered.

Continuity and Change at Komatsudani

Comparing our videos of typical days at Komatsudani Hoikuen in 1984 and 2002 provides us with a picture of how this preschool has changed and stayed the same over the course of a generation. This combination of change and continuity reflects the workings of many factors: the vicissitudes of a family-owned business; demographic and economic shifts; and changing social, bureaucratic, and political contexts.

The clearest sign of change at Komatsudani is the new two-story school building and attached dining hall. The money for the new buildings came in part from the national government and in part from the city of Kyoto. Unlike the space occupied by the preschool in the old temple, Komatsudani Hoikuen's new building was designed as a preschool. Another clear marker of change at Komatsudani is the change in leadership. There has been an orderly and by all accounts successful succession of directors, from Yoshizawa Hidenori, who also recently retired as head priest of the temple, to his daughter-in-law, Yoshizawa Norie, who was the director of the *hoikuen* when we made our video, to her husband Yoshizawa Hironori, who took over in 2004, when Norie had a baby. When we first met Yoshizawa

Norie, she was just six months into her job and still nervous about her ability to keep the venture thriving. A year later she was much more confident. Enrollment was down, but only a little, and that modest decline turned out to an aberration rather than a trend. Yoshizawa Norie explained to us that the main drop in enrollment was due to one small cohort of children moving up through the grades. In 2002 there were twenty-two three-year-olds and twenty-three five-year-olds but, for no discernible reason, only seventeen four-year-olds.

As we will see in chapter 4, American teachers and directors who watched the Komatsudani video consider a ratio of seventeen four-year-olds to one teacher to be much too high. But in Japan, the concern is just the opposite, with many informants telling us that a ratio of seventeen children to one adult borders on being too low for optimal social development. Many American teachers speculated that Morita-sensei is unable adequately to supervise the children in her class and prevent fights because the class size and student/teacher ratios are so high. This is what we call the "little old woman who lived in a shoe" theory of child socialization — that quality of care necessarily deteriorates as the number of children per adult goes up. As we discovered and reported in our original study, most Japanese early childhood educators have a quite different way of thinking about ratios and class size. Instead of viewing teachers' non-intervention in children's disputes as an unfortunate and inevitable by-product of large student/teacher ratios, Japanese early childhood educators view it as a desirable structural feature that functions to preclude preschool teachers from over-intervening. As a child psychologist explained to us, "When the class size falls below twenty children per teacher, it becomes a kind of danger zone, where there are still too many children for teachers to give one-on-one attention, but too few to make it clear to children and to the teacher that it is up to the children to handle their own problems." A class size of twenty-five or so children with one teacher is considered ideal for children to learn to be members of a group, which is the top choice Japanese teachers, directors, and experts gave on our questionnaire which asked "what is the most important thing for children to learn in preschool." It is therefore crucial for Komatsudani to maintain enrollment not just for economic reasons but also for child development ones.

To maintain enrollment, Komatsudani has made accommodations to better serve and attract parents of young children. Recent developments include the addition of hot lunches and of the school bus, which spares parents in the neighborhood having to walk up the hill to bring their children to school and brings the school within reach to parents in adjacent neighborhoods of the city. There also have been some changes in routines and in the curriculum. One is that the school day no longer begins with *rajio taisō* (morning exercise to recorded music). Another is the already discussed institutionalization of the practice of having a group of older children spend some time helping out with the infants and babies.

Since we conducted our original study at Komatsudani in the mid-1980s, new buildings have been constructed, new services have been added, some routines have been modified, and some curricular innovations have been introduced. And yet we suggest that Komatsudani has changed relatively little. The spirit, ethos, and underlying philosophy of Komatsudani Hoikuen, as reflected in the way the adults interact with the children and structure the children's experiences, are unchanged.

How was this continuity from 1984 until now achieved? Yoshizawa Hidenori was at the helm for all but the last four of these years. He facilitated a smooth transition of leadership in a traditional Japan manner, by arranging for his son to marry an experienced preschool teacher, the daughter of a priest who runs another Kyoto *hoikuen*. Yoshizawa senior stayed on during his daughter-in-law's first two years, to help ease her into the role of director. His presence during the transition period no doubt gave not just his daughter-in-law but also staff and parents confidence in the continuity of the most valued aspects of the program. For a field characterized by short careers, Komatsudani has also enjoyed a relatively low rate of teacher turnover. Teachers have left over the years to marry or have children, but the turnover has been gradual, giving time to integrate new staff into Komatsudani's philosophy and routines. In 1984, the current assistant director, Sato-sensei, was a classroom teacher in Komatsudani's infant room and Nogami-sensei was a student teacher with the three year-olds. Continuity at Komatsudani is maintained not by systematic training of new hires or the use of training manuals—the school's philosophy is nowhere written down—but instead through an informal apprenticeship system in which new hires are paired with old hands.

Komatsudani has not changed its core beliefs and practices. If anything, the staff members at Komatsudani believe even more strongly in the program's mission and philosophy because their sense of change in Japanese society gives them a heightened sense of urgency. The changes Komatsudani has made over the last twenty years and the Yoshizawas' concerns for their *hoikuen* have much to tell us about contemporary Japanese society and the challenges facing Japanese preschools as they respond to these

3.10. Madoka's neighborhood of Shinkoiwa.

social changes. Now, even more than a generation ago, many Japanese look to preschools as sites that can hold off undesired social change and preserve endangered cultural values and practices.

Madoka: A Contrastive Case

To put continuity and change at Komatsudani in context we offer a contrastive case, Madoka Yōchien, a private kindergarten/nursery school in Shinkoiwa, a modest middle-class neighborhood on the east side of Tokyo (figure 3.10). We chose Madoka for the second Japanese preschool in our study because it differs in many ways from Komatsudani: Komatsudani is a *hoikuen*, Madoka a *yōchien*. Komatsudani is in Kyoto, the ancient capital city in the west of Japan, Madoka in Tokyo, in the east of Japan. Komatsudani serves more working-class families, who can register with the local ward office for reduced tuition rates; Madoka's clientele is more middle-class. Komatsudani makes no claim to having a particular educational orientation; Madoka is a progressive preschool that is based on *nobi nobi kyōiku* (a "room to stretch" curriculum) and an original architecture designed to promote *dōsen* ("lines of flow") and *anākī* (anarchy/spontaneity) and to provide children with *ajito* (hiding) places. We will provide a brief description of a day at Madoka as captured on our videotape, coupled with the explanations and reflections of the classroom teacher and the director, to highlight differences and similarities with Komatsudani.

A DAY AT MADOKA YŌCHIEN

When we videotaped at Madoka in July 2002, there were 250 students in nine classrooms, three each for the three-, four-, and five-year-olds. The

3.11. Madoka Yochien.

school building is two-story, with slides and ladders (as well as conventional steps) linking the two floors. The grounds are large and beautiful, with a small stream, a hill, wooden climbing structure, and abundant bushes and trees (figure 3.11).

Madoka's twenty teachers arrive at 7:00 each morning and put their brightly colored aprons on over their sweatpants or shorts. They each have desks in the large staff room, where they work on their lesson plans and write in their parent-teacher contact books. At 8:00 a.m. the teachers gather in the staff room with the directors, for a morning briefing. Between 8:00 and 9:45 children, wearing their school uniforms of a white shirt, checked skirt or shorts with suspenders, and a hat, and carrying a colorful tote bag containing a change of clothes, arrive by bus or with their parents on foot or by bike. When a child arrives at school, she first goes to her classroom to tick off her name in the attendance book and change out of her school uniform into a T-shirt, gym shorts, and a cap. She then chooses between playing inside or out.

Teachers at Madoka work in pairs; each has a class of from twenty-five to twenty-eight students who share a large room that can be divided into two with a movable screen. During free play periods one teacher from each pair stays inside, with the screens drawn open making one large room, while the other teacher is outside on the playground.

At 9:45, cleanup time is signaled and children both inside and outside rapidly clean up their playthings. The formal part of the school day begins with the customary morning song ("*Sensei, ohayō, minna-san, ohayō*"), followed by roll call. On this day Kaizawa sensei, the teacher of the Midorigumi (green class), leads her twenty-six *nenchu* (middle year) class of four-year-old children outside for swimming in the above-the-ground pool set up on the playground each July. The (male) swimming instructor offers a

3.12. Kaizawa-sensei interviewing the children.

short lesson, demonstrating and then encouraging the children to blow bubbles and then to stick their heads under the water. The ten minutes of swimming instruction are followed by free play in the pool and on the nearby playground with water guns.

After changing back into their school clothes, the children play with puzzles and blocks and look at books. Next comes lunch, which begins with a song and a series of recitations led by the six *tōban* (lunch monitors), under the guidance of Kaizawa-sensei. Pretending that her fist is a microphone, Kaizawa-sensei tells the children, "Say your name, the name of your group, and your favorite color" (figure 3.12). Leaning toward the pretend microphone in his teacher's hand, the first child in line announces, "I am Ishigawa Keijiro of the Rabbit Group." Moving the pretend microphone back in front of her mouth, Kaizawa-sensei asks, "And what color do you like?" Keijiro hesitates and then responds, in a barely audible voice, into his teacher's hand, "All of them!" Kaizawa-sensei responds, "Kei-chan says he likes all of the colors. Let's clap!" After this routine is repeated with the four other children in line (who all turn out to like all of the colors), Kaizawa-sensei cues the *tōban* to say, in unison, that they will do their best (*"Gambarimasu!"*) serving the food today. Their classmates respond, "Thanks for taking care of us, *tōban*." The helpers distribute the lunch boxes one by one to their classmates. They then return to the front of the room and recite, "Father and mother, thank you for the delicious school lunch. We'll eat everything. Let's eat!" Once lunch is finished the *tōban* return to the front of the room and Kaizawa-sensei says, "Standing straight, with our hands clasped, all of us together say, 'Gochisō sama deshita' ('Thanks for the meal we just ate' or literally, 'It was a feast')."

After lunch there is another period of free play followed by a gathering of the children on the floor in a half-circle around Kaizawa-sensei, who reviews with them an activity they did for the recent Moon Festival.

"Your wishes are written on this paper, right? Onda Miyuki-chan wants to be Sailor Moon! Yuki wants to be Doraemon! I can't read everyone's wish now, but I wrote everybody's wish on this paper." Kaizawa-sensei, reminding the children of what they need to put in their backpacks, then tells them to change back into the uniform they wear going and coming to school. The children run to their cubbies to grab the cloth bags that hold their uniforms. As children scurry about the classroom unloading and loading bags and backpacks and changing clothes, Nobu, in tears, approaches Kaizawa-sensei:

NOBU: Yuki pulled my hair.

KAIZAWA-SENSEI: Why did you do that, Yuki?

YUKI: 'Cuz Nobu pinched me.

KAIZAWA-SENSEI: You say he pinched you first? Is that true?

YUKI: No.

KAIZAWA-SENSEI: That's strange.

NOBU: He walked by and pulled my hair.

KAIZAWA-SENSEI: And then you pinched him? Nobu, did you pinch him or not? You pinched him, right? I don't like this. The gods see everything you do. Do you understand? Think about it. And when you are ready to tell the truth, come talk to me. Think about it. I am more bothered by your lying than by what you did. Think about it. (As Kaizawa-sensei turns her attention momentarily to a girl asking for help with a button, Yuki wanders away). Yuki, come back, we're not done.

YUKI (WITH TEARS IN HIS EYES, WHIMPERING): I did it first.

KAIZAWA-SENSEI: It's really important to say you're sorry when you do bad things. I've done bad things to friends, but then I realized I was wrong, and apologized. If you apologize, you feel much better. Do you understand? Do you have something to say?

YUKI: I'm sorry.

NOBU: That's okay.

KAIZAWA-SENSEI (TO NOBU): You, also, have to say "sorry."

NOBU: I'm sorry.

YUKI: That's okay

KAIZAWA-SENSEI: You'll have to change your clothes quickly. Everyone is waiting for you.

Once the children are changed into their uniforms, they again gather on the floor in front of Kaizawa-sensei, who reads them a book and then leads them in a humorous counting song, with gestures, about a group of swallows. The last verse goes: "The fifth little swallow, from its bottom, came some poop! It smells really stinky!" As the teacher and children sing the last verse, they hold their noses with one hand while pretending to wave away the bad odor with the other.

Kaizawa-sensei then distributes plain white paper, folded in half, and explains that this will be used for letters that will be sent to each of them during the two-week vacation that begins in two days.

> KAIZAWA: You can put something on the paper, like a whale or an elephant. It is sad with nothing on the page. Who is this letter from that's going to all of you?
>
> CHILDREN: The director? Mariko-sensei?
>
> KAIZAWA: Right! I won't see you during summer vacation, which will make me very sad. So I'll write you, "Wakana-chan, how are you? Risa-chan, you aren't eating too much ice-cream, are you?" I'll write a lot of things and send it to you.

Chimes ring out throughout the school, indicating that it is almost time for the buses to load. Kaizawa-sensei leads the children in the good-bye song *("Sensei, sayonara, minna-san, sayonara")* and then dismisses the children, some of whom board buses, others of whom are met by parents or grandparents at the door.

Comparing Komatsudani and Madoka

A comparison of the days we videotaped at Madoka Yōchien and Komatsudani Hoikuen helps to highlight and to contextualize sources of continuity and change in Japanese preschools and consistencies and variations in Japanese early childhood education. One preschool cannot represent the preschools of a country. But neither can two. In *Contested Childhood* (2000) Susan Holloway argues for the need to appreciate the diversity of Japanese early childhood education and care programs and she faults *Preschool in Three Cultures,* among other studies, for presenting an image of early childhood education in Japan that is both too uniform and too rosy. Holloway presents a typology of Japanese preschools based on three ideological/ philosophical orientations, which she labels "relationship-oriented," "role-oriented," and "child-oriented." It is useful to be reminded of the dangers of essentializing, over-generalizing, and idealizing, and Holloway's presentation of ideological variation in Japanese approaches to early childhood education and care is instructive and provocative. But Holloway's typological solution creates a new problem. Just as there is not just one type of Japanese preschool, there are also not three types (Walsh 2003). This Caesar-like dividing of Japanese early childhood education into three parts is a heuristic device, a schema imposed to create distinct categories out of what is in reality an array of positions in Japan about how to educate and care for young children, positions that in turn are followed more or less consistently by preschools, producing a great diversity of program structures, philosophies, and practices. And (as Holloway acknowledges and describes) ideology is just one continuum among many that could be used to chart the variety of Japanese early childhood programs. There is also diversity by region and by social class; there are differences between urban, suburban, and rural programs; between private and public ones; between *hoikuen* and *yōchien*; and between Buddhist, Christian, and secular preschools (Boocock 1989). Each Japanese preschool is the locus where these continua intersect and interact, as mediated by local conditions, institutional histories and politics, and the personalities and predilections of the directors, teachers, parents, and children who collectively and collaboratively give each preschool its particular flavor and feel.

In the Preschool in Three Cultures method, as explained in chapter 1, we address the problem of typicality and the question of diversity not by claiming that the schools where we videotape are representative of those of their country, but by showing the videos in five or more sites in each country to audiences of early childhood educators and soliciting their reactions. In this way we shift the question of the typicality of our focal preschools onto the shoulders of our informants. In the sections that follow, we address the diversity of Japanese early childhood education both by comparing Komatsudani and Madoka and by presenting reactions to our videos of days in both schools from Japanese early childhood educators we interviewed in cities around Japan.

THE CURRICULUM THAT LOOKS LIKE THE ABSENCE OF A CURRICULUM

Both at Komatsudani and at Madoka we at times had a hard time knowing what to videotape because the days seemed less defined by explicit lessons or activities than the days we videotaped in Chinese and American preschools. Much of the day at both Komatsudani and Madoka is spent in unstructured play on the playground and inside the classrooms and in transitions (taking toys out and putting them away, changing clothes, moving inside and outside and back again). This organization of the day is typical of Japanese preschools, both *yōchien* and *hoikuen*, of the "free" type. When we asked Kaizawa-sensei if Madoka's approach could be described as *jiyū asobi* (a literal translation of the English language term "free play"), she explained that she prefers other terms:

> We don't use the term *"jiyū asobi."* We prefer everyday terms such as *"suki na asobi"* ("play that is liked"), *"shitai asobi"* ("play that one wants to do"), and *kodomo shutai* (child-oriented).

Director Machiyama described Madoka's curricular approach as *nobi nobi kyōiku* ("room to stretch" or "feel at ease"), with an emphasis on *dōsen* ("lines of flow"), which he explained to us means organizing the curriculum according to the anticipated routes children will take through the school: "I designed the school building and grounds myself. The central idea is that the school is the children's toy. It was designed to be played with in various ways. In a sense, the design of the buildings and grounds is the curriculum." This concept is explained in more detail in the school's brochure for parents, which emphasizes that Madoka's physical layout offers children the chance to experience *anākī* (anarchy/spontaneity) and *ajito* (hideaways; figure 3.13). This emphasis on choice makes Madoka sound like the play-oriented American preschools we discuss in chapter 4. But we would suggest that there is an important difference between the American emphasis on individual children choosing during "activity center time" which among a handful of activities to pursue and the Japanese emphasis on children choosing what to play with less constraint on the options, less specific learning goals, and less structuring of the activities by teachers.

We can see in Director Machiyama's descriptions of the unique features of Madoka evidence for the heterogeneity of approach to be found among *nobi nobi kyōiku* preschools, with some emphasizing that activities should be child-initiated, while others, like Madoka, emphasize the importance of children's choice. And, as Holloway shows in *Contested Childhood*, in addition to easygoing, play-oriented *nobi nobi kyōiku* preschools such as Komatsudani and Madoka, there are some Japanese preschools that are academically oriented and others that are focused on individualized learning. But this diversity does not mean that there are equal numbers of preschools with these orientations or that all three of these philosophies have equal status in Japanese early childhood education circles. Our sense, borne out by our discussions with informants, is that the majority of Japanese early childhood educators believe that preschools should emphasize social and emotional development over academic preparation; that collective play is

3.13. An *ajito* area (hideaway).

more valuable than individual activities; and that the overall mood should be easygoing rather than strict (Oda & Mori 2006).

Play-oriented *yōchien* such as Madoka and *hoikuen* such as Komatsu-dani are more like each other in curricular philosophy than either is like an academically oriented program. That having been said, there are some differences in Komatsudani's and Madoka's approaches to curriculum. The clearest example can be seen in the swimming activities at the two preschools. At Komatsudani, swimming time was all unstructured play. At Madoka, in contrast, unstructured free play in the pool followed a period of formal instruction, in which a physical education teacher who rotates from class to class led the children in exercises involving blowing bubbles and placing their faces in the water. Other examples would be the greater attention given at Madoka than at Komatsudani to organizing ambitious field trips, putting on class plays and musical performances for the school festivals, and undertaking large art projects and nature-themed science projects.

Structural features of Japanese early childhood education that cut across all preschools create some curricular similarities. The most important is the large (by US standards) class size and student/teacher ratio. Most Japanese *yōchien* and *hoikuen* have a class size of twenty-five to thirty children with one teacher for children four- and five-years-old. Whatever the *yōchien*'s or *hoikuen*'s stated educational philosophy, this ratio and class size support a curriculum that emphasizes children's peer relations, learning to do things as a group, and self-sufficiency in changing clothes and organizing belongings. There are a few Christian and Montessori preschools that reject what they see in Japanese early childhood education and in Japanese society as too much emphasis on the group and too little on the individual. These preschools offer curricula that look more like the learning-center, project approach found in progressive US preschools. But even in these programs, the class size and student/teacher ratios generally are higher than in the US, which makes the overall atmosphere and routines different than those of their American counterparts.

Some Japanese early childhood education experts we spoke with are concerned that preschool teachers are not doing enough to foster children's *chiteki hattatsu* (intellectual development.) Some of these experts have introduced the ideas of Reggio Emilia and other project-oriented curricular approaches that emphasize the importance of teachers organizing cognitively stimulating activities and asking probing questions that support the intellectual development of young children. A group of education faculty members who viewed the Komatsudani and Madoka videos faulted both programs for missing opportunities to scaffold children's thinking and to provide the kind of structure to play activities that would promote the children's intellectual growth.

While we agree with the goal of providing children with cognitively stimulating experiences in preschool, we are not convinced that Japanese early childhood education will be improved by becoming more like Reggio Emilia or by an increase in the explicit attention given to intellectual development. We would argue that in spite of the apparent lack of curriculum or intellectual rigor at Komatsudani and Madoka, the programs at these schools are in fact highly intellectually challenging for young children and reflect what we call the implicit cultural logic of Japanese early childhood education. The approach practiced at Komatsudani and Madoka and many other Japanese preschools of emphasizing free play, physicality, and social interaction and of teachers holding back from intervening too quickly in children's disputes is an approach that is practiced widely in Japan without often being explicitly taught in pre-service classes, described in textbooks for preschool teachers, or prescribed in the guidelines for teachers and caretakers issued periodically by the government, although the core values of this approach are implied in the most recent guidelines, especially for those who know how to read between the lines.

In 1998 the Ministry of Education, Culture, Sports, Science and Technology (MEXT) issued *National Curriculum Standards for Kindergartens*, a document that emphasizes the social and emotional development of young children through play and social interaction. The document is consistent in emphasis and spirit with the "Education Reform Plan for the 21st Century" document issued in 2001 by MEXT for elementary and secondary education. The plan reflects a deep concern about the soul of Japanese society and urges an appreciation for "education of the heart," for critical thinking skills, and for creativity, and calls on teachers to make lessons more enjoyable, worry-free, and easy to understand. It also calls for a reform based on a curriculum of *yutori* (relaxation, latitude, or room for growth), a concept close to Madoka's version of *nobi nobi kyōiku*. At the elementary school level there has been a conservative backlash against the liberalization of the curriculum (Takayama 2007). But even as the pendulum swings back towards academics, rigor, and control in policy debates about Japanese education, there is little sign that preschools in Japan are being pressured by the government to emphasize academic preparation, as they are being pressured today in the United States.

The approaches of Komatsudani Hoikuen and Madoka Yōchien share basic values and assumptions about children and child development with the curriculum reform documents. The days we videotaped at Komatsudani and Madoka were unusually rich in opportunities for children to develop socially, emotionally, and intellectually. For example, the girls' fighting over the teddy bear gave them the opportunity to experience complex emotions (the 2001 *yōchien* guidelines call for children "experiencing enjoyment and sadness together through establishing active relationships with friends"); to employ language to communicate their feelings and understand the feelings of others; and to progress in their understanding of the need for society to have rules (in this case, rules for sharing and turn-taking).

The new guidelines urge teachers to create lessons employing role-playing and simulations that give children an opportunity to develop socially. But we would suggest that it would be impossible for teachers to construct lessons as rich, complex, and authentic as the girls' struggles and negotiations over the sharing of the teddy bear. And what teacher-constructed lesson could be more intellectually rich and stimulating for young children than the opportunity to care for infants and toddlers enjoyed by the older children at Komatsudani? When Kenichi teaches Taro to use the urinal, Kenichi is not only developing his *omoiyari* but his intellect as well. Indeed, empathy requires sophisticated working of the mind as well as the heart, because to feel what another is feeling and then act in a way that responds appropriately to another's needs, one must observe, reflect, and plan. In the urinal lesson we see a five-year-old engaged in high-level intellectual activity, as he must take into account what the younger boy already knows and doesn't know about using a urinal and the younger boy's fears, pleasures, and need for autonomy. No piece of computer software, educational toy, or teacher-orchestrated activity can approach in intellectual or emotional complexity the tasks of sorting out disagreements with classmates or caring for a baby or toddler. This is the core cultural logic of the curriculum of Komatsudani and Madoka and many other Japanese preschools, a logic that requires of teachers great restraint coupled with careful observation, planning, and strategic interventions.

APPROACHES TO HANDLING DISPUTES

Kaizawa-sensei's aggressive intervention in the boys' hair pulling incident seems the antithesis of Morita-sensei's non-intervention in the girls' fight over the teddy bear, suggesting a divide in Japanese approaches to handling children's fighting. But we would suggest that Morita-sensei and Kaizawa-sensei have more similar philosophies than might first appear. An erroneous assumption many readers took from our first study, which we are glad now to have a chance to put right, is that Japanese teachers do not intervene in disputes between children. This was not then and is not now the case. As we have discussed above, there are Japanese educators who disagree with Morita-sensei's non-intervention approach for a variety of reasons. The key point we intended to make in the original study and want to reiterate now is not that Japanese teachers never intervene, but that non-intervention is an option available to Japanese teachers for responding to fights. In contrast to the US, where intervening in children's physical altercations is the rule, in Japan non-intervention is a pedagogical strategy that is employed by many teachers, a strategy that reflects an approach to childhood socialization that is widely, but by no means universally, shared in Japan. Even teachers in Japan who say they would be quicker than Morita-sensei to intervene nevertheless for the most part find the reasoning behind her non-intervention familiar and logical, just as most Japanese teachers who watched our old video readily understood if not fully endorsed the logic behind Fukui-sensei's non-intervention in Hiroki's misbehavior.

It would be wrong to conclude from our descriptions of typical days at Komatsudani and Madoka that Morita-sensei and Kaizawa-sensei routinely handle misbehavior in very different ways. What such a conclusion misses is that there are times that Morita-sensei intervenes and times when Kaizawa-sensei does not. Morita-sensei intervened in an earlier tug of war among the girls over the teddy bear when she became concerned that the tussle was taking place too close to the corner of the piano. And at the height of the big fight captured in our video we hear Morita-sensei call out to the girls from across the room, reminding them with a "Hey!" not to let things get too far out of control. We also observed an incident where Morita-sensei reprimanded Nao for swinging her elbows recklessly out of frustration, hurting another child. Morita-sensei came over and told Nao, "That's how babies behave. You aren't a baby anymore, right?" Kaizawa-sensei's intervention in these cases was one strategy she employs; non-intervention is another, just as her predecessor a generation ago in the four-year-old classroom at Komatsudani, Fukui-sensei, explained to us that she had tried a range of approaches to dealing with Hiroki's misbehavior, settling in the end on a policy of (mostly) not intervening, and letting him and his classmates work things out. Kaizawa-sensei is similarly pragmatic and eclectic. We observed her intervening quickly and aggressively in some disputes (such as the hair pulling) while letting other situations play out without her intervention. The reasoning behind the non-interventionist strategy is to give children ample opportunities to deal with socially complex situations including arguments and fights. This reasoning does not require that teachers never intervene, just that do not always or usually intervene. Kaizawa-sensei's stated policy on intervening in children's physical disputes is almost exactly the same as Morita-sensei's:

> When there's a fight among children, I watch and wait and try to decide if they are really attempting to hurt each other, or if it is just rough play. It's sometimes hard to tell. If it looks like it's getting to be too rough or that it might get out of control, I tell them to be less rough, but I don't tell them to stop.

In deciding whether or not to intervene both teachers say they use the strategy of *mimamoru*, of observing and "standing guard" instead of immediately taking action. This strategy is a component of a larger pedagogical approach called *machi no hoiku* (caring for children by waiting), a strategy that although not formally taught in Japanese colleges of education or stated in the official curriculum guides, is employed by preschool teachers across Japan. As a preschool teacher in Tokyo explained to us: "Japanese teachers wait until children solve their problems on their own. Children know their abilities, what they can do. So we wait. It could be said that we can wait because we believe in children."

Machi no hoiku is not easy to practice. It is not a passive absence of action but instead a strategic deployment of non-action, a strategy, like other Japanese regimens of self-control, that takes years of experience to master. Many of the comments in Japanese focus groups that were critical of Morita-sensei's non-intervention approach came from university students in early childhood education teacher preparation programs, which is consistent with the notion that the Japanese pedagogy of non-intervention requires some years of experience to appreciate and master. When we interviewed Morita-sensei most recently (in 2007), she told us, "After five years of teaching I'm just starting to feel like I know what I am doing and to have confidence that I can make the right decisions about when to act and when to hold back and watch." Retired Director Yoshizawa told us, "It takes a real care professional to tell the difference between rough play and a real fight. It takes at least five years." Director Kumagai of Senzan Yōchien in Kyoto commented on the fighting scene at Komatsudani by saying:

> This teacher can wait because she has three years' experiences of working in a day-care center. First-year teachers can't wait. This is the big difference between an experienced preschool teacher and most young parents. Watching and waiting (*mimamoru*) is very difficult for parents. If most parents were at school and they saw their children in a fight like this, they couldn't stand it. They'd have to do something. So would inexperienced teachers. That's why we need experienced teachers, who can stand back and watch and wait. Children need to be given opportunities to experience life in the gray zone, where things aren't just black and white. When teachers intervene too quickly, it's like they are picking a bud before it has a chance to flower.

Again, the key point here is not that teachers should never intervene, but that they should have the self-control and the wisdom required to watch and wait and then make a strategic decision about whether or not to intervene. And when they do intervene, it should be based not only on their assessment of risk, but also on their developmental goals for the children and their assessment that their intervention will not just stop an unwanted behavior but also contribute to the development of deeper feelings and understanding. Kaizawa-sensei's approach to the hair-pulling incident is an example of just such an intervention (figure 3.14). Her tactics and goals here are consistent with an approach described and analyzed by Lois Peak in her 1992 book *Learning to Go to School in Japan*. Peak describes incidents she observed in *yōchien* where teachers chose opportune moments to frustrate chronically misbehaving, recalcitrant, or babyish children, sometimes to the point of driving them to break down in tears. This, we think, is what Kaizawa-sensei was doing with Yuki. It is not just that she found his lying about hair pulling to be more serious than other misbehaviors—it was, she explained to us, the lying, not the hair pulling, that bothered her most—but also that for this particular problem she felt that provoking an emotional "boiling over" was the best strategy. We would also suggest that the goal of her intervention was not just to get the boys to

3.14. 1. "Yuki pulled my hair."

2. "You say he pinched you first?"

3. "Is that true?"

4. "The gods see everything you do."

5. "I did it."

6. "I'm sorry."

tell the truth and then to apologize but also and perhaps even more importantly to get them to express and acknowledge the sadness that comes from interpersonal distance, an emotion that, as we discuss in the next section, is highly culturally valued. She felt so strongly that this was a valuable teaching opportunity that she invested more than five minutes dealing with the boys during the hectic changing time when many children were asking for her assistance with buttons. It is clear from a careful look at her interac-

3.15. Kaizawa-sensei explains her strategy.

tion with Yuki and Nobu and confirmed in her self-report afterward that although Kaizawa-sensei appears to be emotionally distressed in her talk with the two boys, frowning intensely and speaking in a voice laden with emotion, she in fact was not upset, angry, or frustrated at any time in the interaction. One clue is that we see her take brief time outs from her intense discussion with the boys to remind other children, without any hint of emotion in her voice, to change quickly and to attend to the bus schedule. Her intensity and emotionality with the two four-year-old boys was a carefully crafted technique, a performance that, eventually, had the intended effect. When she reviewed this scene on the videos, Kaizawa-sensei explained her intervention (figure 3.15):

> The boys eventually apologized to each other, but that was not my goal in intervening. With three-year-olds, who don't yet know how to apologize, I might lead them through a process of apologizing and accepting others' apologies so they will know how to do this on their own in the future. But these boys already know how to apologize. So if they don't apologize, it is because they aren't sorry for what they've done. There is nothing to be gained by forcing them to apologize if the feeling isn't there. I wanted them to understand the importance of being truthful and to think about the effects on others and on oneself of hair pulling, hitting, and especially of lying. If, after thinking about the effects of their behaviors, they chose to apologize, that's fine, but it wasn't my goal.

Our screenings of the Japanese videos in the US suggest that many Americans are no more comfortable with Kaizawa's "break him down" interrogation approach than they are with Morita-sensei's standing by while girls wrestle on the floor. But both Morita-sensei's seemingly laissez-faire approach and Kaizawa-sensei's seemingly overly aggressive one need to be understood as thoughtful, intentional strategies that follow cultural scripts that are well known, understood, and employed by other Japanese teachers, even if they aren't written in textbooks or articulated in curriculum guides. The artful, strategic deployment over time of both of these scripts is intended to produce children who are both self-reliant and interpersonally skilled, spontaneous, joyful, and emotionally responsive. As Morita-sensei explained:

> I think children can learn many things from fighting. For example, they can learn that if I say something hurtful to another person, it makes me sad. The person who does something and the person who has something done to her are always changing, right? One day, a girl might hit somebody and the next day she might be hit. During this process of switching positions, people come to understand feelings. People can't come to understand feelings without having direct experience.

TALK AND FEELINGS

In the Komatsudani and Madoka videos we see teachers discussing with children the feelings not only of people, but also of animals and even of inanimate objects. The particular emotion emphasized by both Morita-sensei and Kaizawa-sensei in these scenes is *sabishii*, which carries a meaning somewhere between the English words "sad" and "lonely." Holding up an origami fish, Morita-sensei says to the children, "It looks *sabishii* with no eyes." Explaining to her students that she wants them to make greeting cards to send her during vacation, Kaizawa-sensei holds up a blank piece of folded paper and says that it looks *sabishii* with nothing drawn on it and then says that she will be *sabishii* not to see the children during the summer break. As Kaizawa-sensei says this, she chokes back a pretend sob and mimes wiping her teary eyes, performing for the children a caricature of anguished loneliness (figure 3.16).

Another example of the pedagogy of *sabishii*, observed at a *yōchien* in Kyoto: at lunchtime, the classroom teacher, circulating around the room, notices that many of the children have finished their meat and rice and dessert, but left their carrots untouched. Speaking to a boy in a theatrical voice loud enough for the whole class to hear, the teacher says "Poor Mister carrot! You ate Mr. Hamburger and Mr. Rice, but you haven't eaten any of Mr. Carrot. Don't you think he feels *sabishii*"?

3.16. Kaizawa-sensei pretends to cry.

These observations suggest that in Japanese childhood socialization more emphasis is placed on teaching young children to intuit and respond to feelings rather than, as we will see in the US chapter, to express emotions verbally, or as in China, to express oneself verbally in storytelling, giving a classmate feedback, or debriefing an activity. Japanese educators who viewed the US and Chinese videos were surprised by the emphasis in both countries on young children's verbal expression. In the original study we quoted Japanese preschool teachers discussing a scene in the US video that shows an American teacher asking children who have been fighting to use words to express their angry feelings:

YAGI: Wow—that's amazing. Talking so directly with such young children about their feelings.

TANAKA: . . . .It seems a bit heavy, doesn't it? It reminds me of marriage counseling. (Tobin, Wu & Davidson 1989, 152)

Japanese educators had similarly politely critical reactions to the way the teachers in the new US videos encouraged children to put their thoughts and feelings into words. For example, a teacher from Tokyo said of the new St. Timothy's videotape:

It's impressive how much time and attention those teachers spend one on one with the children, getting them to talk. The smaller number of students makes this possible. But I can't help wondering if it is too much? I felt a bit sorry for that boy who threw the bowling pin and then had to have such an intense conversation with the teacher. And after a child makes a drawing, I wonder if it might be more pleasurable to not have to talk so much about it, but just to have done it.

Many Japanese respondents were surprised by the verbal virtuosity of the Story Telling King and his classmates in Shanghai. A graduate student in early childhood education said:

> Wow, it's amazing. These children are just four years old and they talk so much and explain their positions so clearly with so much detail, and they seem very comfortable talking in front of people. Even as an adult I cannot do that. I don't think I could be voted Story Telling King! There is such a big difference between how well those Chinese children speak in formal situations and the awkwardness of the children at Madoka Yōchien speaking in front of their classmates before lunch, even with their teacher's prompting. The Chinese boy told a story without help that lasted for five minutes and the Japanese children struggled to say their names and their favorite color! I guess we Japanese do not have many opportunities to express ourselves using verbal power. We are more listener oriented, which means as speakers we feel we do not need to put everything into words.

A preschool director offered a similar response: "In our preschool our emphasis is not on teaching young children to express themselves verbally but instead on the development of the heart (*kokoro*) through the encouragement of *yomitoru* (reading other people's thoughts and feelings) and *kumitoru* (understanding)."

In Japanese theories of interpersonal communication, not needing to explain one's feelings or ideas is paired with the responsibility of listeners to intuit the unverbalized feelings and thoughts of others. Komatsudani's emphasis on having the older children care for toddlers and infants and Morita-sensei's strategy of not intervening in the older girls' interactions with Nao can be seen as serving the development of empathy in young children. What babies and toddlers and immature three-year-olds like Nao have in common with carrots and origami fish and blank pieces of paper is an inability to verbalize their feelings. Vegetables, origami fish, sheets of paper, babies who cannot talk, and immature classmates who lack social skills provide Japanese preschool children with educable moments, specifically with the chance to learn *omoiyari*, which means to be aware of the unverbalized and awkwardly expressed feelings of others.

When we asked Morita-sensei what children can learn from fighting, her first response was: *Itte kanashii. Itte* means "say" and *kanashii* means "sad." Together, they produce a phrase that means "Saying something (hurtful) to another person makes you sad." This phrase is a striking twist on phrases outsiders to Japanese culture might expect a preschool teacher to say in this situation such as "Saying mean things to people makes them sad" or "When someone says something mean to me, it makes me sad." The emphasis in *itte kanashii* is on not just emotion, but empathy, and more specifically on using an awareness of one's own emotions (in this case, of the sadness that comes from hurting others) as an undesirable consequence that can be used to motivate pro-social behavior in the future.

We observed teachers at Komatsudani performing for children exaggerated, stylized performances of emotions other than *sabishii*, emotions including *okote iru* (anger, usually performed by sticking out the lower lip, lowering the corners of the eyes, and crossing the arms) and *ureshii* (happiness/excitement/satisfaction, performed by clenching fists alongside your face while smiling, like a gymnast who just stuck a perfect landing). But of these emotions, it is *sabishii* that is given the greatest curricular emphasis in Japan. Why is this so? We speculate that emphasizing feelings of sadness and loneliness with young children is a pedagogical tool known to Japanese mothers and teachers alike; it is a deep cultural script, tied to a particular cultural sensibility—a kind of melancholic longing (*wabi-sabi*) highly valued in Japanese aesthetics and social life (Hayashi, Karasawa & Tobin, 2009). Not purely or even mostly negative, *sabishii*, like shame and guilt, is a pro-social emotion that binds people together in society.

The Changing Relationship between *Yōchien* and *Hoikuen*

The most basic variation in Japanese early childhood education is a structural one: the difference between *yōchien* and *hoikuen,* a difference that must be kept in mind to understand the differences between Madoka and Komatsudani. A key characteristic of early childhood education in Japan described in the original study is the existence of the side-by-side systems of *yōchien* and *hoikuen.* Other countries have two-tiered systems, but usually to serve different aged children, as in France's system of *crèche* for infants and toddlers and *école maternelle* for children ages three to six. *Hoikuen,* like *crèches,* serve infants and toddlers. But they also serve older children. *Hoikuen* and *yōchien* compete for three- to six-year-olds, a competition that has taken on new urgency in an age of shrinking birthrates.

In our original study we described some of the social class and status tensions that divide *yōchien* from *hoikuen.* Historically, the biggest difference between the two systems is one of social class: *hoikuen* historically have served the working classes, whose mothers could not afford to stop working to stay home with young children, in contrast to *yōchien,* which traditionally served middle-class *sarari-man* (salaried, white-collar) families (Wollons 2000). Social change in Japan has worked to blur this distinction (Imoto 2007). With more professional women refusing to quit work when they become parents, there is an increasing need for full-day care for children from middle-class families. Some professional, middle-class parents choose to enroll their children in *hoikuen,* but because *hoikuen* are associated, accurately or unfairly, with daycare rather than with education and with working-class rather than middle-class values, some middle-class parents prefer *yōchien* for their children, even though *yōchien* hours are inconvenient for working mothers. The Ministry of Education (MEXT) is working with *yōchien* to help them compete with *hoikuen* by diversifying their offerings and extending their school day with after-school enrichment classes.

Some *hoikuen* are adding frills and more academic emphasis to their curriculum to compete with *yōchien.* But Komatsudani and many other *hoikuen* see no need to become more *yōchien*-like. Hoikuen have less need to change than do *yōchien* because they have a built-in competitive advantage of taking infants and toddlers and being open all day—*hoikuen* typically are open from 7 a.m. to 6 p.m. while the *yōchien* class day typically runs from 9 a.m. to 2 p.m. Once parents have enrolled their infant in a *hoikuen,* for reasons of schedule, convenience, trust, and a desire for continuity, they are unlikely to move him to a *yōchien* when he turns three. Many *yōchien* now have extended hours (*azukari hoiku*) and after-school enrichment plans, but their schedule and more frequent holidays still make them less convenient for working parents than the year-round, all-day service provided by *hoikuen.*

With *yōchien* feeling pressure from parents to lengthen their school day and with some *hoikuen* feeling pressure to provide more academic preparation, programmatic and curricular differences between *hoikuen* and *yōchien* seem to have grown smaller over the years. Japan thus may be repeating a phenomenon that happened in the US in the last two decades, where half-day nursery school programs changed their names to "children's centers" and extended their hours of operation to serve working mothers, thereby stealing away customers from daycare centers, which carry a built-in competitive disadvantage from their historical association with poverty and low quality. On the other hand, the *hoikuen* have a tradition and an infrastructure for full-day care that they can use to attract children of middle-class working parents. As the traditional ideology of *ryōsai kenbo* ("good wife, wise mother"), an ideology the government used to keep middle-class women at home and out of the workforce, has lost influence over the years, the stigma on middle-class women putting their children in full-time care has largely disappeared. The discourse of responsible motherhood in the service of the nation has been replaced by a national effort to increase the nation's birthrate by reducing the economic, emotional, and social burdens of parenting. As Yuki Imoto explains:

> While the birthrate has been in decline since the mid 1970s, it was in 1989 that the government decided to raise the issue as a "crisis"; the media sensationalized the significant drop in the fertility rate to 1.57 as the "1.57 shock" (Roberts 2002, 54). Henceforth, the government attitude toward childcare policy took a turn to one of active involvement. In 1994, this was officially realized in the Angel Plan, which saw the implementation of a series of policies that "sought to remove the stigma from a mother who worked and replace it with the idea that the state should support such women to ensure they could have a full career and bring up their families" (Goodman 2000, 3). Childcare for infants from birth, extended opening hours at night, and other childcare services were introduced. (2007, 95)

With the availability of high-quality, affordable, full-day early childhood education and childcare officially viewed as a potentially effective incentive to parenthood, *hoikuen* and *yōchien* and the government ministries that sponsor them scrambled to find ways to expand their services and be increasingly responsive to parental needs and desires.

In this context, concluding that it is economically wasteful and inefficient to perpetuate two governmental systems that are running competing programs for an overlapping demographic of children, in the 1990s Japanese policy experts and politicians called for a rationalization of early childhood education and care services and for the combining of the *hoikuen* and *yōchien* systems. However, resistance put forward by *yōchien* and *hoikuen* providers as well as by bureaucrats in the two national ministries blocked progress toward a merger and talks eventually broke down.

This battle took a new turn in 2006 when the government's Central Council of Education and Social Welfare Committee introduced a "third alternative," a new kind of preschool: the *nintei kodomo-en* (literally, "accredited children's garden") or, for short, *kodomo-en* ("kindergarten"). With the hope that these new hybrid early childhood education and care programs might eventually replace *yōchien* and *hoikuen*, the government suggests that *kodomo-en* can be created in four ways: out of the merger of existing *hoikuen* and *yōchien* operating in the same communities; existing *yōchien* taking on *hoikuen* functions; existing *hoikuen* taking on *yōchien* functions; and independent facilities that are currently unlicensed taking on the functions of both the *hoikuen* and the *yōchien* (that is, of full-day care and of early childhood education) and applying for licensure (Imoto 2007). It is too early to tell whether the kodomo-en movement will succeed.

Pathways of Continuity and Change in Public and Private Preschools

More often overlooked but perhaps just as salient as the *hoikuen/yōchien* distinction is the distinction between public and private preschool programs. Approximately 60% of *yōchien* are private and 40% public. But because private programs are on the average larger than public ones, about 80% of children attending *yōchien* are enrolled in private programs. The percentage of public programs is higher among *hoikuen*, which provide a mandated social service of caring for children of working parents.

Public and private preschools in Japan have different employment patterns for teachers, which makes for different institutional cultures and different dynamics of continuity and change. Teachers in public *yōchien* are employees not of the preschool but of the government. As tenured government employees, they tend to stay in the profession for many years, which gives continuity to the profession. But because they are employees of the government rather than of a particular *yōchien* and because MEXT has a policy of rotating teachers every few years to level the quality of education across schools (and, some critics suggests, to weaken the power of the teachers union and of teacher influence), public *yōchien* have high teacher turnover.

Private *yōchien* also have high teacher turnover, but for a different reason. In order to keep costs down and turn a profit, the directors of private *yōchien* use various strategies to encourage teachers to retire after working only a couple of years. In Japan, in both the public and private sectors, salaries rise dramatically with experience. The easiest way for a private preschool to hold down costs is to have a significant percentage of the workforce quit before their salaries rise. Although Japan is thought of in the West as a land of lifetime employment with the same firm, this is true only for work in the public sector and in some elite companies. And even within the public sector and in elite companies, lifetime employment is a policy much more for men than for women, who have for the past fifty years or so followed a career cycle described as a U—most enter the work force after graduation from high school or college, work for a few years, quit when they get married or have their first child, and then return to part-time work when their children are grown. This traditional pattern of women's work has changed recently, with women becoming more independent and less willing to sacrifice their career and salary to be an at-home wife and mother. But despite this change in women's attitudes towards work, private preschools remain a business that depends on employee turnover to keep costs down. Even with high (by American standards) student/teacher ratios, competition and custom prevents preschools from raising tuition above about $300 a month, which makes profit margins slim.

The high staff turnover in the private sector leads to a young teaching force that in turn leads to an energetic teaching style some observers refer to sarcastically but not entirely unkindly as *burikko*, a word typically used to describe female pop stars. The young teachers of most *yōchien* are *genki* (energetic), *akarui* (cheerful), *sunao* (unaffected), and *jounetsuteki* (enthusiastic), characteristics that are also valued in young children. In other words, young *yōchien* teachers, like the young hosts of children's morning television programs, are avatars who model the demeanor and characteristics that their young students are to follow. This modeling of childlike behavior, which takes the form of performing childlike versions of emotions of sadness and excitement and of engaging in physical play, is a style of teaching that is better suited to young teachers like Morita-sensei and Kaizawa-sensei than to veteran teachers.

This is not to suggest that younger teachers are better than older ones, but rather that they tend to have a different style of teaching and therefore that preschools with mostly younger teachers (which is to say private preschools) have a somewhat different look and feel from preschools where most of the teachers are older and more experienced (which is to say public preschools). This point was emphasized to us by Professor Kiyomi Akita of Tokyo University in a discussion we had with her and some of her colleagues about our Komatsudani and Madoka videos. Professor Akita explained that because new teachers are less capable of developing sophisticated pedagogical approaches than are more experienced ones, private *yōchien*, with their relatively inexperienced staff, necessarily rely on a transmission model of practice, with the director and the few experienced teachers each year passing on to their younger colleagues teaching strategies and curricular ideas. As a result, private preschools with a strong director often have a distinctive style and approach, reflecting the vision of the director (Holloway 2000, 209–10). Because directors of private preschools (who are often also the owner) tend to occupy the position for many years, there is considerable consistency of practice in private preschools over the years. In contrast, in public *yōchien* with an experienced, tenured teaching staff who rotate from preschool to preschool every few years, directors (who also rotate) have less influence and the pedagogy and curriculum are less likely to be idiosyncratic or distinctive and more likely to reflect the current notions of best practice of the Ministry of Education and of scholars in schools of education. Early childhood education experts employed by MEXT and university professors of education are much more likely to consult in public preschools than in private ones. Moreover, the ministry has much more leverage over public than over private *yōchien* to get them to adapt the spirit and the letter of reforms, such as the 1998 *National Curriculum Standards for Kindergartens*. Another factor is that experienced teachers who have already mastered strategies for working with large groups of children and have a clear, secure sense of who they are in the classroom are better able than are struggling new teachers to make adjustments to their teaching and to experiment with new pedagogical ideas.

This difference between the employment characteristics of private and public preschool programs in Japan carries profound implications for continuity and change in preschools over time. Both Komatsudani and Madoka are private programs where the directors and a few highly experienced teachers play very strong roles in mentoring new staff, establishing a characteristic, even idiosyncratic approach, and maintaining continuity of practice over the course of a generation despite a high staff turnover. Komatsudani's current system of having older children care for younger ones is a good example of how both continuity and change occur in a private preschool. This approach to mixed-age interaction, a practice found in few other Japanese preschools, reflects the guiding philosophy of a strong long-serving director, the Buddhist priest Yoshizawa Hidenori. Concerned for more than a generation with what he saw as the loss of social complexity in the lives of young children, Director Yoshizawa over the years consistently strove to create a program that would provide children with opportunities for developing empathy and other social and interpersonal skills. Although all but one of the teachers who were working at Komatsudani when we made the original video in 1985 had left the school and indeed had retired from the field when we returned in 2002, the continuity of vision provided by Director Yoshizawa and his daughter-in-law in their tenures as directors, combined with the shared vision of Nogami-sensei, who had come to Komatsudani as a student teacher in 1985 and stayed on for twenty years, created a context for innovation, in this case for what we have called the institutionalization of the mixed-age interactions that had begun spontaneously a generation earlier. Similarly, Madoka Yōchien, under the guiding hand of Director Machiyama, the son of the founder, developed a strong, idiosyncratic curricular approach that has been consistent over the years, despite high staff turnover. Madoka's *nobi nobi kyōiku* curriculum, while not in itself idiosyncratic or unusual for a private *yōchien*, is unique in the way it makes use of the cleverly designed building and grounds, integrated by a system of slides and exterior steps, which encourage the children to move back and forth throughout the day between the inside and outside and to interact with nature in a school located in a gritty urban setting. The building and grounds, designed by Director Machiyama in collaboration with an architect, are an extension of his educational philosophy. It would be impossible for the director of a public program to have a similar influence on a preschool's physical environment or on the curriculum.

Because the staff of public preschools are on the average much more experienced and more professional, because most transfer periodically from school to school, and because public programs are more responsive to new directions and ideas coming from MEXT and from early childhood education researchers, public programs are less varied in quality or in approach than are private programs, which, for better or worse, tend to reflect the predilections of their directors, who often are also the owners. There are high-quality private *hoikuen*, like Komatsudani, and high-quality *yōchien*, like Madoka, that are remarkably consistent in their approach over the years. On the other hand, there are weak and even peculiar private programs that reflect the sometimes odd pedagogical ideas of their long-serving directors; and there are mediocre private programs led by directors with backgrounds in business rather than in early childhood education who are calculating and cynical in their appeals to the insecurities and misplaced priorities of young parents. Such programs change quickly from year to year, as they introduce trendy innovations. Or perhaps it is more accurate to say that they change on the surface while staying consistent in their market-oriented approach to attracting students.

Because public *yōchien* are all under the control of the Ministry of Education and public *hoikuen* under the control of the Ministry of Health and Welfare, and because their teachers and directors rotate, they are much more homogeneous than are private *yōchien* and *hoikuen*, which are heterogeneous in philosophy and quality. The professionalism and experience of the staff at public *yōchien* allow them to function as what Kiyomi Akita calls "communities of knowledge development," in which curriculum and pedagogy are continuously discussed and reworked by experienced teachers, in contrast to the private preschools' "transmission of knowledge" model, in which the director and a few experienced teachers pass on philosophy and practice to an ever-rotating group of young teachers.

Professor Akita's suggestion that knowledge transmission is more characteristic of private programs and knowledge development of public ones makes a lot of sense. But there is a danger of exaggerating the difference between public and private programs in this regard, and of idealizing public ones and denigrating private ones. Although Madoka is private and the majority of the teachers relatively young and inexperienced, as in good public programs, the staff participate each year in after-school *ennai kenshü* (group study) sessions, in which teachers present issues they are struggling with in their classrooms, issues both of how to deal with particularly challenging children and of planning good lessons. Director Machiyama participates as a "commentator" for these discussions, and he pays the teachers four-hours of overtime a week to participate, but he is not the leader or organizer for these meetings, which are teacher-run. The fact that Madoka's teachers and staff participate in *ennai kenshu* demonstrates their professionalism and provides further evidence that what may look like the unstructured and even under-supervised "free play" of the children at Madoka are in fact activities that are carefully observed, discussed, and scaffolded by the staff.

A continuity of philosophy and practice is maintained over the years at both Komatsudani and Madoka through a process of apprenticeship and on-the-job training. These informal modes of training are critical to the passing down of practices that are part of each country's repertoire of implicit cultural practices. For example, as Director Yoshizawa, Director Kumagai, and Morita-sensei told us in their reflections on *machi no hoiku*, the ability to practice *mimamoru* (watching and waiting) takes years to master. This approach is not found in Japanese textbooks or curriculum guides but instead is passed down from teacher to teacher and mastered through the experience of working for several years in a program that has a consistent overall approach. Morita-sensei explained it to us:

MAYUMI KARASAWA: Is holding back and not intervening in fights something you learned at the university? Would you say that this is common in Japanese preschools, or that it is Komatsudani's own approach?

MORITA-SENSEI: I don't know. I can't really say. I only know this *hoikuen*. If I were in another *hoikuen*, it might be different. But here, at Komatsudani, the other teachers do the same thing. They observe children. I think the climate here gives me the foundation for my way of dealing with fighting.

Komatsudani is able to transmit practices from one cohort of teachers to the next in part because it is a private family business. Komatsudani

Hoikuen is a part of the Komatsudani Temple, which is managed by the Yoshizawa family, who live on the temple grounds and hand down control of both the temple and *hoikuen* from father to son. Komatsudani is a private business, but one motivated more by a sense of mission than profit. The curriculum at Komatsudani is not Buddhist in any explicit or obvious way and the teachers and staff, other than the Yoshizawas, are not more Buddhist than the Japanese general population. And yet the spirit and purpose of Komatsudani Hoikuen reflect the values and beliefs of the Yoshizawa family, who direct the temple as well as the *hoikuen*. Ancient temples such as Komatsudani that have significant historical and culture value but few parishioners often run a preschool, which is seen as a use of the temple that is consistent with Buddhist values.

Madoka Yōchien has no religious affiliation, and it is more explicitly a business than is Komatsudani Hoikuen. Director Machiyama is the business manager as well as education leader. He inherited the business from his father, who began it. But although it is a profit-making business, Madoka Yōchien is not run only or even primarily based on economic concerns. Madoka has a clear mission and philosophy and a long-term commitment to providing quality early childhood programs to families in the neighborhood, a mission and philosophy that keeps Madoka from making precipitous changes in approach in an attempt to attract new clients or increase the bottom line.

Contemporary Pressures on Japanese Preschools

THE SHRINKING OF THE JAPANESE FAMILY

Japan has one of the lowest birthrates in the world. Already low in 1984 at 1.6 when we did the original study and even lower in 1989, at the time of the "1.57 shock" discussed above, it is now 1.2. Causes include an increasingly late age of marriage by both males and females and more women deciding not to marry. Many of the changes at Komatsudani between 1984 and 2005 can be attributed in part to indirect and direct effects of Japan's falling birthrate. Because the birthrate was already low and falling a generation ago, many of these changes were anticipated in our original study of Komatsudani. The shrinking birthrate is having similar effects on Madoka, and indeed on most Japanese preschools, the only exceptions being preschools in those few parts of the country that are enjoying population growth, most of which are in new suburbs.

The most direct effect of this birthrate on preschools is their having to compete more aggressively to keep up their enrollment. Some have reduced enrollment and staff, but downsizing carries the disadvantage of a loss of economies of scale; many expenses of preschools are fixed, including administrative salaries, utilities, maintenance, and land taxes. For these reasons, enrollment can fall only so far before preschools hit a danger zone. Drops in enrollment can lead to cuts in programs that in turn lead to the preschool becoming less attractive to potential customers. Enrollment drops also carry the risk of jeopardizing program reputations. To compete in neighborhoods in Japan where birthrates are low, rather than downsizing, many private preschools expand their recruitment area. Like fishing boats that have to go further and further from home port to fill their holds, many *yōchien* and *hoikuen* are sending their brightly colored fleets of buses further and further out to fill their classes. This strategy of recruiting outside their immediate neighborhood exacerbates the problem of competition as more and more preschools attempt to recruit from the same pool of children. For each child enrolled from outside one's neighborhood, preschools risk losing a local child to another preschool that is also sending its buses further and further out. It could be argued that the increasing geographic range of *yōchien* and *hoikuen* recruitment has the benefit of giving families increased choice. But it carries the disadvantage of causing less well-funded programs that cannot afford buses to close down, with a net result of fewer preschools serving children in their local community and more children spending more time each day on buses. It also means that *hoikuen* such as Komatsudani, which did not have buses twenty years ago, now spend money on this service. As Yoshizawa Hidenori explained to us, "We didn't used to need buses because the children were all brought to school by their parents or grandparents. But these days, parents in the neighborhood are too busy to walk up the hill with their children in the morning or they live too far from school to bring their children, so to get enough children, we have to provide bus service."

Japan is not just aging as a nation, but aging unevenly, much more rapidly in the countryside than in the city and in some neighborhoods than in others. Kumagai-sensei, the director of Senzan Yōchien in Kyoto, explained to us that the problem her *yōchien* faces is not an overall population drop in the Higashiyama-ku neighborhood, where both Senzan Yōchien and Komatsudani Hoikuen are located, but a drop in the number of families with young children: "Young parents cannot afford to live here. As housing prices soared in the late 1980s and early 1990s, young families moved to the surrounding suburbs, where land is cheaper and new houses were being built. As a result, this neighborhood became older and older." Director Kumagai was cautiously optimistic that the economic downturn in Japan might paradoxically help their enrollment situation by leading to a decline in urban real estate prices, allowing younger families to return to live in the city. Otherwise, neighborhoods such as Kyoto's Higashiyama-ku risk becoming empty of children.

As several preschool directors explained to us, another effect of declining birthrates on preschools is that many preschools, and, particularly private *yōchien*, are distorting their curricula to woo perspective clients. Some preschools with declining enrollments feel compelled to add trendy programs of little educational or social value. In neighborhoods where ambitious, nervous young parents are seeking an academic fast start for their children, preschools increasingly give in to the temptation to do more explicit academic instruction than they would do otherwise. Computers, tennis, swimming, and English conversation are among the enrichment activities being added to the standard *yōchien* curriculum to attract customers. From a consumers' rights point of view, this could be viewed as a good thing, as increasing competition compels preschools to be more sensitive to the desires of their potential customers. But most of the Japanese early childhood experts and preschool directors we interviewed view the market effects on the curriculum as an unfortunate pressure leading preschools to pander to the sometimes misguided desires of their potential clients and to lose sight of what is good for children.

A change in services that is of more obvious value to parents is extending the school day. To recruit children whose parents both work full-time, many *yōchien* are now offering the option of an extended-day program. Some *yōchien* and *hoikuen*, including Komatsudani, are running after-school programs for primary school children. A few preschools have made the more radical but demographically and economically logical move of changing from being a preschool to an eldercare center.

It is unclear what this increased competition caused by declining birthrates will mean in the long run for the quality of Japanese early childhood education. A Darwinian survival-of-the-fittest/market capitalism model would suggest that competition will improve quality, as weaker programs naturally will die out and stronger programs will become even stronger. Our preliminary hunch is that in some cases this will occur, as weak programs will close first and strong programs will not only survive, but also grow. But we worry that in other cases very good preschools with solid curricula and experienced, caring staff but without working capital or entrepreneurial leadership will lose out to programs run by directors with more business sense than knowledge of young children. Preschool directors in Japan, more than ever before, have to be savvy business managers as well as able educators.

The drop in the Japanese birthrate also means that preschools in Japan have had to adjust, as did preschools in China a generation ago, to the emotional and social needs of single children. In a society where young children have few siblings or cousins and live in urban settings that provide few opportunities to interact with peers, Japanese preschools provide a range of social and emotional experiences that once occurred spontaneously at home and in neighborhoods. In our 1985 study, we found that much of the Chinese preschool curriculum was based on the perceived need to provide special attention to the problems of the single-child family. Unlike China, Japan has no enforced single-child family policy, and yet, because many parents are by choice having only one child, it is facing many of the same problems of dealing with the social and emotional issues of single children and of compensating for the declining opportunities for spontaneous peer interaction. In the Japanese context, the problem is conceptualized less as a concern, as it was in China, with spoiling as with the need to help single children develop *omoiyari* (empathy) and to experience social complexity. Komatsudani's institutionalization of the practice of having older children care for younger ones therefore can be understood in part as a reaction to the shrinking birthrate and to what Yoshizawa Hidenori in 1985 described as the "shrinking world of the Japanese child." He suggested to us that the children's world is shrinking not just because birthrates are down but also because many parents perceive their neighborhoods as too dangerous to allow young children to venture out on their own, as they did a few generations ago. Concern about the growing social isolation of Japanese children is widespread in Japan. As Susan Holloway points out, "gloomy pronouncements" on the falling quality of children's everyday lives in Japan may or may not be substantiated by facts (2000, 12). There are no studies that document differences between children's neighborhood life a generation ago and now. But as a press on Japanese preschool, the perception of deterioration is more important than the fact—if there is a widespread perception that the world of the Japanese child is shrinking, it is this perception with which Japanese preschools must cope.

ECONOMIC DECLINE

Japan's dramatic economic downturn in the 1990s had a profound effect on preschools. Some preschools, like other businesses, went bankrupt for complex reasons including a decline in the value of their assets (their land and buildings) and pressures caused by the loss of ancillary income in a stagnant economy. Another negative economic impact has to do with how a decline in tax revenues affects the government's willingness and ability to fund *hoikuen* and *yōchien*. The Angel Plan called for more investment in early childhood education and care as an incentive to young parents to have children. But some Japanese critics suggest that the Angel Plan produced more rhetoric than actual investment. Bad economic times can also have some positive effects. During a period of economic decline, as companies hire fewer university and junior college graduates, teaching becomes a more attractive career option, perhaps increasing the quality of the labor pool in early childhood education. Hard times may also mean that teachers in private preschools are more likely to resist pressure from directors to retire at twenty-three or twenty-four years of age, when they get married or have their first child, and in this way increase the average number of years of experience of the early childhood education workforce.

In many countries, an economic recession might lead parents to decide to pull their children out of preschool, to save the tuition, or to shift their children from more expensive to less expensive preschools, But there is no indication that this is happening in Japan where preschool attendance remains nearly universal. Some parents who are struggling financially might decide to send their children to *yōchien* for only two rather than three years. But tough economic times can also have the opposite effect, as mothers of young children are more likely to be in the workforce, which means that more families enroll their children at age three rather than waiting until age four and that more families need the all-day schedule provided by *hoikuen* rather than the two-thirds day schedule of *yōchien*.

NATIONAL MOOD

The drop in birthrate and the economic downturn of the past twenty years are easy to quantify. The effects of the decline in the number of young children and of economic stagnation on preschool teachers' employment patterns and on the workings of *yōchien* and *hoikuen* as businesses are relatively easy to track. Impossible to quantify and harder to demonstrate is the increased sense of social and cultural malaise in Japan that in the 1990s and on into the new century replaced the optimism of the mid-1980s. Symptoms include a discourse of pessimism about some social problems, denial about others, and finger pointing about who is blame for what is widely perceived to be a decrease in young children's social, emotional, and cognitive competence. Kato and Takaura, for example, refer to the current sense of crisis in Japan as "a temporary madness of the era. . . fueled by Japan's economic stagnation, a lack of confidence in the nation's political system, and worries about the morals of Japanese youths (in Bjork & Tsuneyoshi 2005, 622). In his analysis of the "crisis discourse" in education in Japan, Keita Takayama cites the "prevailing moral panic over the unruliness of 'today's children, 'classroom collapse' (*gakkyū hōkai*), and 'snap-short [short-fuse] children' (*kireru kodomotachi*)" (2007, 7).

Many of the Japanese teachers who have watched our Komatsudani and Madoka videos explain what they see as the emotionally and socially immature behavior of some of the children as resulting from a decline in the quality of parenting over the past generation, a decline that makes the job of preschool teaching much more difficult. Many of the directors and teachers complain that young Japanese parents are selfish, ignorant about child development, and preoccupied with their careers and hobbies. Preschools, like elementary schools and junior highs, are reporting more behavioral and social problems among their students, problems they attribute to many causes, but usually in the end trace back to parents. In addition to concern about what is perceived to be a general decline in parenting skills and a rising incidence of parenting problems requiring intervention, including child neglect and child abuse, there is even a new psychiatric diagnostic category: *ikuji neurose*—"childrearing neurosis" (Imoto 2007).

It is hard to know for sure if the quality of parenting has become objectively worse in Japan than it was in 1985. Higher (reported) rates of child abuse do not in themselves tell us much about the general state of parenting. But whatever the reality, the perception that parenting is worse is having an impact on Japanese early childhood education. Japanese early childhood educators, believing that parents are unable or unwilling to teach children proper values at home, feel compelled to try to compensate. At the urging of the government ministries, both *yōchien* and *hoikuen* are doing more parent education than they did a generation ago. But there is doubt and even cynicism among early childhood education experts that these efforts will have much of an impact, as we can see in the comments of Kadota Riyo of Seinan Gakuin University in Fukuoka: "Teachers and directors have no particular expertise to do parent education. And parents don't have a lot of respect for teachers' expertise in this area. Teachers tend to be younger and less well educated than parents and to not have children of their own, so why listen to them about parenting?"

Concerns about the declining quality of young parents are mirrored by concerns about the declining quality of young teachers. Professors of education, like their colleagues in other disciplines, complain that the quality of their undergraduate students is falling, and that today's college students come to them less motivated and less well prepared than students were a generation ago. Teacher educators complain that when these early childhood education majors graduate and become preschool teachers, they lack the professionalism of teachers twenty years ago. As Professor Kadota told us: "Preschool teachers today are worse than they used to be. They are worse as undergrads than undergrads were when I went to school and they become worse teachers. As teachers, they are too busy with their personal lives and hobbies to give proper attention to their job."

As demonstrated by both the substance and tone of Professor Kadota's comments, the biggest and most profound difference we find between Japanese society in 1984 and in 2005 can be summed up in one word: pessimism. In place of the optimism about Japanese early childhood education and Japanese society we heard in our Japanese interviews in the original study, in our new study we heard mostly pessimistic stories, stories of the effect of economic decline on preschools as businesses, of the problems caused by a decline in the quality of both parenting and teaching, and in the collective loss of core cultural values and a fraying of the social fabric. We encountered a lot of finger-pointing, blaming, and expressions of a general sense of pessimism that is larger than a loss of faith in any one institution—a loss of faith in the economy, parents, the government, politicians, educators, and, most profoundly, in the future.

The solution to these problems we hear from many Japanese early childhood educators is that now even more than a generation ago preschools must help children develop social skills they are not learning at home or in their neighborhoods. We find a striking similarity of points of view, and even some similar tropes, in the interviews we conducted with Director Machiyama of Madoka, Director Yoshizawa of Komatsudani, and Director Kumagai of Senzan Yōchien in Kyoto (figure 3.17). Machiyama-sensei suggested that children these days lack sufficient opportunities for complex social relations. We asked him how he could explain our observation that there seemed to be a lot of incidents of children crying in the classroom and he replied, "Crying is not a problem. *If there was no crying, that would be a problem.*" He suggested that when children cry at school out of frustration with not being about to dress themselves or to convince other children to play the way they want to, this is both a symptom of the social inexperience of these children and an opportunity to learn. This explanation resonates with something Director Yoshizawa told us in 1985. We see him as something of a visionary, as he anticipated a generation ago the prob-

3.17. Directors Machiyama Yoshio, Yoshizawa Hidenori, and Kumagai Ritsuko.

lems that have now grown more severe: "The world of young children has
grown more and more narrow. Their parents protect them too much from
playing roughly with other children without adult supervision and from
getting dirty from playing in the mud" (figure 3.18). When we asked him if
the fighting we observed at his *hoikuen* were not a problem, he responded,

3.18. Getting dirty.

"Fighting is not a problem. *If there were no fights, that would be a problem.*" He went on to explain that one of the most important things preschools can give young children in contemporary Japan is the opportunity to experience greater social complexity, including the experience of being in a fight. In 2005, when we asked Director Kumagai if she thought that families and children have changed in the past twenty years, she responded:

> Yes. Everyone is running scared. Parents overprotect children and themselves. They fear the world. They fear forming relationships with others, fear that a relationship they might get into will become strained, so they don't form relationships, and as a result are isolated. They fear germs, so they keep their children away from others. They fear dirt, so they keep their kids away from dirt, sand, and nature. They are afraid of encountering problems in life. But *if there were no problems, that would be the real problem.* Life is full of problems. Our job as early childhood educators isn't to protect children from problems, but instead to put them in situations where they can experience problems and struggle to find solutions.

Dealing with tears, fights, and hardships are normal aspects of a healthy childhood that children in contemporary Japan are seen as being at risk of missing out on as result of shrinking family size, a loss of opportunities to interact spontaneously with other children in neighborhood settings, and parents who are either anxiously overprotective or narcissistically too self-absorbed to give their children attention or opportunities for play with others. Today, as in 1985, Japanese preschools are asked to provide young children with the kinds of experiences and the traditional values they learned at home and in their neighborhood in earlier eras.

4 The United States

St. Timothy's Children's Center is located on the grounds of St. Timothy's Episcopal Church, on a hillside in a modest neighborhood of townhouses and apartment buildings overlooking the Pearl Harbor shipyard and the expressway that carries traffic to downtown Honolulu, ten miles to the east. The staff and children at St. Timothy's are racially and culturally diverse, reflecting Hawaii's demographic mix of Americans of Asian, Polynesian, and European descent. In 1984, when we selected St. Timothy's as the focal US preschool for the first Preschool in Three Cultures study, we were concerned that we might be criticized for selecting a program located in a state in the middle of the Pacific Ocean with students and teachers who were mostly nonwhite. Cheryl Takashige, the head teacher in the Rainbow classroom at St. Timothy's, and the director at the time, Colleen Momohara, shared our concern that viewers on the US mainland might think it odd to have teachers in Hawaii representing the US. Our rationale, then as now, is that while early childhood education in Hawaii has some special features, so too do other states where we might have videotaped and that an Asian-American teacher is no more ethnic or less typically American than a teacher of Italian, Irish, or Jewish descent. It turned out that our concern proved, in most cases, to be unnecessary. When we showed the videotapes we made at St. Timothy's to audiences of early childhood educators in various cities on the US mainland, the only practices they found to be exotic were the children removing their shoes when they entered the classroom and the use by children and teachers of the term "shi-shi" for "pee." The responses of US teachers and directors across the US to the 1984 St. Timothy's video showed that the practices and beliefs of the teachers at St. Timothy's were representative of early childhood educational practices found in accredited US preschools and of widely shared American cultural beliefs about how best to educate and care for young children.

It was only after the publication of the original book that we came to appreciate that participating in our study put the teachers at St. Timothy's at risk not, as they and we initially feared, of coming across in our book as insufficiently American, but as coming across as too much so. Just before the first book came out we sent Cheryl Takashige page proofs. Soon after we got a call from her telling us that reading the book made her uncomfortable: "The teacher in your book is me but it's not me. When I saw the videotape, it looked pretty much okay to me, but now that I see the whole thing in print. . . ." After talking with Cheryl we came to see that her discomfort came not just from her discovery that we had used her quotes to build an argument and that we had quoted her selectively (and in a few places, which we corrected in the second edition, misleadingly), but also and more profoundly from the realization that she had been turned into a character in a text, and not just any text, but an ethnography. As she told us: "You make it seem like the reasons I do the things I do in the classroom are because I am an American. But I don't teach the way I do to be American or to make the kids American. I teach the way I do because I think it is the best way to teach."

Reading our page proofs, Cheryl encountered herself as a key informant in an ethnography. Because the genre of our book is comparative ethnography, Cheryl's words read less as the beliefs and perspectives of an individual teacher than as an American cultural discourse. In an ethnography, a teacher's pedagogical theories become a belief system; a well-thought-out approach to classroom management becomes a folkway. Our comparative method put Cheryl into the unfamiliar, uncomfortable role of being an ethnographic subject, a character in a text whose behaviors and worldviews are seen not as natural, individual, and intentional, but as cultural, which is to say, as exotic and arbitrary.

This problem of textualization and estrangement is especially acute in our study for the US participants. In our new study, as in the original one, we see the primary rhetorical task of our project as making, for American readers, the strange (China and Japan) familiar, and the familiar (the United States) strange. Writing primarily with an American readership in mind, our aim in the US chapters of both the original book and the new one is to expose the implicit assumptions that underlie American early childhood education. In our zeal to show that what goes on in an American preschool is no more natural or culture-free than what goes on in China and Japan, we failed in the first study to anticipate the sense of defamiliarization this approach would produce in our American informants.

And now, as we set out to describe and analyze our return to St. Timothy's (as well as our research in a second American preschool, Alhambra),

4.1. Jannie at the gate.

we are about to do it again. Guided by the lessons we learned from the first study, we have taken greater care in the new study to avoid caricaturing the American practitioners' beliefs and practices and we have endeavored to show more of the nuances, tensions, and variations in the American educators' positions. That having been said, the primary goal of the US chapter in the new book as in the original one is to produce a feeling of strangeness and defamiliarization in readers, for whom we aspire to create an appreciation for the cultural and historical constructedness of beliefs and practices that are usually taken for granted.

A Day at St. Timothy's Children's Center

On this Wednesday in April 2003, Jannie Umeda, the head teacher of one of the two classrooms serving four-year-olds at St. Timothy's, arrives at school just before 7:00 (figure 4.1). As she sets up the morning free-play areas, children begin to arrive, most driven to school by commuting parents on their way to work in Honolulu. Parents help their children put their backpacks in their cubbies, chat briefly with Jannie, and then kiss their children goodbye. Noah enters the classroom and points to a chart taped to the wall, explaining to his father that this is a "web" he helped create of things you can do with water. The children then join Jannie on the rug, in front of the large cage that is home to a Jackson chameleon. Courtney takes a live grasshopper out of a jar and places it in Jackie's cage. Jannie, speaking in a whisper so as to not distract Jackie, says to the children, "Look—she's about to eat."

During the next ninety minutes, as the rest of the children in the class arrive one by one, Jannie moves around the room interacting with the children, sitting down on the rug to chat with one group about Pokémon (figure 4.2): "Which is the one that sings and makes you fall asleep?

4.2. Talking Pokémon.

Oh, Jigglypuff. Maybe I should bring Jigglypuff here at nap time." Val Moriwaki, the assistant teacher, arrives at eight, and joins the children in their free-play activities. At 8:30 the day officially begins with circle time, as Jannie leads the children in the morning songs: "Today is Wednesday" followed by "Good morning, Kevin. Good morning, Teddy. Good morning, Abigail. We're glad you're here today." Natalie, this day's morning-opening helper, takes attendance, walking around the circle of children seated on the carpet, counting each with a tap on the head, until she reaches seventeen. Jannie says to Natalie, "You missed Malia, eighteen, and yourself, nineteen, and Colin is absent. That's twenty."

After attendance, Jannie reminds the children of the current curricular theme. "Remember the other day we talked about all the things you do with water. There's something about water that we didn't say." Kevin shouts out, "Surf boarding." "Yes," Jannie continues, "but when you look up, not in here, but when you are outside. . ." "Rain," a child calls out. "Rain, that's right, rain," Jannie replies as she stands up and leads the children in a song: "I'm singing in the rain, singing in the rain, what a wonderful feeling, thumbs up, elbows out, knees together, bottoms up, ticki, ticki, ticki, ticki, do." The song over, Jannie hold up a series of icons representing the options available today for activity center time: "Water table. Drawing. Collage. Water table is available for six. There are a lot of ways to make six. Good, four and two makes six. Zach? Collage. Okay. Neal? Water table. Now water table is closed."

As the children work at the water table and the other activity centers, Jannie and Val circulate, asking questions, giving assistance, and chatting with the children. At the collage table, Jannie listens patiently as Barry tells her a convoluted story of his father misplacing his car keys. She asks about the picture he has put together out of colored squares, rectangles, and triangles, and as he narrates, she writes down each word on his paper: "My

4.3. Jannie writes what Evan tells her.

house, mom's house, dad's house. My, you have a lot of houses, five houses."
Val performs a similar service for Natalie in the drawing area: "What do you
want to say about your picture, Natalie?" "It's for my daddy. My daddy's
turning twenty-four" (figure 4.3)

After about thirty minutes, choice time ends and a thirty-minute playground time begins. Three boys run over to the tall climbing structure and
begin to ascend. Val soon joins them there, saying, "I don't think that's very
safe. You can ask the teacher if she can watch you on the structure. Can
you do that on the structure if there is no teacher there? No. You might
get hurt."

Meanwhile, Jannie approaches Aaron, who has just thrown a plastic
bowling pin in the direction of Barry (figure 4.4):

JANNIE: Do you think it was a good idea to throw two of these? What if when
you threw it, it went over there and hit your friends? What would have
happened to them?
AARON: They'd be hurt.
JANNIE: Would you be happy? Would they be happy? No, so a good idea we
said next time would be, if you want to throw something, what would
you throw?
AARON: A ball.
JANNIE: Yes. There's a ball right there.

In the large sand box area, a lion dance has spontaneously broken out.
Noah, with a plastic milk carton on his head, and Clayton, behind him, play
the part of the lion's body, dancing in a circle as other children beat out a
loud rhythm with wooden spoons on metal bowls. In the garden area in the
corner of the playground Val and a few of the children check the progress
of the crops: "Let's count how much corn we have. One, two, there's a little

4.4. 1. Evan throws a bowling pin.   2. "Do you think it was a good idea to throw these?"

one. Four, five, wow!" Examining a developing ear of corn, Marshall cries out, "It's starting!" Natalie, standing outside the toilets, rings a bell, announcing that playground time is over: "Ai, ai, ai, ai, calling all Rainbows." The girls use the stalls while the boys line up at the urinal. Val, just in the nick of time, gives some needed advice to the boys in Pidgin-inflected English: "When somebody is going shi-shi, not to bother them because they might turn and the shi-shi going to go somewhere else!"

After the snack, Jannie gathers the children in a circle on the rug and introduces a lesson: "Who thinks they know what *absorb* means? Clothes absorb. Every time you folks have an accident [pointing to her shirt] it soaks up all the juice, right? We're going to do an activity about absorb. Val is with the Green Rainbows, so five people go with her." Sitting around a table with a group of children, Jannie holds up a paper towel, which she dips in a bowl of water: "What's going to happen? It's going to get wet. What's happening? It's *absorbing*. See how it all gets wet? Look how much water absorbed." After fifteen minutes of experimenting with paper towels and sponges, the children come back to the rug, where Jannie leads a debrief: "When there is a spill, what do you think we should get, a paper towel or a sponge? Sponge! It sucks up all the water, right?" (figure 4.5).

Jannie announces the options for the second activity period: "Blocks available with the dinosaurs. And big blocks in the dramatic play area. And drawing Mother's Day cards." At the drawing table, Val writes as Brandon dictates: "I love to hug her when I go to school. I play with my mom legos. Happy Mother's Day." When Val is done, she says, "And then you can write, 'Love, Brandon'" (figure 4.6). After thirty minutes, Jannie announces that it is cleanup time. As Aaron sprawls across the large box that the toys go in, three other boys playfully spank him on the butt and Aaron complains, "Spanking! Ow!" Jannie, hearing Aaron's complaint, comes over and says to the boys, "You know what, guys? Is that all right to hurt your friends? Was

4.5. 1. Noah and his dad look at the "What is water?" web the class developed.

2. Demonstrating absorption.

3. Pouring water.

4. Reading a book about tadpoles.

4.6. 1. Val writes Mother's Day card . . .

2. And Brandon signs it.

he saying 'Ow'? What does that mean? Right, it means, 'It hurts.' Do we hurt our friends? Then why are you guys hitting him? Aaron is trying to close the box. It's not funny when you guys are hitting him. It's not fun for him. It hurts his body. And that's making him sad."

Once the toys are put away, Jannie reads a book about how tadpoles become frogs and then asks the children some follow-up questions about how tadpoles and fish breathe. She then sends the children off to wash up for lunch one by one, based on the first letter of their names: "Right, *N* is for *Nicky*. Yes, Noah, you can go too."

The teachers eat the lunches they have brought from home alongside the children, who eat the beef stew, vegetables, and salad provided by the school. "Try a small piece of corn. Try it, Aaron. It's the same kind of corn that you guys eat. Okay. One more piece of meat and you're done." The children go the bathroom to wash their faces and then return to the classroom to spread out their blankets for a nap. The teachers turn down the lights, put on some soft music, give hugs and kisses to the children, and rub the children's backs as they fall asleep. During the nap Jill, the afternoon assistant teacher, arrives. The three teachers work silently next to the sleeping children, wrapping the Mother's Day gifts the children have made. As children awake, they quietly take a book from the shelf and sit on the rug to read. When nap time ends, the lights are turned on and the children put their blankets away in their cubbies. The children read and play with puzzles. Two girls look at one of the many scrapbooks Jannie has made in which she has combined digital photos and pasted pieces of paper to document activities from earlier in the school year.

At 2:30 Jannie says good-bye and heads home. Jill and Val set out the afternoon snack; then after the snack, they help some of the children finish their Mother's Day cards while other children play with blocks and in the dramatic play area. From about 4:30 on, parents and grandparents arrive to pick up their children, The children hug the teachers good-bye, grab their backpacks, walk to the parking lot with their parents, and drive off.

St. Timothy's Then and Now

When Jannie and the other St. Timothy teachers and staff watched the videos we made at the school in 1984 and 2002, most of the differences they identified had to do with changes made in response to licensing requirements: "We had to get rid of that old red climbing structure. It was a safety issue." "Most of the children don't bring lunch boxes these days. Now we offer catered lunch. And if they do use a lunch box, it must be insulated." "No more tooth brushing. It's too hard to keep it sanitary." "We didn't used to have security buzzers that go off when the gates are open."

In contrast to the changes made in response to safety concerns and licensing requirements, the St. Timothy teachers were struck by the consistency in activities and curriculum: "Choice tray is the same." "The family graph." "The songs are the same!" "The same focus on verbalizing." "It looks pretty much the same, except we don't call it 'home area' anymore. Now it's the 'dramatic play area.'" "In the dramatic play area there still tends to be more girls than boys, but the girls now play 'work' as much as they play 'house.' They rarely pretend to cook; they have play pagers and cell phones and keyboards."

Much of the continuity at St. Timothy's can be attributed to the fact that St. Timothy's was guided in 2002, as a generation ago, by the philosophy and quality standards of the National Association for the Education of Young Children and, more specifically, by NAEYC's notion of developmentally appropriate practices (DAP). As the director, Dolores Brockman, explained, "Our curriculum is still based on choice. It is developmental and child centered." The teachers and directors categorize many of the modifications of curriculum and structure St. Timothy's has made over the years as improvements in their implementation of DAP ideas. For example, Ms. Brockman answered our question about what had changed the most at St. Timothy's since our original study by saying: "One big change is that our classrooms are now self-contained. We used to flip-flop. But we learned that the three-year-olds found switching rooms in the middle of the day hard. We realized that it's not really DAP. Little kids don't get a feeling of ownership of the space if they switch rooms."

Jannie explained that the addition to the curriculum of having children keep journals was an extension of St. Timothy's long-standing emphasis, encouraged by NAEYC, on language development: "Now it's not just an emphasis on verbalizing, it's also 'journaling.' We attended a literacy workshop and we decided to do journals rather than computers." Jannie also incorporated her hobby of scrapbooking into her teaching, encouraged by the recent NAEYC emphasis on documentation and "making learning visible," an approach supported by the portfolio assessment movement and the Reggio Emilia preschools in Italy (Katz & Chard 1997; Project Zero & Reggio Children 2001). Jannie explained her scrapbooking approach to documentation, an activity that lies at the heart of her teaching (figure 4.7):

For example, the children may be in the block area building a house with the big blocks and their garage has a leak and they are trying to decide how to fix it. I always have my camera ready so I can take pictures of what they design and construct. The kids have got so used to me taking pictures of their activities that now they say, "Come take a picture!" Usually, right after I take a picture of something like them fixing their leaky garage, I ask them, "Tell me what you are doing. Use your words. Tell me about why you did this?" and I write down exactly what they say. And then each night I put the pictures,

4.7. Looking at a scrapbook in the reading corner.

and their words about the pictures into their folders, which I design kind of like scrapbooks. If there are four kids doing an activity and I take a picture, I make four copies and the picture goes into each of their folders. I do this to show the parents what we do at school, to show them that it's not just play, and that the children are working together, socializing, constructing. And I put scrapbooks of activities we've done in the reading corner. The children love looking at pictures of activities they did before.

Another change at St. Timothy's cited by one of the veteran teachers is that "we now call misbehavior 'mistaken behavior.'" When we asked her to explain the difference, she said, "Calling it 'mistaken behavior' reminds us that the child doesn't mean to behave badly, he's just made a mistake, and he needs guidance on the right way to behave." We can trace this reasoning back to an influential 1995 article by Dan Gartrell, "Misbehavior or Mistaken Behavior," published in an NAEYC journal, and Gartrell's 2003 book, *The Power of Guidance: Teaching Social-Emotional Skills in Early Childhood Classrooms,* which was endorsed by NAEYC. Whether or not this teacher had read this particular article and book, she and her colleagues at St. Timothy would have been exposed to this logic through attendance at workshops offered at NAEYC regional conferences.

Throughout our interviews with them, Director Brockman and the teachers at St. Timothy cited the positive influence NAEYC played over the years in pushing them to improve their practice. But Ms. Brockman also gave some examples of directives from NAEYC that she and the teachers have found more bothersome than useful, such as the NAECY guidelines on lunch: "Because of DAP, we've gone to 'family-style eating.' Kids serve themselves, scoop the applesauce, and so on. We didn't choose to do this, but it's part of accreditation." When we asked her to explain her objection, she said, "Because that's not actually how families eat. Two- and three-year-old kids don't serve themselves at home, and it isn't consistent with the cultures of many of our children." Another NAECY requirement that Ms. Brockman referred to without great enthusiasm was that there must be sheltered spaces in each classroom for children to play: "Something else we've added is a 'private space for one,' which is required by DAP. If you don't have it, you'll get dinged by the accreditors." These last two examples are instructive because they show that NAEYC functions for St. Timothy's not just as a source of progressive ideas but also as a regulatory agency, whose rules and regs must be followed whether or not they make sense to the director and teachers or are appropriate for the local context.

Another source of pressure that staff at St. Timothy's have to deal with now more than they did a generation ago is the parents. St. Timothy's response to parent expectations shows continuity in vision and approach, as the teachers and directors described themselves as striving in the face of mounting pressures for more and earlier emphasis on academic skills to accommodate parents' concerns without compromising the program's core, DAP-based beliefs, and values.

> JANNIE: We have to justify our play curriculum more than we had to before. Parents say to me, "My kid needs to read. My kid needs to get into a private school." We have to explain, justify our approach more than we used to: "Cutting with a scissors and playing with Play-Doh teach fine motor control, which will help for holding a pen."
>
> LOUISE: Parents want something new each year. "Why aren't my kids being more challenged?" If there isn't new stuff, parents think that their kids aren't being challenged. They don't realize kids can interact with the same stuff in new ways.
>
> DOLORES: Our practices are more or less the same as before, but we've had to get more professional at articulating to the parents how and why we do what we do.
>
> JANNIE: At the first parent-teacher conference parents always ask me for more academics. I say to them, "Read the philosophy in your handbook. It explains how we teach the kids through play. That's our learning environment." At the conferences I have a folder with all their child's work and I show them how they are learning through their play. And they're generally okay with that.

The Hawaiian economy is the other key factor cited as a pressure leading to change at St. Timothy's. Hawaii suffered a severe economic downturn in the 1990s, precipitated by Japan's economic crisis—tourism is Hawaii's main business and when the Japanese economic bubble burst, Hawaii suffered. As Dolores Brockman told us:

> Good economic times in the late 1980s led to higher enrollments. Parents in this era could afford high-quality childcare, "something more formal than auntie's." In bad economic times more mothers may have stayed home and parents may have put off preschool entry until their child turned four, so we had to cut one of the three-year-old classrooms. And because Hawaii offers full-day public kindergarten, the enrollment in our five-year-old classes declined, too.

St. Timothy's enrollment fell from a peak of about 130 children in 1990 to about 100 in 2005.

Despite enrollment decline, staff turnover, economic ups and downs, rising pressure from parents, and new requirements from accreditors, St. Timothy's has been able to keep the books balanced while staying true to its core vision. A day at St. Timothy's in 2002 is much like a day in 1984, and the explanations and reflections given by staff in 2003 and 2004 are very consistent with those of a generation ago. If we looked only at St. Timothy's Children's Center, we would have to conclude that over the past twenty years things have not changed much in US early childhood education. But by turning to a second case, a case of a preschool of a type that did not exist in the US when we did our original study, we can see that there have been significant shifts in funding, provision, curriculum and outside influences and pressures. Whereas St. Timothy's Children's Center helps us identify continuity of belief and practice in American early childhood education, Alhambra Preschool points to change.

A Day at Alhambra Preschool

Alhambra Preschool is housed in a cluster of classrooms on the campus of a middle school in a working-class neighborhood of Phoenix (figure 4.8). Run by the Alhambra School District, with the support of the State of Arizona's Early Childhood Block Grant funds that provide a year of preschool to economically disadvantaged children, the preschool serves over 200 three- and four-year-old children who live in the district. Half of the children attend preschool in the morning from 9 to 11:30, the other half from 12:30 to 3, with the teachers working both shifts. The program also operates a "wrap-around" day-care program that is open from 7 a.m. to 6:00

4.8. Alhambra street scene.

4.9. Jamal says good-bye to his dad.

p.m. that children of working parents attend before and after their morning or afternoon preschool session.

On the day we videotaped, four-year-old Jamal, a student in Fran Smith's morning preschool class, arrived at the daycare room at 7:30 a.m. In the video we see Jamal walking hand in hand with his father from the parking lot to the daycare room, where they are greeted by Ms. Shirley, the daycare program's lead staff member in the mornings. Jamal puts away his backpack while his father signs the attendance book. After a series of hugs and kisses and assurances that his mother will pick him up at 5:00 (figure 4.9), Jamal joins the children who had arrived before him on the carpet, where they are playing with blocks and puzzles. At 8:00, the fifteen children who have by then arrived walk in a line behind Ms. Shirley out of the daycare room and through the middle-school campus, through a series of walkways to the cafeteria. Here the preschool children, too small to push trays down the cafeteria line designed for older children, are served a breakfast of scrambled eggs, pork sausages, hash browns, and orange juice by Ms. Shirley, her assistant Guadalupe, and a member of the lunch room staff, all wearing plastic gloves (4.10).

4.10. Breakfast in the cafeteria

Breakfast over, the children retrace their path back to the daycare room, where Ms. Shirley reads them a story. Meanwhile, in the preschool classroom, Fran Smith and her assistant Eva Rangel prepare materials for the morning session. A few minutes before 9:00, Fran walks through the corridors of the sprawling middle-school campus to a parking lot where large yellow school buses are arriving, ferrying preschool students to Alhambra from across the school district. As Fran greets the children in her class and leads them in a line to her classroom, Eva goes to the daycare room to pick up Jamal and several other children and walk them to the classroom, stopping along the way to pick-up the children who came to school on foot and to greet (in Spanish) their mothers and baby sisters and brothers.

As the twenty children enter the classroom they put away their backpacks, wash their hands, and take a seat at a table where Eva and Fran, wearing plastic gloves, pour them juice and serve them graham crackers. As the children eat, Fran takes attendance (figure 4.11):

Jamal. Is Jamal here?

Yes, I'm here.

Miranda?

I still here.

You're still here. Good.

Esmeralda?

Aquí estoy.

Eva, seated at a table with several children, chats with them in both Spanish and English (figure 4.12). As they finish breakfast, the children throw away their paper cups, plates, and unfinished food and get a puzzle, game, or book. In the reading corner, four boys tussle over three seats on a small bench. Fran, seeing the commotion, comes over and says, "Jeremy, three friends can sit on the bench. When you get up to get another book, another friend may sit here." Jeremy responds, *"Porque esto me gusta."* Fran

4.11. Fran takes attendance.

4.12. Eva chatting with Jeremy.

replies, "You like your book and he likes that one and that's okay, but we can share sitting on the couch." When Fran leaves, Jeremy and Ferdie playfully push against each other, and then bump heads accidentally. Cindy, the special education aide assigned to work with Ferdie full time, comes closer to the bench to listen to Jeremy's complaint about Ferdie: "*Yo le dice que aquí tiene cucas and el me pushó*" (I told him that he had crumbs here [pointing to his chin] and he pushed me). Cindy tells Ferdie, "*Debes tener mas cuidado*" (You should be more careful) (figure 4.13).

Fran announces that it is "time for the Pledge," and children put away their books and puzzles and gather in a circle in the center of the room. Ferdie holds aloft a small American flag while the children, hands on hearts, stumbling over the longer words, recite, "I pledge allegiance, to the flag, of the United States of America. And to the Republic . . ." Fran then turns on the cassette player and leads the children in a song, "I'm gonna shake, shake, shake, shake my sillies out. Jump, jump, jump my jiggles out. Wiggle, wiggle, wiggle my worries away." She then asks the children to sit in a circle on the carpet and says, "Why is Jamal standing up? Because he knows it is his turn for the calendar." Jamal walks to the board next to Fran and picking

4.13. Jeremy complains about Ferdie.

up the small wand, points at the word "March" on the calendar. Fran asks the class, "What month is it?" Several voices at once shout out "February." "No, February is all gone. What month is it now?" A voice calls out "March." "Very good. What letter does it start with?" "M." "Good, Phillip, I heard that. And whose name starts with M?" "Miranda." "Right, Miranda starts with M. And Moises. And. . ." "McDonald's," shouts out a voice from the back. Fran and the children then sing, "Sunday, Monday, Tuesday, Wednesday, Thursday, Friday, Saturday, start all over again," as Jamal moves his wand, more or less correctly, across the days of the week on the calendar.

Pulling a well-worn stuffed animal from the cloth bag at her feet, Fran turns to Pablo and says: "You brought Buddy Bear back. Very good. Thank you, Pablo. Let's see, what did Buddy Bear do at your house. Did you have fun with Buddy Bear? Yes. Does he look happy? Does Buddy Bear look happy? Let's ask Buddy Bear. 'Did you have a good time?'" Buddy Bear, in Fran's hands, nods his head affirmatively. "Yes. He had a good time. Did you write in this book, Pablo?" Pablo, shyly, with a hint of a smile, nods. "You did?" Pablo nods again. Opening up the Buddy Bear journal, Fran says, "Wow, Pablo, you drew a lot! Did you do this by yourself?" An affirmative nod from Pablo. "Good job." She asks the class, "Does this look like Buddy Bear?" A girl shakes her head. Fran to Pablo: "Did Buddy Bear help you draw this?" Nod. "He did?" Nod. "Was he sitting with you?" Nod. "And who wrote this?" Pablo, in a whisper, "My mom." Fran, in a louder voice: "Your Mom. Should I read it to everyone?" Nod. "It says, 'My second visit with Buddy Bear. On March 5. Buddy Bear and I had lots of fun today. Buddy met all my friends and family. My sister loved him and she thought Buddy was real cute and funny.'" Fran asks Pablo, "She thought he was funny?" Nod. "We played outside most of the afternoon and I drove Buddy in back of my toy bike. You have a basket on your bike?" Nod. "Wow." Back to reading from the journal: "'I hope Buddy can come over again soon because we had fun.'" To Pablo:

4.14. Fran and Precious.

"You let your sister sleep with Buddy?" Nod. "When she was asleep you took him and you went to sleep with him?" Nod and smile. "Did that make you feel good?" Nod. "Well, thank you for sharing Buddy with your sister. That's really nice. Now who's going to take him home today? Miranda. Okay, Miranda, come up here." Fran puts Buddy Bear and his journal back into the canvas bag and hands him over to Miranda, who puts him in her cubby.

Fran then asks the seated children, "Are you folks ready to play? Today, we have things outside and things inside. So I need Jeremy, Jose—listen, Phillip—Angel, Jonah, Kathleen, and Precious to go with Ms. Eva. Okay, Precious, you can stay." Half of the children go outside with Eva while the other half disperse around the classroom, some to a table set up with Play-Doh and cookie cutters, others to a table covered with plastic animals, others to the housekeeping corner, and Precious to the carpet to play with a school bus loaded with Fisher-Price people. Fran joins Precious on the carpet, pointing to one of the small figures (figure 4.14):

FRAN: What do you think he does?
PRECIOUS: He go to school.
FRAN: What bus is this?
PRECIOUS: A school bus. How come this bus, what is this for?
FRAN: That says "stop." So when the bus stops, to let all the boys and girls off.

Cindy sits at a table, working with Ferdie: *"Cuantos pantalones? Uno. Dos. Tres."*

Phillip and four girls are busy in the housekeeping corner. Alexa wears a black fireman's raincoat with yellow warning stripes. Phillip is wearing a motorcycle policeman's helmet and high heels and carrying a broom. Precious enters the area and loads a shopping cart with a baby doll and plastic groceries. Alexa and Shari are speaking agitatedly. Alexa complains to

Precious: "I'm going to tell Ms. Fran you're taking out all the stuff." Overhearing, Fran comes over and tells Alexa, "Use your words and tell her," and then says to Precious, "All your friends want to play, so what can you do to help them? Give them some things to play with. Did you go shopping and get all of these things? Girls, there's more things over there. Precious is going shopping and when she's done she's going to share with you. Shari, I like the way you are talking to Precious. Thank you."

A few minutes later Precious speaks harshly to Jonah: "Get out. I'm telling teacher. Teacher! Ms. Fran! There's five people in here!" Fran walks over and responds:

> FRAN: There are five people in housekeeping? How many people should we have in housekeeping?
> PRECIOUS: Four. So Jonah has to get out.
> FRAN: Who was here first?
> PRECIOUS: Only me.
> FRAN: Well, Jonah was here, and Alexa was here and Veronica and Shari are here and you're here. Do you think that today maybe you all can play nicely? We'll try it with five.

Outside, Eva helps children get set up to paint at an easel. Three boys are playing with trucks nearby when Jerome complains to Cindy about Ferdie:

> JEROME: He's playing rude.
> CINDY: You have to tell him not to play rude.
> JEROME: Don't play rude.
> CINDY TO FERDIE: *Tiene que jugar bien, si no. . .*

Ferdie's speech teacher, who comes to the classroom once a week to work with him, arrives and takes him back into the classroom to sit with him at a table, where they chat in English as he makes things out of Play-Doh.

An hour or so after the activity center session began, Fran brings it to a close by playing a song on the CD player: "Clean up, clean up, everybody everywhere, clean up clean up, everybody do your share." Once things have been put away, Fran leads the children out of the classroom and across the campus to the playground. After fifteen minutes of climbing, swinging, and playing in the large sandbox, the children come back to the classroom. It's now 11 a.m. The children take their places in a semicircle on the rug facing Fran, who asks, "Who's my big helper today? Alexa. Alexa gets to pick a story." Alexa chooses *There Was an Old Lady*. Fran reads the book animatedly, at the end of each page replacing the words "Perhaps she'll die" with "Oh, my."

When the story is finished, Fran calls on the bus children to get their backpacks and take a drink of water before coming back to the rug. Once the children are resettled on the rug, she says, "Shall we do the Three Pigs." Precious cries out, "The three pigs with the woof." "With the wolf?" Fran asks, "Are you going to help me sing?" Turning on the CD, Fran leads the children in singing along with Raffi, "'Little pig, little pig, let me come in,' 'Not by the hair of my chinny chin chin.'" This is followed by singing along to "He's Got the Whole World in His Hands," complete with hula-like hand gestures demonstrated by Fran (who grew up in Hawaii).

As the song ends, Fran says good-bye to the children: "You're tired, aren't you? You worked hard today. Miranda, you're taking Buddy Bear home. Don't forget." Eva walks Jamal, Precious, Shanelle, and Alexa to meet Ms. Shirley outside the daycare room and then escorts the children who walk home to meet their waiting mothers at the school gate, where Eva chats with the mothers in Spanish. Meanwhile, Fran walks Ferdie and several other children to the bus parking area.

Children from Fran's and the other morning preschool classes enter the daycare room, put away their backpacks, and then walk with Shirley and her afternoon assistant to the cafeteria for lunch, which is again served to them on trays. After lunch they play "Duck, Duck, Goose" on the grass and then take a ninety-minute nap. Meanwhile, back in their classroom, Fran and Eva greet the afternoon preschool children, who are just arriving, and then repeat the morning routine. In the daycare room, after the nap, the children go to the cafeteria for a snack, and then Alicia, the afternoon teacher, leads the children in an art activity. Holding up a bright green shamrock cut from a piece of paper, Alicia tells the children, "This goes along with all of the St. Patrick's Day stuff we're doing about Ireland." A child responds, confused, as if he's never heard of the place, "Ireland?" Alicia, undaunted, pushes on: "Today, we're going to paint our shamrocks green. But we're not using green paint." (Holding up jars of yellow and blue tempera paint). "Look at what we're using! What happens when you put them together?" From 3:00 on, parents arrive to pick up children. By 5:30, when Jamal's mother arrives, there are just six children left in the daycare room. She signs the drop-off and pick-up book, picks up Jamal's backpack, and then mother and son walk out the door to the car.

Teacher and Director Reflections on "A Day at Alhambra Preschool"

We found it difficult to edit the Alhambra videotape because it was hard to define what constitutes the Alhambra preschool day. From the perspective of Fran and Eva, the day begins at eight, when they arrive in their classroom to plan activities and prepare materials for the morning and afternoon preschool sessions, and ends at 4:00 p.m., when the afternoon children have departed and they have cleaned up their classroom. The day begins for Miranda when she arrives on foot with her mother at 9:00 and ends when her mother picks her up at 11:30. For Ferdie the school day begins at 8:30 when he boards the school bus in front of his house and ends at noon when the bus drops him off at home. The school day begins for Jamal at 7:30 when his dad drops him off in the daycare room and ends ten hours later, at 5:30, when his mom comes to pick him up from the daycare room. Children attend preschool at Alhambra for just two-and-a-half hours a day, but teachers work morning and afternoon shifts and many children, like Jamal, spend time in the daycare room before and after their time in the preschool classroom. In addition to the Early Childhood Block Grant (ECBG) preschool classrooms like Fran's that serve income-qualifying children, Alhambra also runs a parallel program at the same site for tuition-paying children, who follow the same schedule and have more or less the same curriculum and whose children mix with the ECBG children on the playground and at the easels and at the sand- and water-play tables during outdoor activity center time. Special education specialists, speech pathologists, and play therapists come into the classroom throughout the week for thirty minutes at a time to work with Ferdie and other children identified with special needs. Further adding to the complexity of the children's day and our shooting, children must walk back and forth across the middle-school campus from the bus drop-off area to the classrooms, from the classrooms to the daycare room, and from the daycare room to the cafeteria for a snack and lunch. Unlike St. Timothy's Children's Center in Honolulu, Daguan and Sinanlu You'eryuans in China, and Komatsudani Hoikuen and Madoka Yōchien in Japan, the day at Alhambra lacks unity of time and place, with children coming and going from daycare program to preschool classroom throughout the day, teachers dealing with multiple groups of children, and children interacting with multiple teams of adults.

Some US early childhood educators who experienced a sense of chaos, confusion, and dislocation from viewing the Alhambra videotape expressed criticism of the Alhambra program. For example, when we showed the Alhambra videotape at a conference of progressive early childhood education scholars, an audience member asked, "Why don't they give the children more consistency, with one set of teachers, in one room, for the full day instead of all of this coming and going? Don't they realize all this moving around is hard for young children?"

The teachers and director at Alhambra are well aware that it is less than ideal for the children to have to move from room to room, for children to spend as many as ten hours a day away from home, and for teachers to work 2.5 hours with one group of children in the morning and then another 2.5 hours with another group of children in the afternoon:

> FRAN: I wish we had a longer day. I wish we had a four-hour program. Then we could help the children a little bit more. Because when you break it down, when you take away all the transition time, we only have an hour of real instruction time. If we had a four-hour program, that would be ideal. With fifteen kids! That's my dream.
>
> EVA (LAUGHING): We don't want any more than that!
>
> TOBIN: Is it tough to deal with two groups of kids and parents?
>
> FRAN: It is. The afternoon class is hard. After lunch, it's like, "We've already done this and we have to do it again." And for the kids who need daycare, it's a very long day. Christine, our office manager, tries to put them in the morning class, so they can nap in the afternoon, but it doesn't always work out that way. An ideal class would be four hours, one class a day, with fifteen kids.

As she watched the last section of the videotape, Alhambra's director of preschool programs, Bonnie Lund, commented:

> The teachers' job in A-OK [the daycare program] is extremely difficult. They have kids coming in at 3:30 in the afternoon who have already been in A-OK all morning. They've already gone to preschool for two-and-a-half hours, and they don't get to go home. Instead, they go to A-OK and wait for their parents to come, which might not be till 6:00 at night. They've already been here for seven hours and now they've still got time before they go home.

Bonnie Lund and her staff cobbled together a comprehensive program of early childhood education and care at Alhambra to serve a variety of student and parent needs in the midst of daunting structural constraints and bureaucratic regulations. The year we videotaped, the program was located in temporary space on a middle-school campus. Bonnie explained that this was the best space available because school districts view their pre-K programs as add-ons rather than as essential services and because school building funds in Arizona can be used only for K–12 classrooms. Department of Education funds can be used for up to three hours a day of early childhood education but not childcare while Department of Economic Security (welfare) funds will pay for up to ten hours of childcare while parents work or go to school, but not for children's education. Children whose family income is below 185% of the poverty line (in 2006, around $37,000 for a family of four) or who have special needs can ride the school bus while children whose parents can afford to pay tuition must come to school by car or on foot. Legal immigration status is required for enrollment in the preschool program, but not in daycare. Department of Health guidelines require adults to wear plastic gloves when serving food, while NAEYC wants food served "family style," by the children. The list of contradictory regulations and restrictions goes on and on, for such are the challenges in many parts of the contemporary US of running a public program that offers a full day of childcare and a preschool experience to children of both poor and working-class families.

The other major theme that came out in our interviews at Alhambra was a struggle over the curriculum. This struggle took the form most specifically of an ongoing philosophical disagreement between Fran and Bonnie, the director, a disagreement that they describe in very similar terms. Fran told us that Bonnie wants her to teach more phonics and to use *The Letter People,* the packaged pre-reading program that is being used by all the other Alhambra teachers, but that she is determined to hold out and stay true to the child-centered, play-oriented beliefs and principles she was introduced to when she entered the field eleven years ago.

TOBIN: Is the preschool curriculum changing?

FRAN (LAUGHING): Well, they're trying to change me.

TOBIN: You feel that pressure from the Bush initiatives?

FRAN: Yeah. And that's hard. How do you deal with that when you don't agree? I don't totally disagree, because I think academics *is* important. But kids need to play. They can't learn if they don't first get to feel comfortable in the classroom, to know how to be in school.

TOBIN: Where does the pressure come from? Is it just kind of in the air or do you feel it directly, from Bonnie?

FRAN: Yeah. Lately.

TOBIN: It's not like she's coming in to your room everyday.

FRAN: Not yet. But, to be honest, it is coming. Like *The Letter People.* Just because a company came up with a curriculum doesn't mean we have to spend all this money and buy it. When it's set in stone and packaged like that, I think that it can really limit your thinking. If Bonnie came to me and told me I had to do *The Letter People*, I guess I would have to do it, but that's not me.

Bonnie told us that she respects Fran's commitment to her beliefs about how and what to teach, that she considers Fran a friend, and that she will not order Fran to change, but that she thinks Fran is stuck in her ways and that her job as director is to push teachers to learn new things and to take advantage of new developments in the field, including such curricular innovations as *The Letter People*. Bonnie's position in this debate was expressed most clearly in her response to our question of how Fran differs from Barb, a teacher in one of Alhambra's classrooms that serves children of tuition-paying parents:

> Their methods of teaching are extremely different. That's what makes the classrooms here so interesting. The teachers are allowed their own creativity. Fran's class isn't nearly as academic as Barb's. Fran is much more into creativity, open play, and working one on one with the children in different activities. She's not as structured as Barb. Whereas Barb has really high expectations for her children and she thinks kids can read by the end of the year. She has 50 percent of her class that's approaching reading, with several already reading. Barb's expectations are academic. Fran's expectations are social. It's personal style. Some teachers have a more academic focus and it goes with their concept of what early childhood education should be. Barb is one of the teachers here who was most enthusiastic about bringing in *The Letter People*. Fran is one of our holdouts.

The Curriculum Wars

The argument between Fran and Bonnie about *The Letter People* is a local skirmish in a national war over the teaching of reading. The front line of this battle is the elementary school reading curriculum, but the argument has trickled down to preschools. This battle is being fought on many fronts, including arguments between the "whole language" and the "phonemic awareness" camps of reading researchers and struggles over textbook selection and methods of instruction fought out by school boards, principals, and teachers. The stakes are high in this debate because in 2000 President George W. Bush made reading the cornerstone of his educational platform and "methods of teaching reading that have a scientific basis" (meaning methods that feature phonics) the law of the land under his No Child Left Behind (NCLB) legislation.

Bonnie and Fran both see themselves as being closer to the middle than to either extreme of this debate. Bonnie sees herself as a centrist and as a pragmatist and those who categorically oppose phonics, packaged curricula, and direct instruction as "purists":

> There are some really purist early childhood people who say that we shouldn't be pushing children into writing and into reading, that it isn't developmentally appropriate, whereas I feel that some children who are three and four years old are ready to read and to learn letters and to sound letters out, and if we don't give them that opportunity then we are really shortchanging them; we're holding them back. The purists would not like *The Letter People*. They'd say it's too challenging for preschoolers. And yet NCLB requires that you need to start teaching preschoolers phonemic awareness, alphabet knowledge, and print awareness. It's really going to be interesting to see how this new direction is going to impact preschools.

Bonnie, who became the head of the Alhambra Preschools in 1995, has been struggling with Fran and some of the other teachers over these issues for almost a decade:

> BONNIE: I came from being a K–8 administrator, so I'm a more academic early childhood person. Some people were upset when I came in because I was expecting counting and writing centers and for the children to perform in a winter concert. There were people saying, "No, this is not developmentally appropriate for preschoolers, they shouldn't be doing calendar and performing." These teachers had been introduced to a very purist philosophy in their CDA [child development associate] credential programs.
> TOBIN: Purist meaning?
> BONNIE: Meaning NAEYC. The person who was training most of them in their CDA was a believer in that early childhood education philosophy where you just keep everything totally developmentally appropriate.

From Bonnie's perspective, Fran is too much under the sway of the purists, which keeps her from moving beyond her training in developmentally appropriate practice and makes her resist teaching phonics. Fran, in contrast, sees herself as an educator committed to child-centered instruction who is also a pragmatist who incorporates phonics and other strategies into her

4.15. Calendar.

teaching to give children the building blocks of reading, as seen in her approach to calendar and her use of Buddy Bear:

FRAN: Basically, the reason I use calendar is just to get the kids used to going from left to right (figure 4.15). That's the main purpose. And it's also about learning the rhythms and patterns of the calendar song, "Sunday, Monday, Tuesday" and then it ends "start all over again." But my main purpose is just to get them going from left to right, which is important for their learning to read.

TOBIN: I notice you are doing a lot of focus on initial sounds, too.

FRAN: Especially after December, I start doing it a little bit more, when they're ready for it. Like for the *M*, they came up with *milk* and *Mom* and *McDonald's* and *Miranda*. I don't do *The Letter People* per se, but we do it in a lot of the things we do, introducing the letter, what letter does your name start with, who else has a name that starts with that letter.

TOBIN: Why don't you do *The Letter People*?

FRAN: I just think that it is too academic. I know where Bonnie is coming from, emphasizing the need to introduce students to the letters and sounds. But I think the more connections we can find that our students can relate to, the more meaningful their literacy experiences will be, especially because so many of my students are still learning English. I encourage reading and writing all the time. But I don't think introducing my students to the letter *A* by saying *A* is for *A'choo* would make any sense to them.

TOBIN: Tell me about Buddy Bear [figure 4.16].

FRAN: I've been doing it for about three years. I noticed that we were having trouble with sharing time, everyone wanted to share about a toy every day and they were getting frustrated waiting for their turn. So I decided to replace sharing time with Buddy Bear. The journal has always been part

4.16. 1. "Who's this?"

2. "Look what Carlos wrote!"

3. "Does this look like Buddy Bear?"

4. "Buddy Bear and I had lots of fun."

5. "You went to sleep with Buddy?"

6. "Who is going to take him home today? Miranda."

of it. Buddy Bear and the journal go home together. In the front of the book I have "My name is Buddy Bear. Share me with your family. And then write in the book. And then bring me back to school to share with my friends." The children can write anything, and they get to color. And sometimes the parents write in there. They'll write a story, what Buddy Bear ate, what he did. Pablo's mom speaks English. She wrote in English.

> But some of the moms write in Spanish, and then I have to pass it on to
> Eva or Cindy, to translate.

Most early childhood educators in the US who watched the Alhambra
video spoke positively about the Buddy Bear activity. Responses were split
on the calendar activities conducted in both Fran's and Jannie's classrooms.
Some respondents praised the use of the calendar to teach preliteracy and
math skills and to get the children used to large group instruction. For example, a preschool director commented: "I know that calendar is out of
fashion in some circles and that NAEYC frowns on it. But I don't think we
should be afraid to teach children things. I like the way the teacher in this
video used the calendar as an opportunity to work on letter recognition
and initial sounds." Others criticized the use of calendar with children of
this age as being developmentally inappropriate, a waste of time, and too
teacher directed. For example, a preschool director commented:

> Calendar has got to be my absolute least favorite activity! It's the default ac-
> tivity morning opening teachers do because it makes them feel like they're
> teachers and this is school. It always reminds me of the way little girls line up
> their dolls and play school. "What letter does *March* start with? *M*. No, try
> again?" Please! I'd like to think as a profession that we've moved beyond the
> teacher tossing out questions that have only one possible answer like "What
> day is it?" and the children answering by rote, "Monday" even if they don't
> understand the concept or have any real interest in the activity.

A professor of early childhood education said of the Alhambra videotape:
"I don't like that calendar activity. It's not as bad as that shamrock thing
they did in the afternoon, but it's a close second. It's the antithesis of developmentally appropriate practice for children of this age."

DAP came on the scene in 1987 with the first publication of *Guidelines for
Developmentally Appropriate Practice in Early Childhood Programs Serving Children from Birth through Age Eight* (Bredekamp 1987). Upon its release, DAP
was hailed by many early childhood educators as a key step in the professionalization of the field and critiqued by others for being too prescriptive,
for an over-reliance on developmental psychology, and for being insufficiently attentive to cultural differences (Bloch 1992; Fowell & Lawton 1992;
Jipson 1991; Kessler 1991; Lubeck 1994, 1996; Walsh 1991). NAEYC leaders
complained that these critiques from the left, while not without substance,
were forcing them to fight a battle on two fronts when the real enemy was

on the right, with the proponents of a pushed-down academic curriculum. As Rosalind Charlesworth explains, "The guidelines were a response to 'a growing trend toward more formal, academic instruction of young children' (Bredekamp & Copple 1997, p. v). Prekindergarten teachers were being increasingly pressured to use a curriculum that seemed more suitable for elementary school" (Charlesworth 1998, 274). For many early childhood educators DAP became a professional code, a source of professional pride, and the call letters in the battle against formal, academic instruction of young children.

In retrospect we can see that DAP was introduced at an opportune time for it to take hold, as the US was beginning to support the increased provision of publicly funded preschool and politicians and educators were calling for accreditation and quality standards at all levels of education. As Charlesworth writes of the first DAP handbook: "The initial impetus for this publication was the implementation of the NAEYC accreditation process, which required accredited programs to exhibit 'developmentally appropriate activities, materials, and expectations' (Bredekamp & Copple 1997, p. v). Centers seeking accreditation, however, could not refer to any published guidelines that outlined developmentally appropriate practice" (Charlesworth 1998, 274). The reasoning here is a bit circular: NAEYC required that centers seeking accreditation demonstrate developmentally appropriate practices, which in turn created a need for NAEYC's materials on developmentally appropriate practices. Circular or not, the strategy worked. Although NAEYC is a nongovernmental organization, the NAEYC guidelines became the basis in many states for preschool accreditation.

As NAEYC's influence on preschool teacher training, curricula, and accreditation grew throughout the 1990s, an opposing force was also building up steam. Phonics proponents critical of the whole-language approach to literacy allied with advocates of "back to basics," academic-skills curricular approaches to form a powerful educational lobby. Their targets included bilingual education, multicultural education, progressive education, university-run teacher education programs, and developmentally appropriate practice.

With George W. Bush's election in 2000, the critics of whole language and of the more play-oriented approaches to early childhood education came into power. Bush made No Child Left Behind his highest-profile domestic policy. Although NCLB does not deal directly with preschools, it has had a dramatic effect on early childhood education, both indirectly in the change in the national discourse on education and directly through Good Start, Grow Smart, the administration's plan for early childhood education, released in 2002. The plan begins with an analysis of three key reasons that many young children receive poor-quality early childhood education:

1   Most states have limited alignment between what children are doing before they enter school and what is expected of them once they are in school;
2   Early childhood programs are seldom evaluated based on how they prepare children to succeed in school; and
3   There is not enough information for early childhood teachers, parents, grandparents, and childcare providers on ways to prepare children to be successful in school. (7)

The solutions offered were to make the curriculum of Head Start and other early care and education programs more academic and more focused on phonics-based approaches to reading; to increase the use of quality and achievement standards and outcome assessments; and to provide "research-based information & training to early childhood educators, child care providers, and parents, with a particular emphasis on effective teaching strategies for early language and pre-literacy development."

Caught Between NAEYC and NCLB

The polarization of the positions on early childhood education of government officials, professional organizations, and professors of early childhood education have left many practitioners confused and beleaguered. In the mid-1980s, the prevailing complaint we heard from early childhood educators in the US was feeling unappreciated and misunderstood: "People think teaching preschool is easy and anyone can do it, like babysitting." In the first decade of the millennium, the prevailing complaint is feeling pressured; teachers feel caught between contradictory pressures to be at the same time more developmentally appropriate and more academically rigorous, to meet NAEYC accreditation standards while satisfying Department of Education expectations for teaching young children to read growing out of NCLB (Fuller 2007, 120). As an early childhood block grant preschool director complained to us, "We are caught between 'Nacey' [NAEYC] and 'Nickelby' [NCLB]."

Most US teachers who watched the St. Timothy's and Alhambra videos tended to empathize with the predicament Jannie and Fran are in and with the burden they are under to meet increasingly demanding and sometimes conflicting standards and expectations. The comments of preschool directors and professors tended to be gently critical of what they see as shortcomings in both Jannie's and Fran's approaches. Looking across the comments made by teachers, directors, and professors, we find a prevailing discourse of teachers trying hard but inevitably falling short of achieving the standards of either NCLB, DAP, or both. For example, a professor of early childhood education who watched the Alhambra tape said of Fran: "This is clearly a caring, well-meaning teacher, so I don't want to come down too hard on her. But her approach is typical of what I see in a lot of play-oriented preschools with teachers who have been introduced to the logic of DAP, but who don't know how to create richer, more cognitively complex activities for their students." A director of a preschool program faulted the staff of St. Timothy's for falling short of developmentally appropriate practices for promoting literacy:

> I see the beginnings of some good, developmentally appropriate pre-reading activities, but not enough follow-through. There are a lot of lost opportunities here to develop children's understanding of word-print relations. Like when that assistant teacher was writing down what the child was saying about his picture, "My house, Dad's house, Mom's house." If I were doing it, as I wrote the words down I would be saying "My *house*. Dad's *house*. Mom's *house*. Look, you've got *house* here all those times." And then the children would see the repetition of the word on the paper and they would start to understand how writing can represent speech.

Early childhood educators on both sides of the reading wars make clear their commitment to early literacy and both sides are acutely aware of the pressure they are under to get children reading. As a preschool teacher explained to us:

> A lot of the kids we teach are from poorer families, and there is a lot of worry about them being at risk for failure when they get to elementary school because they can't read, and we get kindergarten teachers complaining that we send them children who aren't ready for kindergarten because they don't already know how to read. We can say, "I thought that was your job?" But it doesn't do any good to complain, because this is how it is. A lot of our kids don't learn how to read in preschool or even in kindergarten or first grade because of where they start off from, but someone has to take the blame, and it is usually us teachers.

A beginning kindergarten teacher told us, "Our professors gave a lot of emphasis to whole language and making children love books and develop their spoken language. That's all great. But once you get out here in the real world, I mean in a school like where I'm working, it is made very clear to us that our students had better be reading at or above grade level by the end of the year, or else."

The pressure teachers of young children feel to give more emphasis to pre-reading comes not just from directors and experts, but also from parents (Fuller 2007, 87–88). Jannie and the other teachers at St. Timothy's, where most of the parents are middle-class, told us that they must continually justify their play-oriented curriculum to parents and resist pressure to do more direct academic instruction. When we showed the Alhambra video to the parents of the children in Fran's class, the parents, many of whom are recent immigrants from Mexico and all of whom are working-class, were generally very supportive, but some wished that there was more academic emphasis. One father commented (in Spanish), "I like the program very much. But if there were one thing I would like to have changed, it would be more teaching of letters and numbers. In Mexico, the teachers teach more. Here there is a lot of play." A mother added, "I wish the day could be longer than two-and-a-half hours of school so my son could be better ready for kindergarten." Bonnie explained that the pressure she puts on Fran to do more direct reading instruction reflects not just her own beliefs and early childhood education but also the values of parents and the school district:

> This district gives a lot of emphasis to traditional education and back to basics. The Alhambra Traditional School is the most popular school in the district. They have a waiting list and you have to test to get in. A lot of our parents want their children to go to the traditional school. Many of our teachers in this district have a more academic focus and it goes with their concept of what early childhood education should be and the parents in our district appreciate it.

Bonnie's emphasis on academic preparation and her support for phonics-based reading instruction places her in the minority among the directors of Early Childhood Block Grant program directors. In the words of a staff member from the Arizona Department of Education, "Bonnie is a bit of an outlier. She doesn't see things the way most of the block grant directors do. Most of them are more on the DAP side."

The preschool directors who are on the DAP side are also feeling the pressure to respond to NCLB, as the director of one Arizona Early Child-hood Block Grant program told us:

> Believe me, I am no supporter of No Child Left Behind or of phonics. But we are deluding ourselves if we think we can just keep on doing things like we have in the past. I am working with my teachers to give more emphasis to pre-reading and even to do phonics and on getting the kids ready for what they are expected to be able to do in kindergarten. I don't particularly like what they are doing in kindergarten these days, but we can't do anything about that. The pressure to have our kids take high-stakes tests and to have test scores determine if our programs get closed down isn't here yet, but it's coming.

During the past ten years or so, NAEYC's notions of best practice have undergone a subtle but significant shift, a shift described to us by Mary McMullen in a discussion of the St. Timothy's video with faculty at Indiana University:

> In the past few years constructivist preschools like St. Timothy's and the Campus Child Center here at IU have undergone a shift. They've moved away from a very Piagetian approach, which was more hands-off, where the teachers set up learning-rich environments and then stood back, to these days more of a Vygotskian emphasis, where the teachers engage more with the children. The teachers now are doing more to facilitate peer-to-peer in-teractions and adult-to-child problem solving. It's more Vygotskian these days in the sense of scaffolding, to take children to the next level. Either it's from subtle pressure coming from parents, or it's from pressure from society, or maybe teachers just discovered, "Hey, this makes sense."

All of the Early Childhood Block Grant programs in Arizona are accred-ited by NAEYC. Accreditation is a multi-step process that includes com-pletion of an accreditation readiness survey, preparation of a self-study, and a site visit by an NAEYC "validator" who evaluates the degree to which the preschool meets program standards and performance criteria. The vali-dator sends her report to an accreditation panel, which decides whether to award accreditation and gives the program a report listing strengths as well as areas that need improvement. This is an iterative process, with new doc-umentation and site visits required when there is significant teacher turn-over or program change; re-accreditation is needed every five years, and schools are expected to adapt to evolving standards. In 2004, an NAEYC validator who watched the 1984 St. Timothy's video made comments that carry the flavor of a site-visit report:

- Forty-five minutes of learning center time is too short. Ninety minutes, that's recommended. Longer activities. And outside play should not be seen as recess but as extension of classroom space and activities.
- (Commenting on a teacher's intervention in a fight between children): Now we focus not just on "use your words" but on problem solving. "I see two friends who want the same thing. What can we do?" If they can't come up with the words, you help them, prompt them, give examples.
- (Commenting on a cooking activity): That's okay, with proper supervision. I'm kind of fussy. I'd use either all fresh or all canned ingredients. And I would prep the kids with lower-level tasks before they start cutting ingredients for soup. I think ECE is a little more thoughtful about practically everything we do these days.
- (Commenting on the teacher dealing with a child who hasn't put away the blocks he has played with): The teacher's question to the child here, "Did you do this?" is number one on the "don't do list."

Number one on what list? Presumably, the NAEYC list of do's and don'ts.

Many of the critical comments directors and teachers made about the St. Timothy's and Alhambra videos took the form of "that's not DAP." For example, a preschool director commented on the rule found in both Jannie's and Fran's classrooms limiting the numbers of children allowed in an activity center: "It's not developmentally appropriate for children of this age to have a set rule on how many children can be at an activity center. If there are more children than an activity can handle, this is as an opportunity for children to develop their problem-solving skills." A professor of early childhood education in Honolulu said of Jannie's classroom management approach, "I think it's good that she was teaching some science with that lesson on absorption. But it would be a more developmentally appropriate practice if instead of her demonstrating so much she had made the lesson more hands-on and let the children handle the paper towels and sponges." A consistent theme of these comments was praising Jannie and Fran for attempting but criticizing them for falling short of achieving developmentally appropriate practice. This theme can be found on the NAEYC website, which states, "Recent data shows that many teachers who say they believe in developmentally appropriate practice do not have developmentally appropriate classrooms. A recent study of kindergarten teachers found that more than half demonstrated conflicts between their philosophy of early childhood education and their classroom practices" (www.naeyc.org/ece/1998/05.asp).

These comments are characteristic of a discourse of failing that feminist scholars have pointed out is characteristic of femininity, of mothering, and of women's work. In *Gender Trouble*, Judith Butler (1990) argues that being feminine is a performance doomed to fail—one can never be feminine enough (or, for that matter, masculine enough or straight enough) because these categories are simultaneously too vague and too ideal to be achieved. Applying this line of thinking to early childhood care and education, Chelsea Bailey (2003) has written about the "always, already failing" mother and teacher of young children. Listening in on chatroom sites where mothers of infants and toddlers share their horror stories and anxieties, Bailey identifies a consistent pattern of self-blame, as mothers describe themselves as falling short of their notion of being a good mom. Bailey suggests that this same pattern is characteristic not just of mothers but also of preschool teachers. It could be argued that by providing clarity to the definition of what it means to be a good preschool teacher and creating standards for best practice, DAP has professionalized the field and thereby raised teachers' self-esteem and lowered their anxiety and self-doubt. In contrast, it could be argued that DAP functions, like rigid gender expectations, as a standard that can never be met and therefore leaves teachers open to accusations of inadequacy both from others and from themselves.

We suggest that both NCLB and DAP are disciplinary regimes that exert their power over teachers and directors. Because NCLB is backed by the power of the government and by an administration that does not hesitate to wield its authority over teachers and others, it seems much more powerful than NAEYC, a professional organization whose accreditation is voluntary and that presents a gentler face. But as Foucault (1975) has taught us, we need to be suspicious of kindler, gentler, more progressive forms of disciplinary power. Psychoanalysis, social work, and modern education are among the progressive movements that Foucault argues are more effective than the more repressive forms of discipline they replaced because they function by internalization and therefore their power is harder to identify or to oppose. NCLB's power is explicit, external, and threatening and therefore widely criticized and resisted by teachers of young children. The power of DAP, in contrast, comes not just from accreditation pressures but also from the way teachers are encouraged to internalize DAP beliefs and practices and monitor their own progress. In contemporary American early childhood education, NAEYC is functioning as the positive pole, and

NCLB as the negative, with teachers, who are subject to both disciplinary regimes, in the middle.

Evolving Forms of Provision

By comparing Alhambra, a public program located on a middle-school campus in Phoenix, with St. Timothy's, a private nonprofit program at a church in Honolulu, and by comparing both with preschools of a generation ago, we can get a sense of the range of contemporary American early childhood education programs and also of the ways in which early childhood education in the US has changed dramatically in some respects and stayed the same in others.

Placing St. Timothy's in historical perspective, we can define the program type as a hybrid of two disappearing forms: the half-day nursery school and the daycare center. For the first two-thirds of the twentieth century there was a split between nursery school programs for children of the upper and upper-middle classes and daycare programs for children of the poor. Because most mothers of the higher classes did not work, and because their children were not viewed as needing extensive socialization out of the home, nursery schools typically provided children with half-days of center-based play experience, often for just two or three days a week. Nursery schools flourished in the postwar era of the rise of the suburbs, the one-income nuclear middle-class family, and the stay-at-home middle-class wife.

All this began to change in the 1970s, as the women's movement combined with economic change to lead increasing numbers of middle-class mothers of young children to work outside of the home, which created an increase in the need for full-time care. Middle-class parents in the 1970s and 1980s often chose family-home care over placing their children in daycare centers because daycare carried the stigma of being for children of poorer families and the reputation of offering childcare without much education. By the early 1980s, to address the growing demand from middle-class families for full-day programs, nursery schools began to evolve into children's centers by lengthening their hours of operation and changing the descriptor in their name. The rise of the children's center met an important need, but still left a large gap in provision. In 1985, only about one-third of four-year-old children in the US were in center-based care. This included the children of the very poor in Head Start; working-class children in private for-profit daycare programs and not-for-profit church-run programs; and middle- and upper-middle-class children who attended the private, mostly not-for-profit child centers that were the heirs of the old nursery schools. This socially stratified mix of early childhood services left a great number of families without access to center-based programs. Some working- and middle-class parents of young children favored the hominess of "kith and kin care" or family daycare homes, while many others turned to these options because they were not able to find a quality center-based program they could afford. This problem is often conceptualized in the United States in terms of the lack of provision for the "gap" group of families who make too much for eligibility in Head Start and other income-qualifying programs and too little to afford the tuition of quality child centers. The gap between the incomes of parents with children in Head Start and in private programs such as St. Timothy's Children's Center was and is huge. There are also families, both wealthy and of modest means, who choose to raise their child at home until kindergarten (Fuller 2007).

That having been said, the percentage of US children who have a year of preschool before entering kindergarten has risen significantly in the last twenty years—from about one-third to over two-thirds. Part of this increase is attributable to increased Head Start enrollments and to a modest increase in enrollments in private not-for-profit programs. But expansion of Head Start and private preschools has increased provision only for the very poor and for the well-off. What has changed levels of provision most dramatically for the "gap" group is expansion of the for-profit sector (including the rise of national chains such as Kindercare) and the development of public programs such as Alhambra's, which has an income cut off of about $38,000 for a family of four, which is nearly double the Head Start level.

Preschool programs run by school districts with local or state funds is a relatively new development in US early childhood education. Whereas there was widespread opposition a generation ago to the idea of K–12 school districts getting into the business of early childhood education, this concept has gained acceptance in a majority of the states. Several different versions of school-based preschool programs have emerged, with some states providing universal access for all four-year-old children to school-based programs, some providing tuition vouchers to parents, who can then shop around for a private or public program, some providing a year of preschool only to economically qualifying children, and some giving local communities funds to use as they see fit for early childhood education, care, and health programs (Fuller 2007).

The structural and economic differences between St. Timothy's Children's Center and Alhambra Preschool should not keep us from appreciating their similarities. The teachers and directors at both sites talk about their practices in similar terms and are guided by similar philosophies. Some of this similarity can be explained by our selection of the two programs. There are preschools we could have chosen for the new study that are less like St. Timothy's than is Alhambra, but because our method calls for us to select preschools in each country that are defined as being good (our goal is not to conduct an exposé or to embarrass teachers and director), we selected two programs that are accredited by the National Association of Early Childhood Education. As discussed above, the influence of NAEYC was apparent in our interviews with staff from both programs, who explained much of their practice by citing developmentally appropriate practice and other NAEYC core ideas. But we suggest that a more profound reason for the similarities between St. Timothy's and Alhambra can be attributed to the underlying influence of American cultural beliefs on preschool practices and on teachers' reflections on these practices, which take the form of what Jerome Bruner (1990) calls "teacher folk beliefs."

In our original study we identified the core American cultural beliefs and practices of St. Timothy's as free choice, self-expression, individual rights, and the pursuit of happiness. A generation later, our research at St. Timothy's and Alhambra reveals considerable continuity in the cultural values of American early childhood education. This is not to say that nothing has changed. New lines of reasoning are being used to support familiar practices, some old practices have evolved, and some new ones have been introduced, but all in ways that are consistent with the cultural beliefs we identified a generation ago.

CHOICE

Choice remains a key feature of the curriculum and pedagogy of American preschools. When children arrive at St. Timothy's and Alhambra, they immediately are asked by the teachers, "What would you like to do?" The choices are not unconstrained. "What would you like to do?" is followed up by a menu of alternatives: "Would you like to help Alex with his puzzle? Read a book? Draw? Help feed Jackie?" Morning circle provides less opportunity for choice, but it ends at both preschools with the teachers laying out the options for the activity center time that follows. At St. Timothy's,

4.17. 1. Jannie showing options on choice tray.

2. Micah chooses painting.

4.18. 1. Fran and Shanelle at the Play-Doh table.

2. Pablo and Jamal play with farm animals.

Jannie holds up icons representing the available choices, and then calls on the children one by one to choose: "Water table? Drawing? Collage?" (figure 4.17). At Alhambra, Fran divides the children into groups that will begin playing inside and outside the classroom, and then sends them off to choose from among several activities, in some cases with a bit of direction, as she explained to us: "The activity centers are open and the children can choose what they want to do. They have a choice, but sometimes I'll try to direct certain kids to certain activities, where I want them to start. If I let them choose where to start it would be really hard to get them away from that activity to the one I really need them to work at" (figure 4.18).

In the discussions of the videos, Japanese teachers, like their US counterparts, talked about the value of free choice. But whereas the teachers in Japan gave greater emphasis to the children being free, the US teachers put the greater emphasis on choice. We see this difference manifested most clearly in scenes in the US videos of the teachers presenting children with a list of options to choose from, in contrast to scenes at Komatsudani Hoikuen and Madoka Yōchien, where the children are free to roam the classrooms and grounds, choosing activities to engage in without the benefit of a teacher presenting or defining options (Fujita & Sano 1988; Hoffman 2000). The difference also can be found in the subtle difference between the words American and Japanese teachers use to describe similar activities, the Americans favoring the phrase "free choice" and Japanese educators favoring "free play" (*jiyū asobi*).

American preschool teachers not only encourage children to choose, but to develop a meta-awareness and a meta-discourse of the techniques and language of choosing. There are multiple times of the day at St. Timothy's and Alhambra when the teachers announce that it is time to make choices and draw attention to the task: "You're song helper today. Do you know what song you want to choose? Do you need to think about it for a minute? Do you want some suggestions from your friends?" "What center do you want to go to? Don't just point. Say it with words. Blocks? Good choice."

Why the emphasis on choice in US early childhood education? There is no single answer. Choice is wrapped up with the American cultural belief that young children (along with the rest of Americans) have an inalienable right to the pursuit of happiness and fun, and activities that are individually chosen are assumed to be inherently more pleasurable than those that are collectively chosen or assigned. The belief that preschool should be fun and full of choice is in tension these days with growing pressure on young children to learn to read. But even the most zealous advocates of pushing an academic curriculum down into the preschool years take care to present this curriculum as fun and to offer children choices within structured and even scripted lessons.

Choice is also valued because it is believed to foster intrinsic motivation and thereby to facilitate learning. In comments of American early childhood educators on the St. Timothy's and Alhambra videos, we can deduce an underlying cultural or folk theory of learning that links choice to intrinsic motivation and to constructivist pedagogy: learning centers are important for children of this age because children can choose activities within their zone of proximal development; children learn best when they choose the activity; if you choose for them, they resist, they are less engaged, and they learn less.

Choice is also tied up with notions of democracy. Letting children choose between building with Legos and playing at the water table is seen as providing practice in exercising the rights of democratic citizenship and more generally, of "independent decision making" (Lee & Walsh 2005, 63). While most American educators who watched and commented on the Alhambra video were critical of the Pledge of Allegiance as an age-inappropriate display of patriotism that teaches young children no valuable lessons about democracy or citizenship, there was widespread support for the notion that choice and child-initiated activities support democratic values. As a preschool director in Phoenix told us after watching the St. Timothy's video:

> I like the way this teacher lays out the options for learning centers and then patiently gives each child the chance to choose a preferred activity. I am really into Alfie Kohn [1996]. He says that you can't teach democratic values by lecturing about them. You have to organize your classroom as a democracy and let children experience what it feels like to be in a democratic environment where their individual voices and choices matter.

A parallel but more cynical explanation for the valorization of choice in the US early childhood curriculum would be to see choice as crucial to the functioning of capitalism. Capitalist economies require consumers to have strong opinions and preferences about almost identical choices. Seen from this perspective, the times at St. Timothy's and Alhambra when the teachers present alternative activities to the children and ask them to choose become less of a metaphor for the polling place than for the shopping mall. It's not just the case that children *can* choose but also that they *must* choose several times a day from among a list of mostly familiar activities. The drama of the moment of choice is often heightened, as on the Home Shopping Network, by a sense of growing scarcity: "Only one more space at the water table."

INDIVIDUALISM

As a cultural value underlying American preschool practices, choice is closely tied to individualism and to the notion of individualized education (Lee & Walsh 2005, 74). In discussions of the videos, the valorization of individualism and disparagement of its opposites, groupism and authoritarianism, were expressed most clearly in the form of critiques by teachers and directors of whole-group, teacher-directed activities and in the form of praise for activities that were described as "individualized" and "child-centered." Looking across the interviews with US early childhood educators, we find no instance of "teacher-directed" being used positively or of "child-centered" being used negatively. Indeed, the term "child-centered" functions as a metonym for progressive practice and "teacher-centered" as a metonym for regressive approaches.

The origami activity at Komatsudani, in which Morita-sensei stood in front of the class and led the children through a series of steps for making paper fish, was cited by several US teachers who viewed this tape as an example of teacher-directed pedagogy that robbed children of their individuality and creativity. For example, a preschool teacher in Memphis commented: "They did a lot of large-group stuff we don't believe in for young children. We would never expect or try to make them all follow something like that at the same time. That teacher-directed activity did not allow the children to use their own creativity in making the art project." A teacher in Phoenix concurred: "I'm impressed with the children's manual dexterity. And I like the way the teacher let the children choose the color of their paper for making the fish. But in this lesson once they chose their color, I didn't see the children getting to make any other choice or having any other opportunity to exercise their individuality."

American early childhood educators who viewed the St. Timothy's and Alhambra videos routinely faulted both programs for having too many large-group activities and too few opportunities for free play and individual choice. For example, a Honolulu early childhood education professor commented on the St. Timothy's tape: "We encourage a higher ratio of child-directed to teacher-directed activities. Take that lesson on absorption. From the beginning to end the lesson was orchestrated by the adults. That sort of teacher-directed pedagogy has been shown to be ineffective for promoting children's learning. Young children learn best when they have say about what they learn and how, with some scaffolding, but not direction, from adults."

SELF-EXPRESSION

Another core belief of contemporary American early childhood education is that children should not only have opinions about what they want to do, but they should verbalize them. In both of the US videos we see teachers being patient about giving children time to respond to queries about what they'd like to do next. When children make their choice silently, by pointing to an activity, the teachers say to them, "Tell me with your words." "I can't tell what you want to do if you don't say it." This emphasis on verbal expression takes on a special urgency at Alhambra, where most of the children are learning English as a second language.

The phrases "Tell me" and "Use your words" are heard throughout the day from the teachers at both schools, not only to encourage children to verbalize their choice of activities, but also for mediating disputes, narrating and recapitulating play, and dictating stories. We hear Jannie tell Aaron, "Tell him that it hurts when he hits you"; Val encourages Kylie to "tell me what's in your picture so I can write it down"; Fran urges Precious to talk about her play with the toy bus ("Can you tell me who is on the bus? Is it stopping for more children to get on?"). Jannie explained why it is so important to record the children's utterances verbatim on their papers: "When they do a drawing, I ask them, 'What did you make? Tell me with your words what you made.' I write whatever they say, word for word, even if it doesn't make sense. Those are *their* words."

This belief in the power of words and the value of verbally expressing feelings runs deep in American early childhood education (Tobin 1995) and seems unchanged from a generation ago. In the original Preschool in Three Cultures study, Cheryl Takashige, the head teacher in the four-year-old class at St. Timothy's, used the same phrases to encourage children to speak that we now hear from Jannie, Val, Fran, and Eva in the new study. The cultural dimension of this practice is highlighted by the contrast between the emphasis in the US preschools on verbally expressing feelings and the emphasis in Japanese preschools on children learning to be sensitive to the unverbalized feelings of others.

DISEMBODIMENT

Over the past twenty years there has been a heightening of concern about danger and risk in US early childhood education, with much of this concern centered on threats of disease, injury, and sexuality. Preschools have become sites where the bodies of children and the adults who care for them fall under increasing scrutiny and discipline. A shift in emphasis in the US early childhood curriculum over the last generation from a focus on play to academic readiness has brought with it a decline in attention to physical expression and the body. The ratio has shifted in the preschool day towards less dancing and more reading, less time on the playground and more time in learning centers, and less prominence of blocks, toys, and "manipulatives" of the type championed by Froebel at the beginnings of the kindergarten movement and more prominence of printed materials, worksheets, and time spent on the computer.

No Child Left Behind and its allied government initiatives have been a direct source of pressure behind this shift from an emphasis on the body to the mind. Good Start, Grow Smart (the White House's 2002 early childhood initiative) has the effect of increasing support for the provision of preschools, but only if those preschools emphasize academic over social and physical development. Specifically, No Child Left Behind orders school districts and federally funded preschool programs to focus on using phonics to teach reading:

> The new Early Reading First program will make competitive 6-year awards to support early language, literacy, and pre-reading development of preschool-age children, particularly those from low-income families. Recipients will use instructional strategies and professional development drawn from scientifically based reading research to help young children to attain the fundamental knowledge and skills they will need for optimal reading development in kindergarten and beyond. (USDOE 2002)

The effect on the life of the body of this redefinition of the preschool as a site for reading instruction for children from low-income families can be seen at Alhambra Preschool. As Fran lamented, "The kids have so little instructional time that we decided not to go out to the playground every-day." Another Alhambra teacher told us, "To get the children from where they are to where they need to be for kindergarten next year I feel I should keep them in the room with me working on their skills instead of sending them out to the playground."

Neurological research does not support a de-emphasis on physical activities for preschool-aged children. But the sense of urgency pushed by proponents of applying brain research to early childhood education, who suggest that children's brains that are not properly supported will miss out at a critical stage on the chance to develop optimally, is heard by many preschool directors and teachers as a directive to de-emphasize the life of the body and throw all available resources into the needs of the brain, the favorite organ of the new American millennium.

The gloved hand of the caregivers at Alhambra serving snacks to the children can be seen as a metaphor for the heightened concern about contamination and disease. Because Alhambra Preschool receives government subsidies for food and because they are housed within a public elementary school, the program must follow the health and safety standards of the Department of Health, which requires food servers to wear gloves. Other examples cited by the staff at Alhambra and St. Timothy's of the proliferation of rules and regulations that are intended to prevent disease but which are burdensome for the programs include the prohibition against tooth-brushing in the bathrooms introduced at St. Timothy's and the barriers to serving lunch family-style (with children passing and serving food to each other) at Alhambra.

Heightened concerns about injuries can be seen in both US videos, where assistant teachers closely monitor the children's play on the climbing structures ("You can ask the teacher if she can watch you on the structure. Can you do that on the structure if there is no teacher there? No. You might get hurt.") Teachers in Japan and China were puzzled by this level of concern and supervision. As the director of a kindergarten in Kyoto commented, "I wonder if having a teacher standing so close actually makes the children safer? Might this not confuse the children, and prevent them from developing and using their own judgment about what they can do and not do?" Japanese teachers raised similar questions about why the teachers in the US videos felt compelled to intervene so quickly in the children's rough-and-tumble play and physical squabbles, as Jannie did when some of the boys were playfully spanking Stu during cleanup time ("It's not funny when you guys are hitting him. It's not fun for him. It hurts his body,") and as Fran did when several children were jostling for seats on the reading bench. In contrast, many US teachers who viewed the Madoka video expressed surprise that children were allowed to climb so high and freely, with little apparent supervision and that teachers at Komatsudani allowed children's fights to proceed with such little intervention. As a director in Phoenix told us, "Even if we wanted to give children more freedom to climb and to have rough-and-tumble play, we couldn't because the regulations wouldn't allow it. We'd get sued." Several US educators told us that they were impressed with the logic of the older children at Komatsudani caring for babies but that concerns of risk and liability would preclude them from introducing such mixed-age interaction in their programs. As one director commented, "I can really see the value of this. But if had our older children carrying around toddlers or an older boy touching a younger boy's penis, we'd get sued in a heartbeat."

Which brings us to the specter of dangerous sexuality that has come to haunt contemporary US preschools. In the late 1980s and early 1990s, a series of cases of purported sexual abuse of children by caretakers in childcare settings received extensive news coverage in the US. Most of these cases, which typically included allegations that multiple children in a childcare setting were systemically abused by more than one staff member, sometimes in ways that included satanic rituals or the production of child pornography, crumbled in the courtroom or were later overturned. But although the high-profile legal cases turned out to lack merit, they had the effect of establishing in the consciousness of the nation the twin characters of the pedophilic preschool teacher and the sexually vulnerable preschooler. Since we conducted our research in the mid-1980s, a moral panic about dangerous sexuality has swept through US preschools, leading to a proliferation of "no touch" policies (Johnson, 2000; Jones 2001), safe-sex workshops, and the flight of men from the field (Silin 1995; Tobin 1997). When the panic began, concern first focused on gay male teachers and then spread to all male teachers, many of whom were encouraged by administrators to change jobs "for their own protection." Soon women preschool teachers also become suspect, with rules instituted that prohibited teachers from cleaning up children who had bathroom accidents or holding them on their laps in any position other than "side-saddle."

This panic about sexuality in preschools hit home for us the day we visited a public preschool located in an elementary school in Phoenix to conduct a focus-group interview with the teachers and director about our videotapes. The director greeted us with tears in her eyes. When we asked what was wrong, she told us that "I just got a phone call saying I am being given an official letter of reprimand for being too lenient on my teachers because of the way I handled a health issue." When we asked what kind of health issue, the story came pouring out:

One afternoon last week, when I was off campus at a meeting, a three-year-old child complained to his teacher, Karen, that his "pee-pee hurt." Karen and another teacher, Lisa, took him to the preschool bathroom and asked him to pull down his pants to show them. They said that his penis looked red, so they phoned his mom, who took him to the doctor—it turned out that he had a urinary infection. The teachers told me the next morning what had happened. Later that week a bunch of us directors met with a trainer from the Department of Education who asked us if we had any training needs or tricky problems we had to deal with. I told the story of the boy with the sore penis. The trainer responded with alarm: "You can't do that. You're in big trouble." The trainer then told on me to my superintendent, who sent the letter of reprimand. When I met with the superintendent, she said that the teachers shouldn't have asked the boy to pull down his pants and the teachers shouldn't have looked at his genitals. I decided to take responsibility for this rather than place the blame on my teachers. I pointed out that these rules may be appropriate for primary and secondary education, but they make no sense with three-year-olds, who frequently need help in the bathroom and sometimes have toileting accidents that require help to clean up and change clothes. But the superintendent, who has no background in early childhood education, wouldn't listen to me and she gave me an official reprimand. The letter in my file makes me feel like over twenty years of working in this field to build my reputation have been wiped out. I guess that in the future, instead of following my training and instincts I will strictly follow the district's rules. I told them from now on I want everything in writing, spelling out exactly what we can and can't do with children.

This event reflects a structural problem of locating a preschool program within a K–12 bureaucratic structure that lacks understanding of young children and early childhood education. More generally, it reflects the moral panic about sexuality that has arisen since we did our original study. Even more generally, this event, when placed alongside the rise in suspicion of teachers and concerns about risk and the de-emphasis of the body, reflects a creeping bureaucratization, surveillance, and routinization of preschools, phenomena that while characteristic of contemporary US culture and society, are by no means unique to the US.

TARGETED PROGRAMS AND INDIVIDUALIZED SERVICES

Another culturally and socially characteristic aspect of US early childhood education is the emphasis on providing extra support for children most in need. The aspects of Alhambra's program that received the most praise from Japanese and Chinese as well as US viewers of the video are the services provided for children with special needs and for English-language learners. Viewers in all three countries commented positively on the support we see in the video being given to Ferdie, a boy with special needs who speaks both Spanish and English. In addition to help from his classroom teachers, we see Ferdie getting help from Cindy, who is assigned to him as a full-time aide, and from the special education specialist who spends time in the classroom with him each week. (Ferdie also received weekly visits from the speech and occupational therapists, but they were not in the classroom on the day we videotaped.) Many Japanese and Chinese viewers were surprised and impressed with the range of services brought to the classroom and with the investment made in helping a single student. In contrast to the unqualified support our US informants gave to Alhambra's full-inclusion approach to helping children with special needs, comments on the mixture of Spanish and English at Alhambra were more ambivalent, with praise mixed with concern. This concern took several forms: There was some concern that a bilingual approach at Alhambra might impede children's learning of English; one viewer commented, "I worry that the time these kids who speak Spanish at home are speaking Spanish at school might be better spent having them speaking English, to get them up to speed for kindergarten." On the other hand, there were criticisms that the Alhambra program was unbalanced and too English dominated; one teacher said, "I'm sorry, but I have to disagree with your description of this as a bilingual program. There's a big difference between a real bilingual program and a program that is taught in English with some Spanish words thrown in." There were more positive than negative comments on Alhambra's bilingual approach. Many of the US teachers and directors who viewed the Alhambra video were impressed with the way the children and teachers switched back and forth throughout the morning from English to Spanish. A preschool teacher in Indiana commented, "I wish I could speak two languages! It's great that the children are in an environment where both languages are being supported." The director of an early childhood block grant preschool in Phoenix said:

> The approach to language in this video looks very much like our program. Whenever possible we hire staff who can speak Spanish. We make sure that at least one of the two teachers in each classroom is bilingual. A bilingual approach is valuable for several reasons. In those first few weeks of school it allows the children who come to school speaking only Spanish to be understood and to make their needs known. As the year goes on, we gradually shift to more and more English, to get the children ready for kindergarten, which is English-only, but we keep using Spanish, too, because we believe in supporting home language retention.

Examples of targeted early childhood education programs include special education services for children like Ferdie; Head Start and other publicly funded programs (like Alhambra's) that provide a year or more of preschool to income-qualifying families; and bilingual programs intended to get children who speak a language other than English at home ready for kindergarten. Targeting programs to at-risk and special-needs children is a feature that, as the OECD report makes clear, is a hallmark of the US approach to early education and care:

> Publicly funded pre-school programmes for children below kindergarten age are not considered to be a universal entitlement for all children of the population. Instead, they typically serve children from low-income families and children considered to be 'at risk' as a result of biological, socio-economic or psychological circumstances, or combinations of these. (OECD 2000, 10)

In Japan and in urban areas of China, as in Europe, low-cost early childhood education and care is universally available and a relatively small percentage of public funds spent on early childhood education goes to children with special needs or who live in special circumstances. In the US, in contrast, early childhood education and care are not universally available and the great majority of the public funds spent on early childhood education are used for children identified as at risk and for programs located in the most needy communities. The question is, why? Why is the US so much more willing to invest heavily in servicing targeted populations than in providing universal services to young children? Political scientists, policy analysts, and legal theorists would approach this question by providing analyses of the political struggles that led to the creation of Head Start and the court fights and congressional negotiations that resulted in the passage in 1975 of the Education for All Handicapped Children Act (later renamed the Individuals with Disabilities Education Act). But such policy-oriented explanations, while instructive, do not address the central question we ask as comparative ethnographers: What are the cultural beliefs behind the targeted programs that make the US approach so unlike the "blanket" approaches being followed in China and Japan and in many other countries?

We would suggest that the first of these cultural beliefs is a focus on equal opportunity. As the National Education Association states on its web site, "Access to a free, quality education is the key to the uniquely American promise of equal opportunity for all." The statement, while jingoistic, captures a core cultural truth, a truth first described almost two centuries ago by Alexis de Tocqueville in his comparative analysis of French and Anglo-American societies: the French are willing to give up some freedom (*liberté*) in order to have greater equality (*égalité*), while the Americans and English will give up some equality for greater individual freedom. "Equal educational opportunity" is a very different thing than "equal education" or equity. Japan, like France and other nations with national systems, would score high on measures of equity in the provision of early childhood education services. The US, in contrast, emphasizes equality of opportunity, which means not the same education for all, but education tailored to the needs of individuals and communities. The cultural logic is that in order for young children with special needs or living in especially difficult circumstances to have an equal chance at success in life, they must be offered targeted (that is, unequal) services.

In addition to the belief in equality of opportunity, another cultural value that underlies support for special education, Head Start, and early childhood education programs for immigrants is a belief in fairness. The logic, which is often stated using the very American metaphors of poker, baseball, and horse racing, goes something like this: "Life is not fair. We need to even the playing field. Everyone is not dealt the same starting hand. Some kids get a raw deal. But everyone deserves a fair shake. Some need help to get up to speed and to be ready to succeed at the next level." In other words, American society is built on competition, and for society to work, this competition must be fair, which means that everyone has to start out with at least some chance of success. The intent of Head Start is to give poor children whose families lack cultural capital a better chance of closing the achievement gap and catching up with their middle-class peers; of special education services to give children with special needs educational access comparable to their "typically abled" classmates; and of bilingual preschool programs to give children who speak a language other than English at home a transition year to get "up to speed for kindergarten." This is the logic used to justify the Good Start, Grow Smart early childhood dimension of No Child Left Behind. Marian Wright Edelman, the founder of the Children's Defense Fund, complains that the Bush administration coopted her organization's rallying cry, "leave no child behind," which she says the administration employs as a smokescreen, without any real commitment to helping poor children (Edelman 2004). The fact that this concept of leaving no one behind can be used by both the left and right to justify social programs attests to its cultural resonance.

In the political struggles to expand the provision of early childhood education in the US the cultural belief in equality of opportunity at times clashes with the cultural belief in fairness. Calls for fairness can be used to justify compensatory, targeted programs, but also to argue that it is unfair to use public funds to offer a program to the few that is not being offered to the many (Fuller 2007). As the FPG Child Development Institute puts it:

> When resources are limited, targeted prekindergarten programs offer the benefits of preschool education to those children in greatest need. The evidence of the effectiveness of prekindergarten programs is also most solid for children at risk of school failure. However, public opinion polling shows that targeted programs receive less political support than universal prekindergarten programs because many middle-class families (and especially those who vote) believe their children should also have access to high-quality prekindergarten programs. (http://www.fpg.unc.edu/-npc/framework/framework.cfm?section_num=6&subsection_num=1, 2006, 9)

These beliefs in fairness and equality of opportunity in turn are tied to the cultural belief in individuality, which in the US takes the form both of a focus on individual rights and a belief in the importance of individual difference. The discourse of individual rights plays a central role in special education, where parents of children with special needs go to court, when necessary (a high level of litigiousness is another American cultural characteristic), to compel a school district to develop an IEP (Individual Educational Plan) for their child that will provide an FAPE (a Fare and Appropriate Public Education) in an LRE (Least Restrictive Environment). In practice, this alphabet soup of rules and regulations means, for example in the case of a four-year-old child with a suspected language delay, physical disability, or emotional disorder, that the school district provides testing and assessment, which leads to a formal diagnosis, which in turn qualifies the child for free access (and free bus transportation) to an early childhood program such as Alhambra's A-OK daycare classroom or to a "self-contained" special education preschool class and to an individualized educational plan that may include a full-time aide and a range of specialist services.

The focus in US education on individual differences (in intelligence, temperament, and ability) and of offering individualized services has spawned the development of professional specializations such as the speech pathologist, the occupational therapist, and the special education teacher; to diagnostic categories including language delay, autism, and ADHD (attention deficit/hyperactivity disorder); and to evolving technologies of individualized intervention, including IEPs and behavioral treatment routines. Combined, this interpenetration of categories of disability, assessment instruments, and interventions constitutes a huge and growing industry that both serves and, some cynics would suggest, necessitates an ever-expanding population of young children needing special services. Does the US have so many special educators because there are so many special education students or so many special education students because there are so many special educators?

A positive view of targeted programs is that the United States invests more public money per capita on young children with special needs and children living in difficult social circumstances than do China, Japan, and many of the countries in Europe known for their quality early childhood education services. Beyond the investment of funds, the US is widely hailed as a global leader in the fields of special education for young children and in the development of bilingual and bicultural programs. On the other hand, a more critical take on targeted preschool programs would be that they stigmatize those they aim to help and create a separate and unequal educa-

4.19. 1. Ferdie playing with Cindy.   2. Ferdie leads the Pledge of Allegiance.

tion system in which private preschools provide children of wealthy parents with constructivist approaches that emphasize creativity and higher-order thinking and public programs provide children of immigrants and the poor with skill-and-drill programs, emphasizing basic skills and rote learning. From this perspective, the overrepresentation of black, Hispanic, and Native American children in special education preschool programs would be viewed not as laudatory extra services for those most in need but instead as a mechanism of segregation and distinction, which relegates people of color to unequal treatment and lowered expectations (Skaggs 2001; Artiles 2003; Klingner et. al. 2005).

These are important criticisms. But they do not reflect the quality of the education and care Fran and Eva provide to the children at Alhambra or the value of the professional services the classroom teachers, aides, and specialists provided to Ferdie during his two years there. Three years after we shot our videotape at Alhambra, we invited Ferdie and his mother, Esperanza, to meet us at the school for a follow-up interview. At this session, Ferdie and Esperanza were reunited with Fran, Eva, and Cindy. Esperanza cried as she reflected on Ferdie's experience at Alhambra Preschool and contrasted the attention and care Ferdie received from Fran, Eva, and Cindy and the rest of the Alhambra staff from the difficulties she has faced trying to get a comparable level of assistance for Ferdie in his new elementary school (figure 4.19):

> The problem for him is he's very hyper. When he started preschool he couldn't stay in a chair or hold a pencil in his hand. Now he's better. Fran's a great person. And Miss Eva, a very caring person. [Imitating Eva] "Ay, *mijo,* how are you this morning?" For me it was very, very special here. Every morning, I'd come in the classroom and stay and Fran and Eva and Cindy would

talk to me about Ferdie. I remember when he started here they got him playing on the table with the shaving cream. Oh my God! I liked it so much. I love this school. It was very beautiful, all his years here.

Fran also reflected on Ferdie's time at Alhambra:

Ferdie has really come a long way. At the beginning of the year Ferdie had trouble controlling himself. He was very aggressive, and he would just take things from other children, and his first response was to hit. When Ferdie first started, he didn't like to touch things or for anybody to touch him. He hadn't been exposed to other children before; it was a sensory thing, as well as a problem of language and behavior. We first worked on the sensory thing. Esperanza mentioned the shaving cream. That was very hard for him to do. The shaving cream and Play-Doh. As he got used to those sensory activities, his behavior changed and he wasn't so frustrated. He started making more sounds. We couldn't understand him at first, but by the end of the year, he was speaking in both Spanish and English. He was able to reason a lot more with other children. It was nice to see the growth.

IS PRESCHOOL GOOD OR BAD FOR CHILDREN?

This is a very American question, or actually two questions, that need to be placed in both cultural and historical contexts. When we conducted the original research in the mid-1980s, there was widespread opposition to full-day center-based early childhood education. This opposition came in various forms. Psychoanalysts and developmental psychologists, in a tradition dating back to Anna Freud's condemnation of orphanages, the Harlows' studies of mother-deprived monkeys, and John Bowlby's research on the importance of maternal-child attachment, wrote books and articles about the deleterious emotional effects on young children of institutional care and of being separated prematurely from the bosom of the home. Republican politicians and conservative activists opposed funding preschools, based on the stated position that out-of-the-home education and care for young children undermines the family. Democrats tended to be more supportive but, with a couple of rare exceptions (Senate bills that failed introduced by Patricia Schroeder and Christopher Dodd), did not exert much effort beyond supporting continuing funding for Head Start. NAEYC, the Children's Defense Fund, and other early childhood education and care professional organizations lobbied for increased public spending on early childhood, but for the most part their arguments failed to attract support from politicians, policy makers, and the business community.

This has changed dramatically over the past twenty years. Although there continues to be an anti-childcare lobby on the far right, it has become a much less influential voice, as the political establishment has shifted to a pro-preschool stance. Another significant development is the entry of the business community into the early childhood education and care debate. For example, the Business Roundtable, an association of corporate chief executive officers, has become a key player in drumming up support for early childhood education initiatives. Their policy statement succinctly captures the logic of linking preschool education with the nation's economic competitiveness:

> America's continuing efforts to improve education and develop a world-class workforce will be hampered without a federal and state commitment to early childhood education for 3- and 4-year-old children. In today's world, where education and skill levels determine future earnings, the economic and social costs to individuals, communities, and the nation of not taking action on early childhood education are far too great to ignore, especially when the benefits far outweigh the costs. (Business Roundtable 2003, 1)

Another new voice in the preschool policy debate is the Federal Reserve Bank. Art Rolnick and Rob Grunewald (2003), economists working for the Fed, make an argument for the economic sense of investing public economic development funds in preschools rather than in projects such as sports stadiums:

> Early childhood development programs are rarely portrayed as economic development initiatives, and we think that is a mistake. Such programs, if they appear at all, are at the bottom of the economic development lists for state and local governments. They should be at the top. . . . Studies find that well-focused investments in early childhood development yield high public as well as private returns (p.1).

In the years since we conducted our original study, researchers and research institutes in the US have conducted analyses of the developmental, mental health, educational, and economic impacts of early childhood education projects. The studies Rolnick and Grunewalk are referring to include the Frank Porter Graham Center's analyses of the long-terms benefits of their Abecedarian Project (2006) and the High/Scope Foundation calculations of the payoffs of its Perry Preschools:

> The data show strong advantages for the treatment group [over a randomly assigned control group who did not participate in High/Scope programs] in terms of higher lifetime earnings and lower criminal activity. For the general public, gains in tax revenues, lower expenditures on criminal justice, lower victim costs, and lower welfare payments easily outweigh program costs. At a 3% discount rate the program repays $12.90 for every $1 invested from the perspective of the general public; with a 7% discount rate, the repayment per dollar is $5.67. Returns are even higher if the total benefits—both public and private—are counted. (Nores et. al. 2005, 245).

This advocacy from the Federal Reserve Bank, the Business Roundtable, and research foundations is providing political cover for politicians to support early childhood education initiatives while dodging the accusations they threw at each other in the past of intruding government into family matters and investing tax dollars in frills. We suggest that such justifications of the value of early childhood education in terms of return on investment should be viewed as an aspect of culture, a reflection of a worldview, and a discourse that is characteristically (though not uniquely) American.

Another new argument being advanced for preschool in the US comes from neuroscience, or what is more popularly called brain research. Beginning in the mid-1990s politicians and policy makers seized on studies of neurological development in infants and young children to justify the importance of expanding financial investment in preschool programs. For example, in 1997, William and Hillary Rodham Clinton convened the White House Conference on Early Childhood Development and Learning. Neuroscience had a featured role, as a statement on the White House website summarized:

> The White House Conference focused on the practical applications of the latest scientific research on the brain, particularly for parents and caregivers. The conference was also a call to action to all members of society—including the health, business, media and faith communities, child care providers and government—to use this information to strengthen America's families. (http://clinton2.nara.gov/WH/New/ECDC/About.html)

Early childhood education advocates where thrilled by this new attention. The prestige of neuroscience as a hard science carries much more weight than studies coming out of the lower-status fields of psychology and education. This has given advocates for expanding the provision of early childhood education leverage they never had before to convince politicians and the public at large.

The application of neuroscience to the preschool policy debate has not come without controversy. Throughout the 1990s brain research was increasingly cited as a source of guidance for early childhood development and early childhood educational practice. Perhaps the high point in public attention was the 1996 cover story in *Newsweek*, "Your Child's Brain," which contained such passages as:

> It is the experiences of childhood, determining which neurons are used, that wire the circuits of the brain as surely as a programmer at a keyboard reconfigures the circuits in a computer. Which keys are typed—which experiences a child has—determines whether the child grows up to be intelligent or dull, fearful or self-assured, articulate or tongue-tied. Early experiences are so powerful, says pediatric neurobiologist Harry Chugani of Wayne State University, that "they can completely change the way a person turns out." (Begley 1996, 55)

Few would argue with the claim that early experiences are powerful. The problem, however, is that neuroscience research provides no specific direction for either good parenting or for good preschool practice, as John Bruer argued in an influential 1997 essay:

> We can't choose preschools based on neuroscience. Nor can we look to neuroscience as a guide to improve educational practice and policy. . . . The neuroscience and education argument may be rhetorically appealing, but scientifically it is a bridge too far. (5)

Bruer went on in 2000 to publish the controversial best seller, *The Myth of the First Three Years*, which expanded his argument, as he suggested that too much focus on investing resources in the first three years of life carries the danger of shortchanging investment in the years that follow. Many groups responded angrily, seeing Bruer's book as undermining long-standing efforts to increase funding for everything from maternal leave policy to early childhood nutrition and inoculation programs to preschool education. An unfortunate dimension of the furor surrounding Bruer's book was the opening of a divide between the groups who were most concerned with the well-being of infants and toddlers and the groups who were most concerned with preschool programs for three- to five-year-olds over the allocation of public resources. The National Academies of Science's 2000 report, *From Neurons to Neighborhoods: The Science of Early Child Development* (Committee on Integrating the Science of Early Childhood Development 2000), weighed in on the controversy: "The recent focus on 'zero to three' as a critical or particularly sensitive period is highly problematic, not because this isn't an important period for the developing brain, but simply because the disproportionate attention to the period from birth to 3 years begins too late and ends too soon" (7). Arguments about whether birth-to-three or three-to-five is a more critical age range, and which period is more deserving of the investment of public funds, reflect the overall inadequacy of funding and the lack of integrated services and planning that characterize early childhood education and care in the United States at the turn of the millennium, as they did a generation ago.

Another characteristic of scholarship on early childhood education and care in the United States that distinguishes it from research in many other countries is the focus on the question of whether center-based early childhood education and care is good or bad for children. Research that compares home-reared children with those attending preschool and that asks whether preschool has a net positive or negative effect is much rarer in Japan and China and in European countries such as France and Italy than it is in the United States, chiefly, we suggest, because only in the United States among these countries is not attending preschool seen as an option for a four-year-old child and only in the United States is the universal provision of preschool the subject of a policy debate.

One way to understand the continuing attention US scholars are giving this question is to see it as a residual effect of the anti-preschool discourse of the 1970s and 1980s. During this period both conservative development psychologists (most notably, Burton White 1975) and Phyllis Schlafly and other anti-feminist social activists argued that the women's movement was harming children by leading women to value their own careers and interests over the best interest of their children. These arguments set the terms of the debate and provoked both researchers concerned about the effects of non-parental care as well as scholars supportive of the cause of expanding the provision of early childhood education and care into conducting studies on the effects of preschool.

Over the years this line of research evolved from an initial focus on whether preschool is harmful or beneficial to children to attention to the interaction of program quality with outcomes (Rosenthal 1999; Mc-

Cartney 2004; Fuller 2007). The new wave of studies, which are much more sophisticated than the earlier phases of this research, are producing nuanced analyses. But these nuances tend to get lost in the policy debates that continue in the US on the question of the costs and benefits of center-based early childhood education and care. Moreover, in the current wave of the research we can still read traces of the terms of debate set by the anti-childcare movement of the 1970s and 1980s and the continuation of the central assumption of that debate that early childhood education and care programs, good or bad, are a choice for many parents rather than a necessity. Research on the effects of preschool on children's learning and socio-emotional development and the economic payoffs of an early investment in early childhood education is a characteristically American research agenda, reflecting American social tensions, political divides, and cultural concerns (Rosenthal 1999, 487). Japan and China as well as countries in Europe that have comprehensive systems of early childhood education and care would no more fund major studies on whether preschool is good for children or a wise social investment than they would fund studies on whether children should attend primary school or have access to medical care.

Over the past twenty years the political, social, and academic discourse on early childhood education and care has changed in some ways and stayed the same in others. On the one hand, there is now considerable support that was not present a generation ago from both political parties and the business community for the public provision of preschool, often under the heading of "Universal Pre-Kindergarten" or "UPK" for short (Fuller 2007). On the other hand, a deep ambivalence about non-parental care of young children remains. Lacking the taken-for-grantedness that the idea of center-based early childhood education and care enjoys in Japan, China, and many other countries, in the United States the costs and benefits of out-of-home early childhood education and care continuously must be studied and debated. Research by biologists on early neural development, by economists on the multiplier effects of public investment in preschools, and by psychologists on the child development outcomes of spending one or more years in preschools of varying quality are all employed in debates on policy questions settled some time ago in other countries. In our new research we seem to have caught American society at a moment of disequilibrium in which the necessary conditions for change are in place but in which a new, more comprehensive system of early childhood education and the will (and funding) it will take to create such a system have yet to fully emerge.

Care and Education

Alhambra's struggle to integrate its daycare and educational programs is characteristic of a tension in early childhood education and care that is found in many countries. In Japan, as we describe in chapter 2, this tension takes the form of the politically charged separation of the *hoikuen* and *yōchien* systems. In Western Europe, as the OECD report (Bennett 2003) makes clear, many countries have huge disparities in funding, quality, staff training, and salaries between the educational and care sectors. As Bennett explains, these disparities reflect the very different histories of the education and care sides of what is now a field called "early childhood education and care," the "and" marking the divide that continues to cause problems for the field.

At Alhambra, this divide is physically enacted throughout the day as children move from the daycare to preschool rooms and back again. Fran, a certified professional early childhood educator, teaches the children for 2.5 hours a day. The rest of the day, the children who do not go home at lunchtime are in the daycare room, where they are supervised by Shirley and Alexa and other staff members who have no formal training. The reasons Bonnie Lund and the teachers cited for the separation of the daycare and education functions of the Alhambra program are financial, structural, and bureaucratic. The Early Childhood Block Grant funds that support the preschool side of the program come from the Arizona Department of Education and can be used only for education, not for care. The Department of Economic Services (welfare) funds that reimburse parents for the time their children spend in the daycare room are intended to pay for childcare so parents can work and go to school, rather than for the education of young children.

At St. Timothy's the divide is subtler, but still very much present. Jannie, who at the time we videotaped in her classroom had an A.A. degree in early childhood education and was working on her Bachelor of Education degree, worked from 7 a.m. to 3 p.m. Her assistant teachers, who have no formal training in education, take over in the afternoon. The morning is structured around two extended learning center periods designed to develop children's understandings of literacy, science, social sciences, and the arts. On the day we videotaped, in addition to introducing and orchestrating the learning center activities, Jannie also taught a lesson on absorption, read a book about fish and frogs, and led the children in a song about rain. The morning activities were all tied together around the theme of water;

the afternoon schedule of nap, snack, and free play, in contrast, has no particular theme or content.

One explanation for the difference between the structure of the morning and afternoon at St. Timothy's is that it would cost too much to have trained early childhood educators on duty from 7 a.m. until 6 p.m. In most child centers in the US, as at St. Timothy's, the head teachers go home before the students, leaving the students in the care of afternoon aides. But there is also a deeper reason: few early childhood educators see a need for more than half a day of preschool. In many states, even kindergarten is only a half-day program, as the research literature is mixed on the educational merits of a full day of kindergarten (Olsen & Zigler 1989; Fusaro 1997). In the absence of compelling evidence for the added value of a full-day program for children under five, a half-day of preschool therefore is all public educational funds will pay for in most states.

Culture and Class Differences

The Alhambra teachers take pride in their work and in the service they are providing children and families:

> FRAN: I came to Alhambra from a tuition-supported preschool where the parents had to pay, and I feel that this is a much more satisfying because the parents are so grateful for anything. Sometimes, when parents pay, they just expect so much, and they don't appreciate what they get.
>
> TOBIN: Your other preschool was more middle-class?
>
> FRAN: Yes, but this is more satisfying. These kids here may have more problems, but you can understand it, where the other kids were just, well, spoiled. They got too much.
>
> EVA: I can understand where the children here are coming from, coming from my background. These parents are more grateful for what we do.
>
> TOBIN: I notice you call the children *mija* and *mijo* [short for *mi hija* and *mi hijo* or "my daughter" and "my son"].
>
> EVA: To me, it's a closeness. It's comfortable. It's like home. Because that's how we call children at home, that's what they're used to.

Impressed with the dedication and professionalism of Fran and Eva and aware of the appreciation and support of the Alhambra parents for the program and the range of services offered, we were not prepared for the critical reactions our videotape of a day at Alhambra provoked in some audiences. For example, in January 2002, at the opening session of the Reconceptualizing Early Childhood Education conference held in Tempe, we held a premiere screening of the Alhambra, Komatsudani, and Sinanlu videotapes. Criticisms of the Alhambra video included disapproval of the saying of the Pledge of Allegiance, the morning calendar time, and the absence of a multicultural curriculum. Positive comments noted the obvious kindness and good spirit of the teachers and the presence of Spanish in the classroom. And yet even those commentators who expressed pleasure in hearing children and teachers speaking Spanish in the classroom wished that the program were more explicitly bilingual, rather than privileging English as the language of instruction.

Several months later we showed the Alhambra videotape to a meeting of the directors of Arizona Early Childhood Block Grant preschools, a gathering that included directors of programs that, like Alhambra, are NAEYC accredited. The comments were at first more positive than those made by the professors at the Reconceptualizing conference, but as the discussion progressed, Alhambra Preschool was criticized for being too teacher centered and allowing too little time for free play; for the Pledge and calendar activities; for food not being served family style; and for the teachers being too directive in mediating disputes between children.

Not everyone, however, who has watched the Alhambra videotape has been critical. In 2003 we invited Alhambra parents to come to school for a screening and discussion of the 2001 videotape. In the two intervening years the percentage of children of Mexican background in the program had risen from about two-thirds to nearly 90%. About thirty parents came to the evening screening. After showing the video, we held a discussion in Spanish and English. Parents were uniformly supportive of the Alhambra program, the teachers, the director, and the office staff, who were praised and thanked for being responsive and helpful, not just with questions and concerns relating directly to preschool, but also with helping parents fill out government forms, directing them to social services, and creating a welcoming atmosphere. We then asked parents to discuss the specific features of the program critiqued by the reconceptualizers and the NAEYC-accredited preschool program directors. Parents expressed comfort with the saying of the Pledge: "We are in the United States, so it is appropriate that our children should show respect to the flag. If we were in Mexico our children would be doing a lot more patriotic activities." Some felt that the focus on pre-academic skills was just right; others wanted more academic emphasis. All praised the teachers, with some noting the respect Mexican parents expect children to show towards their *maestras*. Parents generally were satisfied with the mix of English and Spanish in the classroom, saying they appreciated having teachers who could talk to them and to their children in Spanish. There was a debate on the question of whether the preschool should give more emphasis to Mexican culture, with one father saying that it would be nice if his children were taught a bit about Mexican holidays and cultural traditions so he could talk more easily with relatives back in Mexico, but most parents arguing that they wanted the school to emphasize academic and social readiness and the learning of English, and stating that teaching Spanish and Mexican culture is parents' responsibility.

There are several ways to think about why the Alhambra parents spoke so much more positively about the program than did the scholars and directors who watched the tape. One of things the Alhambra parents most appreciate about the program is the respect and help they get from the teachers, director, and office staff, something that our video of a day at Alhambra does not convey and that therefore was not apparent to outsiders who viewed the video. It also could be argued that the Alhambra parents have an investment in believing that their children are attending a good program; that parents routinely overrate their children's schools and teachers; and that as laypeople they lack the knowledge and perspective to distinguish a high-quality program from a mediocre one.

An explanation we find more convincing is that the Alhambra parents rate the program more highly than do early childhood education experts because their values and concerns are different. What we found in our discussion with immigrant parents at Alhambra is consistent with the findings of other studies on immigrant communities in the US that show that many immigrant parents hold ideas about early childhood education that differ from notions of quality and best practice held by early childhood educators and their professional organizations (Valdéz 1996; González, Moll & Amanti 2004; Adair & Tobin 2008). The Alhambra parents, for example, want teachers to be teacherly and to be directive in dealing with children's disputes. More concerned about their children learning English than about the possible loss of their Spanish or their Mexican identity or cultural patrimony, most of the Hispanic parents at Alhambra, unlike progressive American early childhood education scholars, are not strong proponents of bilingual or multicultural education.

One could ascribe these positions taken by parents to their being misinformed or ignorant—if these parents better understood DAP, bilingual and multicultural education, and constructivist, child-centered approaches, they would support them more enthusiastically. We suggest that a better way of making sense of differences between how the Alhambra parents and progressive early childhood educators evaluate the Alhambra Preschool videotape is to view them as ideological disagreements reflective of a divide found in many domains of American public life. Ethnicity plays a part here, but so does social class. As Bonnie Lund points out, the Alhambra Traditional School, an elementary school offered by the district that features a "back to basics" approach, is a popular choice among this working-class district's African-American and white as well as Hispanic parents. This preference among working-class parents for more structured programs is consistent with the work of Lisa Delpit (1986), who, drawing on her experience teaching in urban Philadelphia, discovered that her students' working-class African-American parents and most of her fellow African-American teachers were not keen on the progressive curriculum she was offering, a finding that may have as much or more to do with class than with race or culture (Lareau 2003).

Working-class white, African-American, and Hispanic parents are on the whole more conservative on a range of social issues, including education, than are professors of early childhood education and the leaders of NAEYC. But while class, ethnicity, and religion play a role in determining the two sides, the disagreement transcends class, culture, and religious divides. We suggest that the divide is less one of class, race, ethnicity, or immigration status than of ideology, what some commentators on US society call a "culture war," referring here not to disagreements between people from different cultural backgrounds, but instead to people who hold dissimilar and even antagonistic views on questions of morality, politics, economics, and education.

As we traveled across the United States showing the videos from all three countries to teachers and directors, we encountered a range of reactions that reflect not regional differences but ideological ones. Early childhood educators working in progressive, NAEYC-accredited programs in Honolulu, Phoenix, Bloomington, Indiana, Memphis, and New York had very similar reactions to the preschool practices seen in the videotapes. Teachers and directors working in non-NAEYC-accredited church-based and for-profit preschool programs raised different concerns about the videotapes than did their counterparts in the NAEYC-accredited programs.

Our argument here can only be speculative because only four of the twenty-four preschools where we showed our videotapes in the US were in non-NAEYC-accredited programs. This is because we relied heavily on personal contacts to locate programs in each city willing to participate in our focus groups, and our contacts, who for the most part are professors of early childhood education, had closest connections with progressive, NAEYC-approved programs. The exception was in Memphis, where we were able to show the videotapes in a range of programs: daycare centers as well as preschools; for-profit as well as not-for-profit; secular as well as religious; in African-American as well as white neighborhoods. Looking across the six Memphis programs where we conducted the research we can identify some suggestive differences in reactions to the videotapes between staff working at the more progressive and more conservative preschools.

For example, commenting on what she perceived to be a lack of structured academic learning at Alhambra Preschool, a teacher at a mostly black working-class daycare center in Memphis commented:

> I thought every preschool does worksheets. It helps them learn. Children need to learn to sit down and do work at the table. We have a certain time during the day where we are sitting at the table. When we have the worksheets we sit at the table and do the art project together instead of doing it one on one.

At a mostly white, non-accredited Christian preschool across town, the teachers also supported a more academic, structured approach, as they expressed approval of the Sinanlu children's writing ability: "We have a pretty aggressive curriculum for our four-year-olds, but they can barely write their names. And those Chinese kids know all their characters!" They also criticized Komatsudani for its play-orientation: "They focused more on playing, and letting them go about on their own. Here it is more structured." At several of the NAEYC-accredited Memphis programs, in contrast, teachers praised Sinanlu for its extended dramatic play activity and Komatsudani for giving children unstructured time to play.

Classroom management was another area of ideological disagreement. After watching the Komatsudani videotape, teachers and directors in Memphis across the range of the programs were critical of what they saw as Morita-sensei's failure to intervene in Nao's fight with the other girls. But they expressed their disapproval in different terms. The director of an NAEYC-accredited, middle-class, church-based program commented: "If I walked by as a director, if I walked by the classroom and saw that much antagonism going on between the children, and the teacher was not trying to at least give the children some feedback, I would be concerned." A teacher at the same school added,

The way we look at how children socialize, we would probably worry about the children's self-esteem if they weren't getting any direction in how to have positive social interactions. For instance, the child who was crying had the doll taken away from her repeatedly without having any help knowing how to deal with that. We would feel like her self-esteem would be hurt by that.

In contrast, teachers at the non-NAEYC programs were more direct in their critiques, focusing not on self-esteem issues but on the need for decisive intervention and for teachers to monitor children's behavior:

TEACHER A: When the children were beating up the little girl, no one stopped them. The girl was tortured!

TEACHER B: There were several times in the video that nobody was around. The teacher seemed to be nowhere.

TEACHER C: The teacher across the room yelled, "Stop." But she didn't go over there.

TEACHER A: But even when she said, "Stop," and the little girl came out from the table, still no teacher went over there and said, "What happened?"

This same group of teachers also criticized the Alhambra staff for not more aggressively supervising the children outside at pickup time:

TEACHER A: Talking! They should be looking out for the children instead of running their mouth.

TEACHER B: I didn't like that at all. It wasn't organized. We say, "You stay right there. Don't you move until somebody comes and gets you." It was like the children were on their own.

These accusations are reasonable, given what these teachers saw in our video, but inaccurate, given that we know from the time we spent at Alhambra that Fran and Eva do in fact give a lot of attention to supervising children during transition periods as they move to and from the classroom. Nevertheless, the point we want to emphasize here is that these and other preschool teachers who watched our videos who work in more socially and educationally conservative programs did not hesitate to speak in terms of the need for teachers to be not just vigilant but firm in their control of the class and administration of rules. An appeal for firmness was also made by a teacher at a corporate-sponsored program who criticized Fran for being too willing to bend the rules of the housekeeping corner:

When they were in the home center and the rule was four children at a time, the teacher said, "Today, if you play nicely, it is five." I think that it is confusing for children when you set up rules for the classroom and the teacher overrules the rules. It is okay to be flexible about some things. But when you set rules, I don't think you should change them.

Saying the Pledge of Allegiance in preschool is another issue where the teachers in Memphis were divided along ideological lines. Some criticized this activity as not developmentally appropriate for children of this age, while others praised it. Teachers at the corporate-sponsored preschool combined their appreciation for the value of saying the Pledge as moral education with a wish that prayer could be brought back into the curriculum:

TEACHER D: We used to do that all the time. You didn't have all the violence in the schools that you have now. It may not be the opinion of all teachers, but we should have never taken that out.

TEACHER E: We used to do that in our daycare; every morning we would sing the good-morning song and say the Pledge, but they don't do that anymore.

TEACHER D: Honoring your country; there is nothing wrong with that.

TEACHER E: We said the Pledge, and when I was growing up we started with prayer. They have taken all that out.

TEACHER D: If you try to institute it, they can have a lawsuit, which they are having, which is terrible.

A generation ago, when we conducted the original study, the ideological battle was being fought between proponents and opponents of out-of-home care for children. A generation later, the terms of the debate in the United States have shifted, but the ideological divide remains. Now that both political parties have endorsed the value of early childhood education and conservative groups have dropped their organized opposition to out-of-home care, the fight is no longer primarily about whether children should be sent to preschool but about what they should experience once they get there. Educators on opposite sides of the ideological divide disagree not only about the teaching of patriotism and prayer but also, as we have seen, about teaching about the calendar; classroom management; the need for children to show respect to teachers; direct instruction; and phonics. These are characteristically American debates and concerns.

Postscript

At the end of the 2005 school year both Dolores Brockman and Jannie Umeda turned in their resignations at St. Timothy's, Jannie taking a higher-paying job with better benefits teaching preschool at a private school with a large endowment and Dolores taking a kindergarten teaching position at a private elementary school that could pay her more to be a teacher than St. Timothy's could pay her to be a director.

During the 2007–2008 school year rumors circulated that some parents and staff were unhappy with the new director and there were problems with the school's finances and the aging infrastructure. Then early in the summer of 2008, as the school year was coming to an end, there was a sudden announcement that St. Timothy's Children's Center was closing its doors. As Alexandre de Silva of the *Honolulu Star Bulletin* reported on June 5, 2008:

> St. Timothy's Preschool in Aiea will indefinitely shut down at month's end as administrators search for funds to tackle overdue repairs, officials said yesterday. The 30-year-old school, which opened in 1977 and enrolled about 110 students ages 2 to 4, is laying off about 18 staff and administrators, said Kathy Takemura, administrator at St. Timothy's Episcopal Church. . . . The preschool "was having some management" problems, and its accreditation expired in February, said Kathy Murphy, executive director of the Hawaii Association for the Education of Young Children. Murphy said she was saddened to hear about the demise of what was once regarded "a very high-quality program," with some teachers holding master's degrees. Murphy said she has been calling preschools to check whether they have space to accommodate St. Timothy's students and teachers. (archives.starbulletin.com/2008/06/05/news/story06.html)

In the wake of this news a group of St. Timothy's parents and teachers began scrambling to find openings at other preschools while others worked on a plan to keep St. Timothy's going, in a new location, with a new administrative structure and business model. By late summer, a new version of St. Timothy's had risen from the ashes, as Chris Aguinaldo reported in the *Honolulu Advertiser*:

> When Cheryl Cudiamat awoke on June 3, she had no idea she'd soon be on the path to opening a preschool. That night, she and other parents would learn that St. Timothy's Children's Center in Aiea, founded in 1977, was abruptly shutting its doors. "There was no explanation with the closure," said

the Aiea mom, whose son Tyson was going to be enrolled at St. Timothy's in the upcoming school year. "All of us—parents and teachers—were just shocked." That disbelief was quickly replaced by the urgency to find new educational arrangements for 80 youngsters. As other parents scrambled to find openings at other preschools, MBA-armed Cudiamat formulated her own solution. . . (http://www.honoluluadvertiser.com/apps/pbcs.dll/article?AID=/20080910/COMPUB04/809100344/1225)

The solution Cheryl Cudiamat and her husband Jeoffrey came up with was to lease space from another church in the neighborhood and to open their own preschool, which they did, in time for the 2008–2009 school year. The new preschool's website explains the vision and mission:

Keiki Care Center of Hawaii, Inc. (KCCOH), a preschool care facility for children ages 2 to 4 years old, has been created to perpetuate and foster the philosophy and values that have been developed and carried on throughout the many decades of years of teaching by its highly trained, experienced and dedicated teachers and staff. . . . KCCOH was opened due to the closure of St. Timothy's Children's Center (STCC) in Aiea, since the hope was to employ as many of the teachers and faculty to keep the "ohana" together, as well as to continue to provide a great preschool education for those families that were displaced due to the closure. STCC was the only nationally accredited preschool on this side of the island, and KCCOH will definitely follow suit and strive for accreditation during this next year. (http://www.keikicarehawaii.com/homepg.htm)

This latest episode in the history of St. Timothy's Children's Center is consistent with the story of preschool in the United States that we have told in this chapter: preschool programs over the past twenty years have hung on to a core set of beliefs while at the same time incorporating new ideas and struggling with daunting economic, logistical, and administrative challenges that have compelled them to change and adapt or go under. We look forward to seeing how Keiki Care Center of Hawaii, Inc. fares in the years to come.

5 Looking Across Time and Cultures

Given the assumption that four-year-old children around the world have similar abilities, needs, and interests, one might expect preschools in different countries to be much the same. The major contribution of the original *Preschool in Three Cultures* was to make clear that Japanese, and US preschools, circa 1984, were very different and that much of the difference could be attributed to culture. The central question that has driven our new study is whether a generation later we would find in these three countries' preschools a persistence of these cultural differences or whether with increased globalization Chinese, Japanese, and US preschools would have become more alike and lost some of their cultural distinctiveness.

As the previous chapters have described, we found that much has changed, but much has also stayed the same. A simple version of our findings would be that over the past twenty years Chinese preschools changed a lot, Japanese preschools not very much, and the US is somewhere in between, with dramatic changes in provision and funding but relatively little change in teacher beliefs and in classroom practices. The more complicated, nuanced version of this story is that there is more continuity than meets the eye in China's early childhood educational change; more dynamism and angst in Japan's continuity of preschool practices and beliefs than is conveyed by the term "continuity"; and more class and ideological tensions in the US contemporary situation than is conveyed by the narrative of a country inching towards creating a national system of pre-primary education.

In this book we have discussed impacts of political, economic, and demographic changes on each nation's systems of early childhood education, but our central concern has been with culture. Most comparative international studies on education foreground social and political forces. Our approach, in contrast, foregrounds culture. Our thesis is that culture acts as a source of continuity and as a brake on the impacts of globalization, rationalization, and economic change. Preschools are institutions that both reflect and help to perpetuate the cultures and societies of which they are a part.

In this chapter we look across the three countries in this study, examining the impact on preschools of economic change, modernization, and globalization. We then turn to the concept of "implicit cultural logic" as an explanation for continuity in the face of pressure to change, arguing that cultural practices are more resilient and resistant to change than is predicted by theories of economic determinism, modernization and globalization. We conclude with some reflections on our method, and the challenge of combining history with ethnography and looking simultaneously across time and space.

Economic Change and the Logic of Modernization

In the years since we conducted our original study in 1985, China has become an enthusiastic and strikingly successful player in the global capitalist economy. The economic and social reforms put forward in the 1980s by Deng Xiaoping, who is widely credited as "the architect of China's economic reforms and China's socialist modernization," featured a strategy of unequal development encouraging the growth of an entrepreneurial class in the largest cities who would create wealth and jobs that would eventually trickle down to benefit the rest of the society. The logic that ties these economic changes in China to changes in the early childhood education curriculum is explicit: To become a modern nation China must participate successfully in the global economy. To succeed in the global economy, China needs a new kind of citizen, who is more creative, risk taking, and adaptive as well as bright and well-educated. To produce this new citizen, China needs a new educational approach that begins with preschools, which need to shift their curriculum and pedagogy, becoming less didactic and controlling and more child centered and personalized.

Most of the Chinese early childhood educators we interviewed, though well aware of this reasoning, say that their embrace of the new educational paradigm was based less on the desire to produce little venture capitalists than on their belief in the wisdom and correctness of the new ideas. Therefore, instead of viewing a shift in economic strategy as preceding and causing the changes in Chinese early childhood education philosophy we have documented in this book, we suggest that it is more useful to conceptualize the educational changes as a shift of values, beliefs, and strategies that has occurred simultaneously across multiple social domains, from economics, to politics, to child rearing. The causality goes both ways: a change in economic philosophy and material well-being in the larger society impacts what goes on in preschool classrooms and what goes on in preschool classrooms exerts an impact, down the road, on the larger society.

In China the demands of economic change are often expressed in terms of the imperative of modernization. The term "modernization" is widely used in China in discussions of plans for reforming many domains of society, including preschools. As it was a generation ago in the era of the Four Modernizations campaign of Deng Xiaoping, "modernization" is used to refer to the need for China to develop a social and economic system that can compete with and yet remain distinct from the capitalist societies of the West and its neighbors in East Asia. As Deng wrote in his essay "On Building Socialism with Chinese Characteristics":

> Education is the most fundamental undertaking of a nation. The realization of the four modernizations depends on knowledge and on a skilled workforce. An error in policy can be rectified fairly easily, but knowledge cannot be acquired at once, nor a skilled work force trained in a few days. This is the reason education must be conducted in real earnest, and started from early childhood. (quoted in Education For All, 2000)

In contemporary China, modernization of early childhood education means more individualized education, with a focus on the rights of the child and on promoting independence and creativity. The primary concern about young children in China that we found in the mid-1980s was with spoiling, a concern that the single-child family policy would produce a generation of overly individualistic, selfish children who would lack respect, will power, filial piety, and social responsibility. Individualism in this period was viewed as an undesirable trait that needed to be corrected by *guan* (loving control). In the interviews we conducted with Chinese early childhood educators in the first years of the new millennium, we heard little concern about single children's spoiling, or the dangers of individualism. The creative, individualistic, and even self-oriented child who was feared a generation earlier had become the norm and even in some sense the ideal, the child with the characteristics needed to succeed in entrepreneurial capitalism.

However, in our last round of interviewing in China in 2006 and 2007, we sensed that perspectives were once again shifting, as we began to hear concern from educators and social commentators that the focus on promoting individualism and a child-initiated curriculum had gone too far, and that the time had come to balance the new emphasis on creativity and self-efficacy with older Chinese values such as social responsibility and filial piety (Zhu & Zhang 2008, 176). Spoiling has returned as a child-development concern, but now this is ascribed not to the single-child family policy as the root cause, but to the side effects of rapid prosperity and the errors of parents preoccupied with their business interests and made dizzy by their pursuit of wealth. As a result, there is concern that a generation of children is being raised that lacks a moral grounding in either traditional Confucian or Chinese socialist values.

Wang Xiaoying points to "the publication of a huge number of books on the problems, crises and serious challenges that have arisen in the course of China's reforms," books with titles such as *Lost Dignity* and *The Trap of Modernization* (2002, 10). Concluding that "the problems presented in these books add up to a picture of profound social and moral crisis" (2002, 11), Wang argues that China is suffering from having abandoned its old socialist values in advance of developing new ones: "It is of course debatable whether the introduction of a capitalist market economy in China is a good thing, but there is no denying that the advent of the free market without the simultaneous emergence of a sustaining moral order is a recipe for social problems of gigantic proportions" (2002, 1). Wang goes on to suggest that China's capitalist reforms have produced a new kind of Chinese personality structure, one lacking in altruism and aesthetics and characterized by hedonism and egoism.

Wang and many other Chinese intellectuals are pessimistic about contemporary Chinese society's ability or willingness to produce a new kind of citizen who can function in capitalism while also being socially minded. But our interviews with Chinese early childhood educators and our many visits to Chinese preschools make us guardedly more optimistic. Many of the new approaches in Chinese preschools that we have described in this book including, for example, the Story Telling King and sociodramatic play activities at Sinanlu You'eryuan are concerned with producing not just children who can grow up with the attributes they will need to succeed in a competitive market economy, but also children who will grow up to be socially minded and recognizably Chinese. Wang suggests that discussion of values is lacking and that hedonism is rampant. But we would argue that we hear in the comments of our Chinese informants a determination to forge a new approach to early Chinese childhood education, an approach that by fusing Confucian and socialist values with the values of the Enlightenment (under the banner of "the rights of children") will produce a new kind of citizen with a new kind of subjectivity, an individual, but one with Chinese characteristics. How this bold social experiment will turn out is impossible to predict. We look forward to finding out when we do another sequel to *Preschool in Three Cultures* in about 2025!

When we asked Japanese early childhood educators to describe what had changed the most for them and why since 1985, most focused on the impacts of economic and demographic changes on preschools. The economic decline in Japan from the boom times of the mid-1980s has made the business of running a preschool increasingly precarious. The decline has impacted preschools in direct and indirect ways, dropping the value of their land holdings, limiting the rate at which they can raise tuition, and changing patterns of women's work, including the career trajectories of teachers, who are less likely to retire from teaching while still in their early twenties as they did a generation ago when the economy was much stronger and they could live more comfortably during their child-rearing years on their husband's income and then re-enter the labor market. The decline in birthrate compels preschools to compete to fill their classrooms and stay in business. To attract customers, preschools extend their hours; diversify their services (with, for example, after-school care for elementary school children, classes and activities for parents, and programs for the elderly); add such frills as English conversation and tennis; and in some cases go to extremes to stand out in the marketplace by emphasizing their rigorous academic preparation and success rate placing students in prestigious primary schools, their unique philosophy (e.g., "naked education"), or (like Madoka Yōchien) the unique design of their playground and school building.

The precipitous economic decline Japan suffered in the 1990s when "the bubble burst" and real estate and stock prices plummeted also had a less direct but in some ways more profound effect on the overall national mood, creating a climate of pessimism, blame, and recrimination, a climate, for example, in which teachers and parents blame each other for the perceived character flaws of the current generation of children. When a country's economy is going well, its social institutions, including its schools, generally are viewed positively, and even given partial credit for the nation's prosperity. When Japan's economy was booming in the 1980s, the whole world, including many Japanese, found much to praise about Japan's education system. Conversely, an economic crisis leads to harsher analyses of social institutions and to an eagerness to assign blame. In Japan some of this blame has been placed on education.

Today in Japan, the term "modernization" is most often used pejoratively, in reference to the costs that modernization and too narrow a focus on economic development have exacted on the Japanese soul. There is a widespread feeling in Japan that the country modernized so quickly and thoroughly, catching up with and then passing the West, that core cultural values were compromised or lost. In our 1985 study we concluded that preschools in Japan are new institutions mandated to pass on to young children values, perspectives, and social skills that are believed to be at risk in the contemporary, hyper-modern society. This mandate is even more explicit today. Unlike in China and the US, educational reform movements in Japan put little pressure on preschools to rationalize or modernize their core practices because there is a general consensus that preschools have an inherently conservative function, which is to protect children from the negative effects of (post)modernization.

Over the past twenty years economic considerations and the imperative to rationalize social institutions, including education, have been a driving force for change in early childhood education in the US. Over the past generation, as the earning power of working-class and middle-class workers has declined against the cost of living, more mothers of young children have joined the workforce, creating an increased need for preschools. Welfare reform begun under President Clinton and continued under the second Bush administration pushed poor mothers of young children into training programs and jobs outside the home, increasing the need for early childhood care and education slots. In the 1990s the business community adapted a pro–early childhood education stance based on the logic that investing in educating young children is a good investment in the future labor force of a community and on calculations that show that every dollar invested in early childhood education yields a significant economic and social return.

Politicians of both parties justify the current emphasis in early childhood education on literacy and academic readiness in terms of the need to keep the United States economically competitive. What is most striking here is that China, Japan, and the United States each justify their curricular reforms with arguments for making their future workforce competitive, but the directions being followed by the three countries in their approaches to early childhood education are strikingly different. China is using the argument of preparing citizens for the new global economy to justify making the early childhood curriculum more free and student centered, to encourage the kind of creativity and initiative that are assumed to be required to succeed in global capitalism. Over the past thirty years or so Japan has followed a similar logic, based on the belief that because the emerging information economy requires increasingly creative, flexible workers, education needs to be made less didactic and freer. The recent decline in Japan's performance on international educational achievement tests has led to calls to follow American's lead and push for more emphasis on achievement and accountability in Japan's primary and secondary education (Bjork & Tsuneyoshi 2005; Takayama 2007), but so far such calls have not led to a shift away from the constructivist, play-oriented curricula found in a majority of Japanese preschools. Meanwhile, the United States is using the logic of national economic competitiveness to push early childhood education away from constructivism towards an emphasis on academic readiness accompanied by calls for higher levels of accountability, more frequent assessment, and a turn to scientifically based practice.

In the US, in the last fifteen years or so, an unlikely commingling of voices of conservative and progressive politicians, business leaders, children's advocacy organizations, and academics have joined NAEYC and the White House in calling for the professionalization of the early childhood education workforce, for learning standards for preschool and kindergarten, for a unified accreditation system for all early childhood education and care programs, and for the extension of publicly supported education down to the preschool level. The common thread behind these initiatives is the imperative of rationalization (Fuller 2007). In contemporary discussions in the US of domestic social policy, including policy for early childhood education, the word that is used most often in place of the now antiquated sounding terms "modernization" and "rationalization" is *reform*. The key terms in the discourse of reform are accountability, assessment, standards and standardization, outcomes, professionalism, consistency, articulation, and science- and evidence-based practice. The current education reforms in the US call for standards-based curricula, scientifically supported pedagogy, the professionalization of the labor force, systematic assessment of student learning, and accountability of schools, with a mixture of support and sanctions for schools that are failing.

The logic of modernization, rationalization, and reform of early childhood education in the US seems inexorable. In 1985, preschools in the United States, for better or worse, were largely free to teach as they wished, emphasizing play or learning, setting their own cognitive, academic, and social outcomes for children, arranging their classrooms and choosing what to put on the walls without needing to follow a set of guidelines, and hiring teachers with or without degrees in early childhood education. Today in the US, as teachers and directors complained to us, preschools are

5.1. McDonald's sign from sociodramatic play at
Sinan Road Kindergarten.

increasingly under pressure to comply with external governmental and
professional organization standards in their curriculum, their classroom
setup, and their learning outcomes and for all of their teachers and directors to have degrees in early childhood education from accredited programs. The play-oriented curricula, whole language approaches to literacy,
and child-centered pedagogies that were seen as best practices when we
conducted our original study a generation ago are now critiqued in some
quarters as old-fashioned, ideologically driven, and unscientific.

Globalization

Critics as well as proponents of globalization suggest that as goods, ideas,
and people are exchanged among nations at an ever-increasing pace, nations are becoming more similar and cultural differences less salient (figure 5.1). The world systems theory version of globalization suggests that as
the world increasingly becomes one system, ideas (including ideas about
education) from the most powerful, culture-exporting countries come to
dominate those of other countries. This is also the prediction of the mod-
ernization/rationalization version of globalization, which would suggest,
following the logic of social Darwinism, that over time the most rational,
effective educational approaches spread, replacing tradition-bound local
approaches that are believed in for reasons other than their rationality and
functionality. The result is an ever-growing global convergence of education practices and ideas.

Is this the case for approaches to early childhood education over the
past generation in the three countries in our study? Since the mid-1980s
have Chinese, Japanese, and US preschools become significantly more

alike? Our answer, in a word, is "No." Our conclusion is that despite modernization and globalization, Chinese, Japanese, and American approaches to early childhood education are no more alike in their core practices and beliefs than they were a generation ago. Or rather we should say that over time they have become more alike in some ways and more different in others. Our study has shown that some cultural practices have been replaced by practices borrowed from abroad, but other cultural practices have emerged unscathed from their encounter with globally circulating ideas, still others have evolved into hybrid forms, and along the way some new cultural practices have been invented.

In 1985 and 2005 Chinese and American early childhood educational goals and practices were dramatically unalike, with China emphasizing control and regimentation and the US play and choice. Twenty years later, China's early childhood educational goals have shifted towards child-initiation and creativity while early childhood education in the US has shifted in the opposite direction, toward more emphasis on academic outcomes and the teacher's role in instruction. This could be taken as evidence of the convergence predicted by some schools of globalization. But we would argue that the fact that US preschools have become more academic and Chinese preschools more play oriented suggests not that they are converging toward a common end point but instead that they may be passing like two ships in the night.

The globalization of early childhood educational ideas does not flow evenly over time and space. Instead, in each country periods of greater openness to outside ideas alternate with periods of turning inward (Schriewer 2000; Steiner-Khamsi 2000; 2004). The 1990s was one of those outward-facing eras in US early childhood education, with the outside influence coming largely from the preschools of the Italian city of Reggio Emilia. In our interviews across the US, when asked about what has changed the most since 1985, directors and teachers often cited the influence of "Reggio," as they almost always call it. When pressed, they specifically mentioned Reggio's emphasis on the arts and aesthetics and on the documentation of children's learning.

Why has Reggio Emilia's approach to early childhood education had so much influence on the consciousness (if not on the classroom practices) of American early childhood educators? What's going on here is more complex than a straightforward process of one country borrowing cutting-edge ideas from another. Reggio Emilia no doubt has excellent preschools. But so do lots of other preschools in other Italian regions and in other countries, including Japan and China, whose preschool practices are not emulated abroad. This raises the question of what has made the early childhood education system of Reggio Emilia so exportable while other potentially useful early childhood educational ideas have failed to catch on in the US.

Rebecca New, who knows Reggio as well as any non-Italian, points out that the Italian take on all this foreign excitement about Reggio Emilia is that the citizens of Reggio Emilia are proud of their preschools, but so are the citizens of other Italian cities. She argues that Italians in other cities would no more try to copy Reggio Emilia's preschools than they would give up their local cheeses or wines for those made in Parma or Umbria. What makes Reggio Emilia's system of childcare and education so special is the same thing that makes Italian wines and cheeses so special—each reflects the locale where it is made. This does not mean that they cannot be consumed or enjoyed outside their region. But it does mean they cannot be mass-consumed without the risk of losing what makes them special in the first place and that they should be consumed alongside of rather than in place of locally made products. New writes, "Each of these interpretations—whether of a good cheese, a good wine, or the proper way to make a certain pasta dish—is associated with a particular place and its people, with both the benefits and the burdens of responsibility shared by the stakeholders" (2001, 212).

An irony of the international spread of Reggio Emilia (which we take from New) is that one of the core ideas, perhaps *the* core idea, behind the Reggio Emilia preschools is that they are based on a deep connection between the school staff and the larger community. Parent and community involvement is intense and ongoing. And this involvement reflects the socialist political beliefs of the city, the parents, and the teachers and administrators. But what happens to the socialist principles that provide the moral foundation to Reggio Emilia's approach when Reggio comes to the US? Reggio Emilia gets stripped of its politics, of its socialism, of the elements that are objectionable to many Americans, and what gets embraced are those parts of Reggio Emilia most attractive to American middle-class sensibilities, namely a focus on aesthetics and on the documentation of children's thinking and learning. This suggests that educational approaches that successfully travel abroad and take hold in other cultural contexts inevitably are either, in Bruno Latour's (1987) terms, systems that are designed to be contextless and universal (like Linnean botany and High/Scope and other packaged curricula) or systems that become stripped of their localness—what Koichi Iwabuchi (2004) calls "their cultural odor"—and their contextually specific features when they go abroad, as is the case for Reggio (Tobin 2005).

Early childhood education in the US is weak compared to that in many other countries in provision and in average program quality (as the 2001 OECD report makes clear); but this does not keep the US from being among the world's leaders in the global dissemination of early childhood education ideas and curricula. Exporting educational approaches is a lucrative international business (Steiner-Khamsi 2004, 204–7). As the US struggles domestically to create a quality, coherent system of early childhood education and care, High/Scope, the Project Approach, and other curricula developed in the US circulate globally. We suggest that this is no accident. The incoherence, fluidity, and contentiousness that characterize the early childhood education and care system in the US provide an inexhaustible domestic market for early childhood education research, training, and curricular innovation efforts. High/Scope and other American research and development centers have been able to use their subsidized research and their contracted work in the US domestic market as building blocks for taking their products overseas. This is an argument that has been used in economic analyses to explain the role a robust domestic market plays in the development of an export industry, as, for example, in the development of the Japanese consumer electronic industry, where domestic consumers push Japanese companies to compete with each other to develop cutting-edge products that get developed and tested in the Japanese market before going overseas.

China is among the nations that are currently consumers of American early childhood education programs. After a long period of turning inward, for the past two decades China has been borrowing early childhood education ideas eclectically, incorporating ideas, for example, from High Scope, the Project Approach, Reggio Emilia, and Japan (Zhu & Zhang 2008). This borrowing has been focused on bringing to China progressive educational ideas and practices that are believed to produce the kind of creative, individualistic, entrepreneurial citizens needed by China's new economy. This drive has led some preschools in the large cities not to selectively incorporate bits and pieces of foreign early childhood educational practices but instead to import the whole progressive early childhood education paradigm, lock, stock, and barrel, albeit overlaying the imported ideas on a preexisting structure of Chinese practices and beliefs. As a result, it is easier to find a state-of-the-art, child-centered, constructivist preschool in Shanghai than it is in many cities in the US. The emphasis now in China is on expanding the new model to the rest of China, a process, considering China's huge size, that can be described as a within-country globalization effort.

Chinese early childhood education is in the midst of a period of heavy borrowing from the West, but this does not mean that it will continue to do so and in fact our last round of interviews in China suggests that the hunger for outside ideas is already abating. Globalization, though a relatively recent term supported by a young set of theories, is not a new phenomenon. Nor is it continuous and always expanding. China has been receiving progressive education ideas from Europe and the US for over a century (Rappleye 2007). Perhaps the high point of this process was John Dewey's visit to China from 1919 to 1921. While Chinese scholars debated at the time and continue to debate today the value Dewey's ideas hold for China, no one doubts the central role he played in introducing Chinese early childhood educators to the concepts of child-centeredness and "learning by doing." Dewey's ideas were influential in Chinese education from approximately 1920 to 1940 before coming under attack in the 1950s by Marxist educators as being dangerously bourgeois, individualistic, and counter-revolutionary (Zheng 1988; Su 1995). This in a sense is ironic because, as Di Xu (1992) points out, there are significant areas of agreement between Dewey's theories and Mao's, specifically in the relation of the school to the society and on the role of experience in learning. In the 1960s and 1970s, during the years of the Cultural Revolution, as Su Zhixin writes, "there was an eclipse of interest in Dewey even as a target of criticism" (1995, 314). When we conducted our interviews in China in 1985, we heard no mention of Dewey from teachers and directors, although around that time his name was once again beginning to be cited positively by scholars. In the years since then Dewey has returned to favor in early childhood education circles.

The fluctuation over time in John Dewey's influence in China is a good example of the unevenness and nonlinearity of the global circulation of educational ideas. Moreover, the story of Dewey in China illustrates how nations alternate between turning inward and outward to reform their education systems. We draw here on the work of Jürgen Schriewer (2000; 2004) and Gita Steiner-Khamsi (2000; 2004), who suggest that there are alternations between periods of closing off to the outside (as, for example, China did from 1950 to 1978 and especially during the Cultural Revolution) and periods of systematically importing ideas from abroad (as China did in the 1920s and again in the late 1980s and 1990s). There are also alternations between periods when the externality of educational ideas from abroad is used to justify their value, periods, that is, when nations explicitly cite the need to progress through importing ideas from other nations that are acknowledged to be more advanced, and periods when educational ideas from abroad are internalized, their foreign origins masked, and their value justified in terms of traditional beliefs. In some periods, the externality of globally circulating educational ideas increases their domestic value; in other periods, the externality is played down or even erased, and imported ideas are re-made (in Steiner-Khamsi's phrases, "indigenized," "recontextualized" and "reterritorialized") in a form that makes them seem like a local invention that is entirely consistent with traditional beliefs and national values.

Applying this logic to Dewey's vicissitudes in China, we see that those who championed his educational ideas in the 1920s did so by emphasizing the need to import ideas from abroad that, once adapted to the local context, would help China modernize and become more democratic. From the 1950s through the 1970s, when China turned inward, the externality of these ideas made Dewey a dangerous and unwelcome foreign element. In the 1980s, Dewey re-emerged, again associated with the cachet of being borrowed from abroad, but this time in more indigenized form, tied to Deng's vision of a uniquely Chinese version of modernization and entry into global capitalism. In the past few years, even as the goals of early childhood education in China have become increasingly child-centered and, in a sense, increasingly Deweyian, Dewey's name is less often cited (Schriewer & Martinez 2004) and the value of the new approach has been indigenized, justified less in terms of being something imported from the West than as something that reflects the values of China's new vision of society.

Our last round of interviews in 2006 and 2007 with Chinese early childhood educators suggests that the aggressive push toward progressivism and child-centeredness that characterized Chinese early childhood education from about 1990 to 2005 has begun to be counterbalanced by an acknowledgment of the value of traditional Chinese pedagogical practices and theories. This leads to the prediction that the period of intense borrowing will soon be replaced by a period of consolidation, localization, and hybridization of foreign and domestic educational ideas. A hybrid form of progressivism will emerge that combines Dewey, Vygotsky, the Project Approach, and Reggio with Confucianism, Chinese socialist principles, and Chinese educational traditions that give importance to memory, performance, mastery, content knowledge, and critique. Professor Zhu Jiaxiong of East China Normal University suggested to us that the globalization of education in China works like a pendulum, swinging back and forth between periods of looking outwards and inwards. But unlike a pendulum, there is no final, fixed, predetermined resting place. Instead, the pivot point of the pendulum is constantly shifting, as new hybrid forms of education emerge, mixing once external with internal elements, producing a new center. After more than a century of being on the consuming end of globally circulating ideas, China seems poised to become a producer. Perhaps in the years ahead the US, Japan, and other countries will look to Chinese early childhood education for innovative ideas. Perhaps Sinanlu You'eryuan will be the next Reggio, and preschool directors from around the world will make their future pilgrimages to Shanghai to study a newly emergent hybrid model of early childhood education that fuses constructivist, child-centered principles with Chinese traditions of large class size, social mindedness, skill and subject mastery, and the use of critical feedback for self-improvement.

During the last twenty years, as China has aggressively imported progressive ideas about early childhood education from the US and Europe and as the US has been borrowing ideas from Reggio and exporting High/Scope and other curricula to third-world nations, Japanese early childhood education, curiously, has stayed largely outside of this circuit of global borrowing and lending. Japanese early childhood education during this period has had relatively little apparent influence on the rest of the world and been relatively little influenced by others. There are two questions here, which we will address one at a time: Why isn't the Japanese approach to early childhood education spreading globally? And why is Japanese early childhood education relatively impervious to influences from abroad?

Japanese early childhood education's lack of visible impact on other countries is all the more surprising considering Japan's growing role in the global circulation of cultural products and ideas. Japan became a major global exporter of goods in the 1960s. In the 1980s, as Japan's economy boomed, Japan made the jump from exporting goods to exporting ideas and cultural products and Japanese management practices provided models for the rest of the world. After years of importing popular cultural products from the West, Japan became an exporter of lifestyle and media products, including high-fashion clothing, computer software, comics, and video games (Iwabuchi 2004). Japanese educational approaches also are widely studied abroad. Envy of Japanese results on TIMSS (a test of mathematics and science knowledge) and other international measures of academic achievement led educators from Europe and the US in the 1980s and 1990s to attempt to imitate elements of Japanese primary and secondary school mathematics and science curricula, classroom organization, supplementary education programs such as Kumon math and *juku* (private after-school tutoring and exam-prep programs) and teacher training and development (especially *kenkyū jugyō* or "lesson study").

If the rest of the world has borrowed little from Japanese early childhood education in the last twenty years, it is not because of a lack of information about what goes on in Japanese preschools. In the years since we conducted our original study, scholars from outside Japan have published books and articles that have pointed out some of the strengths of Japanese early childhood education. In addition to *Preschool in Three Cultures*, there are Merry White's *The Japanese Educational Challenge* (1987), Joy Hendry's *Becoming Japanese* (1989), Lois Peak's *Learning to Go to School in Japan* (1992), Catherine Lewis's *Educating Hearts and Minds* (1995), Eyal Ben-Ari's *Body Projects in Japanese Childcare* (1996), Susan Holloway's *Contested Childhood* (2000), Daniel Walsh's "The Development of Self in Japanese Preschools" (2002), and Diane Hoffman's "Individualism and Individuality in American and Japanese Early Education" (2000). This scholarship has led to some questioning of taken-for-granted assumptions in the West about what is possible and desirable in preschools, but not to any borrowings of Japanese early childhood practices: no opening of *yōchien* or *hoikuen* in the US or Europe; no calls from politicians to emulate the Japanese approach of thirty children with one teacher; no workshops at NAEYC on how to implement the Japanese approach to non-intervention in children's fights; and no pilgrimages to Komatsudani.

The high student/teacher ratios that make Japanese early childhood pedagogy difficult to export to North American and Europe make it potentially a useful model for China and other Asian countries that have a similar tradition of large class size and ratios and elements of a shared philosophical and moral tradition (Rappleye 2007). As we reported in the China chapter, there is evidence to suggest that the Japanese Ministry of Education's 1998 *National Curriculum Standards for Kindergartens* influenced the 2001 Chinese *Guidelines for the Reform and Development of Education in China*. But given the Chinese anger toward Japan for its refusal to own up to and to apologize sincerely for its actions during the occupation of China in World War II, it is no surprise that the contribution of Japanese early childhood educational ideas to the *Guidelines* goes unacknowledged in the report and that there is a general reluctance in Chinese educational circles to use Japan as an explicit model. Understanding why educational ideas from another country get taken up or not domestically requires attending not just to factors of attraction, but also of repulsion. In many of our focus-group discussions of the Japanese videotapes in China there was a level of implicit if not explicit underlying acrimony toward Japan that was characteristic of the resurgence of anti-Japanese sentiment that recently swept the country, acrimony that we suggest led in the discussions to an only grudging acknowledgment of Japanese early childhood educational strengths and an eagerness to pounce on perceived weaknesses.

Our more general explanation for why Japanese early childhood educational ideas have had relatively little impact outside Japan is that Japanese early childhood education is deeply contextual and resistant to decontextualization and, therefore, to global circulation. We suggest that early childhood education systems can be categorized as either self-consciously constructed or implicit. The constructed systems can travel abroad because they are readily packaged. They have authors who can articulate their core beliefs (Montessori for the Montessori method; Lilian Katz for the Project Approach; Loris Malaguzzi for Reggio Emilia; David Weikart for High/Scope). Most have training manuals, or, if they are against manuals, they have a less didactic but nonetheless systematic approach to popularizing and marketing their program, such as Reggio Emilia's system of study tours, traveling shows of student art work, workshops, websites, books and journal articles, and even a liaison for dissemination of its ideas in the US.

In contrast, the core features of Japanese early childhood education have no author, no core text, and no mechanism for dissemination. For the most part, they are not explained in Japanese textbooks and they are not taught systematically in pre-service teacher education programs. The core features of the Japanese preschool are implicit, reflecting a deep cultural logic. Values such as social-mindedness, liveliness, creativity, appreciation for nature, perseverance, and empathy are emphasized in government statements of goals for *yōchien* and *hoikuen*, but without clear directions on how to achieve them and without the kind of codification found in DAP in the US or in China's early childhood education curriculum revision. The characteristic qualities and strengths of the Japanese preschool system include the alternating periods of chaos and order in the classroom (Sano, 1989); the reluctance to intervene too quickly in children's disputes; the high student/teacher ratios that encourage peer interaction; and the emphasis on emotion and especially on the development of empathy. These are not spelled out in curriculum guides, found in training manuals or program descriptions, taught in schools of education, or much discussed by

Japanese scholars in academic publications. They are passed on from one generation to the next less via the principles taught in university courses and written down in textbooks and curriculum guides than via an apprenticeship model, in which new teachers learn what to do from more experienced teachers (some of whom have only a year or two on the job). Because these key features of Japanese education are implicit and emergent rather than constructed, they do not have much explicit support but neither do they have much opposition. They are for the most part unmarked and, from the Japanese perspective, unremarkable, not needing explanation, justification, or codification and therefore unamenable to being packaged for export.

Another reason the Japanese approach to early childhood education is difficult to take abroad is that the central goal is to make Japanese children Japanese. We have suggested that the core structural features of Japanese preschools work to support the development in young children of such traditional Japanese values as *omoiyari* (empathy), *kejime* (the ability to change one's behavior according to the context), and *shūdan shugi* (social-mindedness). These values have equivalents in other cultures, but they are not the same thing and they are not equally prioritized in those other cultures. In other words, you cannot import Japanese early childhood educational means without getting Japanese early childhood educational ends.

The Japanese emphasis on children's free play and de-emphasis on academic readiness are consistent with Euro-American progressivist notions. But the Japanese version of early childhood educational progressivism is made up of too many structural components that are incompatible with Euro-American progressivist beliefs to allow for easy transfer. The Japanese preschool's large student/teacher ratios break one of the core commandments of progressive early childhood education, which equates small class size and low student/teacher ratios with quality. A ratio of thirty students to one teacher immediately places Japanese early childhood education beyond the pale and impossible to import to the US context. Not intervening in children's fights could be conceptualized as a practice that is constructivist and therefore progressive, but most American teachers find children's fighting counter to their generally pacifist orientations and to their belief that teachers should intervene to provide scaffolding to support children's moral and social development.

The cultural embeddedness of the Japanese approach to early childhood education also makes for little borrowing from outside. Because in the contemporary period China is self-consciously trying to change rapidly as a society, Chinese preschools are open to borrowing from globally circulating ideas. In contrast, because many people in Japan are concerned that their society has already changed too much and become too Westernized, Japanese preschools do little borrowing of outside ideas. Japan looks to its preschools as a source of cultural continuity rather than as a source of change. The preschools, though not a traditional Japanese cultural institution, are looked to as a site for children growing up in a postmodern world to be given traditional values that are believed to be endangered. The more Japanese perceive their world as changing and the more their everyday lives are lived in globalization, the more pressure on preschools to stay the same. Contemporary Japan is by no means a xenophobic or isolationist society. Japanese science, business, and other levels of education borrow ideas freely from other countries. Some Japanese professors of early childhood education attend international meetings and follow the international literature. There are attempts by scholars to introduce Reggio Emilia and other foreign ideas to Japanese early childhood education, and practitioners at professional meetings listen to these ideas with interest. But for the most part these external ideas lead to little change in everyday preschool practice. Tellingly, there is little support for reducing student/teacher ratios to the levels found in Europe and the US, levels that would be necessary to implement Euro-American educational practices that feature individual attention and intervention from teachers. There are a handful of Japanese preschools that are modeled on Montessori and other foreign approaches. But these programs tend to think of themselves and be thought of by others as self-consciously non-Japanese alternatives to the usual Japanese approach.

Japanese early childhood education begins with core assumptions that are quite different from those of programs in the US, Europe, and China. Diane Hoffman (2000) argues that early childhood education in the US and most of Europe is based on a developmental model of childhood while Japanese early childhood education is based on a notion of preserving and supporting the childishness of young children and of not focusing on developmental outcomes. Japanese early childhood education also differs from the European and North American systems in viewing the preschool as an institution that takes the place primarily not of the mother but of the traditional urban neighborhood or village square, therefore emphasizing not dyadic interactions but instead social complexity. These fundamental differences in understandings of childhood and the goals of early childhood education make it difficult for Japanese preschools to participate in the global exchange of ideas and practices.

To summarize, we argue that Japanese early childhood education reflects an implicit cultural logic that, because it is implicit and deeply cultural, is resistant to change as well as to borrowing and lending. This deep cultural logic makes Japanese early childhood education unique among world systems and well attuned to the desire of contemporary Japanese parents and policy makers for institutions that can preserve Japanese cultural values in an era of rapid social transformation. Because so many other traditional Japanese institutions have been so thoroughly modernized and postmodernized, preschools are looked to as islands of cultural continuity in a sea of social change.

Marked and Unmarked Beliefs and Practices

We propose that beliefs and practices that are implicit are less open to scrutiny, criticism, and reform efforts than are beliefs and practices that are mandated in government documents, written down in textbooks, taught in schools of education, given a formal name, and otherwise made explicit. In each country's approach to early childhood education, we find beliefs and practices that are unmarked and unremarkable and therefore not subject to policy debates. The unmarked beliefs and practices are supported not by formal documents or explicit policies but instead by what we are calling "an implicit cultural logic."

Examples in Japan of unmarked, culturally implicit beliefs and practices about early childhood education include *mimamoru* (watching and waiting) and other strategies that allow teachers to hold back before intervening in children's fights; the emphasis on the development and cultivation of empathy (*omoiyari*) and emotions (and particularly of the emotions of loneliness and sadness); a valuing of the "childishness" of children (*kodomo rashii kodomo*); and the practice of older children playing with and caring for younger ones. The large (by US standards) student/teacher ratios of between twenty and thirty children with a single teacher found in Japanese preschools are a special case of implicit cultural logic, in that these ratios were originally imported from the West and they are explicitly mandated by the national ministries, but not viewed, as in the contemporary US, as an important program quality factor and therefore generally not studied, debated, or subject to reform efforts. In other words, although a 30/1 student/teacher ratio is a marked and explicit feature of Japanese early childhood education, the pedagogical goals and practices that are tied to and facilitated by such a ratio are based on a cultural logic that is implicit. This logic assumes that higher ratios better support the development of social mind-edness (*shūdan shugi*) and group-living skills (*shakkai seikatsu*) than would the 10/1 student/teacher ratios typically found in US preschools.

Because this logic is implicit, it has a taken-for-granted nature that makes it both unnecessary and difficult for most Japanese insiders to explain. When asked why they have such large classes, Japanese teachers' and administrators' first response tends to be, "Because of money. With our low tuition we cannot afford smaller numbers of students per teacher. We are barely getting by as it is." But this begs the question of why in a country as wealthy and with as much emphasis on education as Japan, preschools choose to hold the line on tuition and maintain much larger student/teacher ratios than are found in American and European preschools.

In the original Preschool in Three Cultures study, it was only when we showed Japanese preschool teachers the videotape of the American preschool with sixteen children and two teachers that they were able to articulate the logic behind their preference for larger class size and high student/teacher ratios. Watching the St. Timothy's videotape of a classroom with a student/teacher ratio of eight to one, a teacher in Kyoto sighed, "It must be great to teach in America. Such small classes!" But when we followed up by asking, "So you think it would be better to have a class size of ten or twelve instead of twenty-five or thirty?" she responded, "No, I wouldn't say better. Well, maybe you could say better for the teacher, but not better for the children. Children need to have the experience of being in a large group in order to learn to relate to lots of kinds of children in lots of kinds of situations" (Tobin, Wu & Davidson 1989, 36–37). A teacher in Tokyo said of our videotape of an American preschool, "A class that size seems kind of sad and underpopulated." Another Tokyo teacher wondered, "In a class that size wouldn't a child's world be too narrow?" Yagi-sensei commented:

> I understand how this kind of small class size can help young children become very self-reliant and independent. But I can't help feeling that there is something kind of sad or lonely about a class that size. Don't American teachers worry that children may become too independent? I wonder how you teach a child to become a member of a group in a class that small? (37–38)

We can infer an implicit cultural logic or "folk pedagogy" (Bruner 1996) at work here: very small classes and low student/teacher ratios produce a classroom atmosphere that emphasizes teacher-student over student-student interactions and fails to provide children with adequate opportunities to learn to function as members of a group. In the US and other countries where student/teacher ratios are marked as an important indicator of program quality, student/teacher ratios are a frequent battleground in policy and funding debates. In Japan, in contrast, student/teacher ratios are an unmarked, implicit cultural practice that rarely become the focus of discussions of quality or of reform efforts.

As discussed in the China chapter, in contemporary Chinese education there is a growing "nativization" (*bentuhua*) movement that overlaps with new Confucian movements. Critical of what they see as overzealous attempts to import foreign ideas without sufficiently localizing them and of failing to appreciate the unique virtues of Chinese thought, these movements are explicit about their goal of restoring to the curriculum traditional Chinese values and pedagogical approaches. These self-conscious, explicit efforts to preserve and reintroduce clearly marked Chinese cultural practices are a growing force in Chinese education. But we are suggesting that most of the characteristically Chinese beliefs and practices that we have identified in our study of contemporary Chinese preschools have been preserved and passed down less through self-conscious effort or political struggle than through the workings of informal, unmarked mechanisms of transmission. Practices that follow an implicit cultural logic in Chinese early childhood education include the emphasis on mastery and performance (Paine 1990), as seen, for example, in the Story Telling King activity; on shared daily bodily routines, as seen in the daily physical exercise activities conducted across Chinese preschools and other domains of Chinese society (Farquhar & Zhang 2005); and the emphasis on critique as a strategy for self-improvement, as seen both in the Story Telling King activity and in the practices of professional development for teachers based on critiques by experts and by peers (Paine 1990; Paine & Fang 2007). Even as Chinese early childhood education goes through dramatic and sometimes wrenching processes of reform, traditions of performance and mastery, a belief in the power of exemplars and the utility of critique, and a commitment to shared social activity are beliefs and practices that are implicit, unremarked, unremarkable, and therefore not subject to debate.

In the US, while debate is centered on questions of provision (for example, in bills calling for universal, publicly supported, pre-kindergarten programs) and on paradigm wars between proponents and opponents of developmentally appropriate practice and of direct instruction in literacy and mathematics, other practices can be found in US preschools that are unmarked and that reflect a core cultural logic that is largely shared across the philosophical/ideological spectrum. These practices include an emphasis on choice, self-expression, and the quality of the dyadic relationship between the teacher and each child in her class. An effect of the power of these shared cultural beliefs, for example, is that the 30/1 student/teacher ratios in preschool classrooms that, as we have seen, are consistent with Japanese cultural logic would be unimaginable and abhorrent if they were introduced to the US preschool context. Unlike in Japan, lower student/teacher ratios in the US are associated in people's minds with higher quality at all levels of education, from daycare for infants to doctoral seminars. The cultural logic/folk pedagogy here is explicit: lower ratios mean more individual attention for each student and fewer classroom management problems. What constitutes a suitably lower ratio varies by children's age and grade level.

We suggest that the implicit cultural logic behind this belief and practice in preschools, a logic that is unspoken and even sometimes actively denied, is that a low student/teacher ratio, by allowing for more frequent and more intense dyadic interactions between each child and the teacher, allows the teacher to be more mother-like. This logic is generally resisted by American early childhood educators because, when said out loud, it works to deprofessionalize a profession that is still struggling to escape the popular perception that preschool teaching is a form of childcare. But we suggest that those who defend the profession by denying the connection between parenting and preschool teaching protest too much and that a key cultural feature and perhaps even a strength of the US approach to early childhood education is its emphasis on dyadic interaction between teacher and child, an emphasis that reflects a hybridity of the roles of mother and teacher and of nurturance and mentoring (Goldstein 1997). The dyadic intensity of the teacher-child bond along with the emphasis on choice (as seen, for example, in the way children are encouraged and sometimes even required to express a preference for which activity center to play in during "choice time") and on self-expression (as seen, for example, in the logocentric approach to resolving disputes, where children are encouraged to put their feelings into words) is characteristic of the beliefs of American early childhood educators that are more implicit than explicit and therefore relatively impervious to policy shifts and reform efforts.

Locating Preschools in Time and Space

To make sense of similarities and differences in preschools of three cultures while also making sense of continuity and change in preschools over the course of a generation, we need to think simultaneously in terms of space and time or, to borrow a phrase from physics, in terms of a "spacetime continuum." The argument of this book is that we have to be historians as well as ethnographers, sociologists as well as anthropologists, paying attention to economic, political, and cultural issues as they play out across places and eras. For thinking about educational continuity and change, a spacetime continuum would mean that 2002 in Kunming both is and is not the same time as 2002 in Shanghai. A wave theory of educational change would suggest that innovations begin in core areas such as Beijing and Shanghai and then spread out like a wave, reaching a peripheral provincial capital such as Kunming several years later and then villages in the countryside much later still. Our findings are largely consistent with this notion, with Daguan You'eryuan in 2002 just beginning to implement changes that Sinanlu You'eryuan had made five or ten years earlier. On the other hand, sometimes political and economic change happens everywhere, all at once. Living in the Internet and wireless phone age means, for example, that the announcement of a new educational policy by the Chinese Ministry of Education reaches Kunming at almost the same moment it reaches Shanghai.

All preschools are moving through history, but not necessarily following the same trajectories or moving along the same temporal lines. Global events impact everyone everywhere but not in the same way or the same time. Core power centers, globally as well as within nations, attempt to influence peripheries, and they usually succeed, but their power is by no means limitless. Remote locations are hungry to consume the latest ideas from the core, but this eagerness does not guarantee that they faithfully reproduce what they copy. The power of the global meets the power of the local each day in every preschool classroom, where practitioners make decisions on what lessons to teach and what to do the next time a fight breaks out among children. We have shown in this book how these decisions must be understood as playing out in both time and space, and to view them as contingent and emergent, reflecting a complex interaction of cultural traditions with social pressures, local and national as well as global. Daguan You'eryuan will never become just like Sinanlu You'eryuan because it exists in its own unique spacetime continuum; Daguan is moving along a path of change, but not the same path on which Sinanlu is traveling. Similarly, we suggest that the systems of early childhood education of China, Japan, and the US, though buffeted by many of the same global forces and events, respond in unique ways, reflecting their unique combination of cultural traditions, social structures, and contextual features.

By asking our informants to reflect on how their contemporary practices are different from both those of their counterparts in other countries and those of teachers in their country a generation ago, we challenged them to engage in both historiography and ethnography. Often, our informants found our questions odd and difficult to answer. They could generally provide reasons for their practices, but most often these reasons were not explicitly cultural or historical. In general, practitioners do not think of themselves or their preschools as cultural exemplars or of their beliefs as reflecting or being based on cultural values (Tobin & Davidson 1991). Nor do practitioners tend to think of themselves historically, as moving through time. When we asked them how they and their preschool had changed over the past generation, most preschool teachers and directors found the question a bit puzzling. They tended to talk about how the field has changed while arguing that they have mostly stayed the same. Some of our informants, like Bonnie Lund, the principal of Alhambra, made sense of differences over time using a narrative of progress ("We know so much now we didn't know before"). Others, like Fran Smith, the head teacher at Alhambra, used a narrative of nostalgia to compare the present with the past, as she reflected on the good old days when she was trained, in play-centered pedagogy, before No Child Left Behind and other forces were pushing programmed instruction into her classroom.

Such narratives of progress and nostalgia reflect the paired pitfalls of linear historical thinking and call for us to rise to the challenge of conceptualizing change over time without viewing the past as either categorically better or worse than the present. Just as the cultural relativism that lies at the core of ethnography demands that we not view one culture as superior to another, so should historical relativism warn us to steer clear of the dangers of narratives of both deterioration and linear progress (Tobin 2008). Just as cultural relativism is a corrective to ethnocentrism, historical relativism requires us to not judge—positively or negatively—one era from the perspective of another. Preschools in China, Japan, and the US have changed in some ways and stayed the same in others, but we cannot say that they have become better or worse, just that they each now, as a generation ago, reflect their culture, their society, and their time (Anderson-Levitt 2002, 81–82).

In 1999, when we decided to launch this new study, we were primarily motivated by the idea of describing and understanding what seemed to us to be an extraordinarily dramatic change since 1985 in Chinese early childhood education. But change, like beauty, is in the eye of the beholder. As Wang Xinglan, the retired director of Daguan You'eryuan, put it after watching the 1985 Daguan video in 2002: "When I look at these images I realize that of course many things have changed. But I feel proud of how we taught then. In the video I see us all working very hard and doing the best we could do with what we had to work with. Those were different times. Then, as now, the staff of Daguan You'eryuan was guided by the same sense of professionalism, hard work, and concern for children."

References

Adair, J. & Tobin, J. (2008). Listening to the voices of immigrant parents. In C. Genishi & L. Goodwin (Eds.), *Diversities in Early Childhood Education: Rethinking and Doing* (pp. 137–150). London, UK: Routledge/Falmer.

Adams, J. (2006). Community matters in China. In E. Hannum & B. Fuller (Eds.), *Research in Sociology of Education 15: Social Organization of Childhood in Developing Countries* (pp. 15–42). Amsterdam/Boston: Elsevier.

Alexander, R. (2000). *Culture and Pedagogy: International Comparisons in Primary Education.* Oxford, UK: Blackwell Publishing.

Anderson-Levitt, K. (2002). *Teaching Cultures: Knowledge for Teaching First Grade in France and the United States.* Cresskill, NJ: Hampton Press.

——— (2003). A world culture of schooling? In K. Anderson-Levitt (Ed.). *Local Meanings, Global Schooling: Anthropology and World Culture Theory.* New York: Palgrave Macmillan.

Artiles, A. J. (2003). Special education's changing identity: Paradoxes and dilemmas in views of culture and space. *Harvard Educational Review, 73,* 164–202.

Bailey, C. (2003, January 6). *Love and loss in the landscape of pedagogical desire: Provocations from early childhood.* Paper presented at the annual Reconceptualizing Early Childhood Education: Research, Theory and Practice Conference, Tempe, Arizona.

Bakhtin, M. (1941/1984). *Rabelais and His World.* Translated by Helene Iswolsky. Bloomington, IN: Indiana University Press.

Begley, S. (1996). Your child's brain. *Newsweek 127* (8), 55–61.

Ben-Ari, E. (1997). *Body Projects in Japanese Childcare: Culture, Organization, and Emotions in a Preschool.* London, UK: Routledge.

Bjork, C. & Tsuneyoshi, R. (2005). Educational reform in Japan: Competing visions for the future. *Phi Delta Kappan, 86* (8), 619–626.

Bloch, M. (1992). Critical perspectives on the historical relationship between child development and early childhood education research. In S. Kessler & B. B. Swadner (Eds.), *Reconceptualizing the Early Childhood*

Curriculum: Beginning the Dialogue (pp. 3–20). New York, NY: Teachers College Press.

Boocock, S. (1989). Controlled diversity: An overview of the Japanese preschool system. *Journal of Japanese Studies 15* (1), 41–65.

Bredekamp, S. (Ed.). (1987). *Developmentally Appropriate Practice in Early Childhood Programs Serving Children from Birth through Age Eight.* Washington, DC: National Association for the Education of Young Children.

Bredekamp, S. & Copple, C. (Eds.) (1997). *Developmentally Appropriate Practice in Early Childhood Programs* (rev. ed.). Washington, DC: National Association for the Education of Young Children.

Bruer, J. (1997). Education and the brain: A bridge too far. *Educational Researcher, 26* (8), 4–16.

—— (2000). *The Myth of the First Three Years: A New Understanding of Early Brain Development and Lifelong Learning.* New York, NY: Free Press.

Bruner, J. (1990). *Acts of Meaning.* Cambridge, MA: Harvard University Press.

—— (1996). *The Culture of Education.* Cambridge, MA: Harvard University Press.

Business Roundtable (2003). Early Childhood Education: A Call to Action from the Business Community. www.businessroundtable.org/sites/files/2003.05.05_Early_Childhood_Education-A_Call_to_Action

Butler, J. (1990). *Gender Trouble: Feminism and the Subversion of Identity.* New York, NY: Routledge.

Caudill, W. (1962). Patterns of emotion in modern Japan. In R. J. Smith & R. K. Beardsley (Eds.), *Japanese Culture* (pp. 115–131). Chicago, IL: Aldine.

Charlesworth, R. (1998). Developmentally appropriate practice is for everyone. *Childhood Education, 74* (5), 274–282.

Che, Y. (2007) "Preschool Teachers' Reactions to Top-down Educational Reform: A Chinese Perspective." Reconceptualizing Early Childhood Education, Madison, Wisconsin, December.

Clark, S. (1994). *Japan: A View from the Bath.* Honolulu, HI: University of Hawaii Press.

Clifford, J. (1983). On ethnographic authority. *Representations, 1* (2), 118–146.

Committee on Integrating the Science of Early Childhood Development. (2000). *From Neurons to Neighborhoods: The Science of Early Childhood Development.* Washington, DC: National Academies Press.

Connor, L., Asch, T., & Asch, P. (1986). *Jero Tapakan: Balinese Healer.* Cambridge, UK: Cambridge University Press.

D'Andrade, R. & Strauss, C. (1995). *Human Motives and Cultural Models*. New York, NY: Cambridge University Press.

Delpit, L. (1986). Skills and other dilemmas of a progressive black educator. *Harvard Educational Review*, 56 (4), 379–385.

Dewey, J. (1889/1956). *The School and Society*. Chicago, IL: University of Chicago Press.

Doi, T. (1967). *Anatomy of Dependence*. Tokyo: Kodansha International.

Edelman, M. (2004). Five questions for: Marian Wright Edelman, Front Row—Interview. *Ebony*. Retrieved on January 10, 2008 (http://findarticles .com/p/articles/mi_m1077/is_3_59/ai_111850281).

Education For All (2000). EFA Assessment, Country Report, China, at http:// www.unesco.org/education/wef/countryreports/china/rapport_2_3 .html

Embree, J. F. (1939). *Suye Mura: A Japanese Village*. Chicago: University of Chicago Press.

Fabian, J. (1983). *Time and the Other*. New York, NY: Columbia University Press.

Farquhar, J. & Zhang, Q. (2005). Biopolitical Beijing. *Cultural Anthropology*, 20 (3) 303–327.

Foucault, M. (1975). *Discipline and Punish*. New York, NY: Pantheon.

Fowell, N., & Lawton, J. (1992). An alternative view of appropriate practice in early childhood education. *Early Childhood Research Quarterly*, 7, 53–73.

Frank Porter Graham Child Development Institute (2004). *Universial or targeted programs: Prekindergarten policy framework*. Chapel Hill, NC: Frank Porter Graham Center. http://www.fpg.unc.edu/-npc/framework/ framework.cfm?section_num=6&subsection_num=1

——— (2006). How FPG got its groove. *Early Developments, 10*, no. 1 (Spring), 5–10. Chapel Hill, NC: Frank Porter Graham Center. www.fpg.unc.edu/ assets/products/ed10_1.pdf.

Fujita, M. & Sano, T. (1988). Children in American and Japanese day-care centers: Ethnography and reflective cross-cultural interviewing. In H. Trueba & C. Delgado-Gaitan (Eds). *School and Society: Learning Content through Culture* (73–97). New York, NY: Praeger.

Fuller, B. (2007). *Standardized Childhood: The Political and Cultural Struggle over Early Education*. Palo Alto, CA: Stanford University Press.

Fusaro, J. (1997). The effect of full-day kindergarten on student achievement: A meta-analysis. *Child Study Journal, 27* (4), 269–277.

Gartrell, D. (1995). Misbehavior or mistaken behavior? *Young Children, 50* (5) 27–34.

———— (2003). *The Power of Guidance: Teaching Social-Emotional Skills in Early Childhood Classrooms*. Clifton Park, NY: Delmar Learning.

Geertz, C. (1983). *Local Knowledge: Further Essays in Interpretive Anthropology*. New York, NY: Basic Books.

Goldstein, L. (1997). *Teaching with Love: A Feminist Approach to Early Childhood Education*. New York, NY: Peter Lang.

Gomi, T. (1993). *Everyone Poops*. La Jolla, CA: Kane/Miller Books.

González, N., Moll, L., & Amanti, C. (2004). *Funds of Knowledge: Theorizing Practices in Households, Communities, and Classrooms*. Hillsdale, NJ: Erlbaum.

Goodman, R. (2000). *Children of the Japanese State*. Oxford, UK: Oxford University Press.

Grunewald, R. & Rolnick, A. (2001). A proposal for achieving high returns on early childhood development. Minneapolis, MN: Federal Reserve Bank of Minneapolis.

Hannum, E. (2003). Poverty and basic education in rural China: Villages, households, and girls' and boys' enrollment. *Comparative Education Review, 47* (2), 141–159.

Hannum, E. & Wang, M. (2006) Geography and educational inequality in China. *China Economic Review, 17* (3), 253–265.

Hayashi, A., Karasawa, M., & Tobin, J. (2009). The Japanese preschool's pedagogy of feeling: Cultural strategies for supporting young children's emotional development. *Ethos, 37* (1), 32–49.

Hendry, J. (1989). *Becoming Japanese: The World of the Preschool*. Honolulu, HI: University of Hawaii Press.

Henry, W. (1956). *The Analysis of Fantasy: The Thematic Appreciation Technique in the Study of Personality*. New York: John Wiley & Sons.

Hoffman, D. (2000). Individualism and individuality in American and Japanese early education: A review and critique. *American Journal of Education, 108* (4), 300–317.

Holloway, S. (2000). *Contested Childhood: Diversity and Change in Japanese Preschools*. London, UK: Routledge.

Hsueh, Y., Tobin, J., & Karasawa, M. (2004). The Chinese kindergarten in its adolescence. *Prospects, 34* (4), 457–469.

Imoto, Y. (2007).The Japanese preschool system in transition. *Research in Comparative and International Education, 2* (2), 88–101.

Iwabuchi, K. (2004). How Japanese Is Pokémon? In Joseph Tobin (Ed.), *Pikachu's Global Adventure: The Rise and Fall of Pokemón* (pp. 53–79). Duke University Press.

Jipson, J. (1991). Developmentally appropriate practice: Culture, curriculum, connections. *Early Education and Development, 2* (2), 120–136.

Johnson, R. (2000). *Hands Off: The Disappearance of Touch in the Care of Children.* New York: Peter Lang.

Jones, A. (2001). *Touchy Subjects: Teachers Touching Children.* Dunedin, New Zealand: University of Otago Press.

Katz, L. G. (1993). *Distinctions between Self-Esteem and Narcissism: Implications for Practice.* Urbana, IL: ERIC Clearinghouse on Elementary and Early OECD Childhood Education. ED 363 452.

Katz, L. G. & Chard, S. C. (1997). Documentation: The Reggio Emilia approach. *Principal, 76* (5), 16–17.

Kessler, S. A. (1991). Early childhood education as development: A critique of the metaphor. *Early Education and Development, 2,* 137–152.

Klingner, J., Artiles, A. J., Kozleski, E., Harry, B., Zion, S., Tate, W., Zamora-Durán, G., & Riley, D. (2005). Addressing the disproportionate representation of culturally and linguistically diverse students in special education through culturally responsive educational systems. *Education Policy Analysis Archives, 13* (38), http://epaa.asu.edu/epaa/v13n38/.

Kohn, A. (1996). *Beyond Discipline: From Compliance to Community.* Alexandria, VA: Association for Supervision and Curriculum Development.

Kurosawa, A. (1951) *Rashomon* [film]. Triad Productions.

Lagemann, E. (1989). The plural worlds of educational research, *History of Education Quarterly 29* (2), 185–214.

Lareau, A. (2003). *Unequal Childhoods: Class, Race, and Family Life.* Berkeley, CA: University of California Press.

Latour, B. (1988). *Science in Action: How to Follow Scientists and Engineers through Society.* Cambridge, MA: Harvard University Press.

Lee, K. & Walsh, D. (2005). Independence and community: Teaching Midwestern. *Journal of Early Childhood Teacher Education, 26,* 59–77.

Lewis, C. (1995). *Educating Hearts and Minds.* Cambridge, UK: Cambridge University Press.

Li, J. (2003). The core of Confucian learning. *American Psychologist, 58,* 146–147.

Liu, Y. (Ed.) (1999). *Shanghai Renkou Fu Zengzhang Yu Jihua Shengyu* (The Negative Population Growth and Family Planning in Shanghai). Shanghai: Shanghai Kexue Jishu Chubanshe (Shanghai Science and Technology Press).

Liu, Y. & Feng, X. (2005). Kindergarten educational reform during the past two decades in mainland China: Achievements and problems. *International Journal of Early Years Education, 13* (2), 93–99.

Lubeck, S. (1994). The politics of developmentally appropriate practice: Exploring issues of culture, class, and curriculum. In B. Mallory & R. New (Eds.), *Diversity and Developmentally Appropriate Practices: Towards More Inclusive Theory, Teaching, and Social Policy.* (pp. 17–43). New York: Teachers College Press.

——— (1996). Is developmentally appropriate practice for everyone? *Childhood Education 74* (5), 283–292.

Marcus, G. (1995). Ethnography in/of the world system: The emergence of multisite ethnography. *Annual Review of Anthropology, 24*, 95–117.

McCartney, K. (2004). Current research on child care effects. In R. E. Tremblay, R. G. Barr, & R. DeV. Peters (Eds.), *Encyclopedia on Early Childhood Development.* Centre of Excellence for Early Childhood Development. Retrieved on May 26, 2008 at www.excellence-jeunesenfants.ca/documents/McCartneyANGxp.pdf.

Meyer, J & Ramirez, F. (2000). The world institutionalization of education. In J. Schriewer (Ed.), *Discourse Formation in Comparative Education* (pp. 111–132). New York, NY: Peter Lang.

Munro, D. J. (1975). The Chinese view of modeling. *Human Development, 18,* 333–352.

NAEYC (1998). *Accreditation Criteria and Procedures of the National Association for the Education of Young Children.* Washington, DC: National Association for the Education of Young Children.

New, R. (2001). *Quando c'e figli* (when there are children): Observations on Italian early childhood. In L. Gandini & C. Edwards (Eds.), *Bambini: The Italian approach to infant/toddler care* (pp. 200–215). New York: Teachers College Press.

Newkirk, T. (1992). *Listening In.* Portsmouth, NH: Heinemann.

Nores, M., Belfeld, C., Barnett, W., Schweinhart, L. et al. (2005). Updating the economic impacts of the High/Scope Perry preschool program. *Educational Evaluation and Policy Analysis, 27* (3), 245–261.

Oda, Y. & Mori, M. (2006). Current challenges of kindergarten (*yōchien*) education in Japan: Toward balancing children's autonomy and teachers' intention. *Childhood Education, 82* (6), 369–373.

OECD (2000). *OECD Country Note: Early Childhood Education and Care Policy in the United States of America.* Paris, France: Organization for Economic Co-operation and Development.

Olsen, D. & Zigler, E. (1989). An assessment of the all-day kindergarten movement. *Early Childhood Research Quarterly 4,* 167–186.

Paine, L. (1990). The teacher as virtuoso: A Chinese model for teaching. *Teachers College Record, 92* (1), 49–81.

Paine, L. & Fang, Y. (2007). Reform as hybrid model of teaching and teacher development in China. *International Journal of Educational Research, 45* (4–5), 279–289.

Peak, L. (1992). *Learning to Go to School in Japan*. Berkeley, CA: University of California Press.

Postiglione, G. (Ed.) (2006). *Education and Social Change in China*. Armonk, NY: M. E. Sharpe.

Project Zero & Reggio Children (2001). *Making Learning Visible: Children as Individual and Group Learners*. Cambridge, MA: Reggio Children.

Rappleye, J. (2007). *Exploring Cross-National Attraction in Education: Some Historical Comparisons of American and Chinese Attraction to Japanese Education*. Oxford, UK: Symposium Books.

Roberts, G. (2002). Planning hopes on angels: Reflections from an ageing Japan's urban landscape. In R. Goodman (Ed.), *Family and Social Policy in Japan* (pp. 54–91). Cambridge, UK: Cambridge University Press.

Rolnick, A. & Grunewald, R. (2003). Early Childhood Development: Economic Development with a High Public Return, *Region 17*, no. 4 supplement (December 2003), 9.

Rosenthal, M. (1999). Out-of-home child care research: A cultural perspective. *International Journal of Behavioral Development, 23* (2), 477–518.

Sano, T. (1989). Methods of social control and socialization in Japanese daycare centers. *Journal of Japanese Studies 15* (1), 125–138.

Sargent, T. & Hannum, E. (2005). Keeping teachers happy: Job satisfaction among primary school teachers in rural northwest China. *Comparative Education Review, 49* (2), 173–204.

Schriewer, J. (Ed.) (2000). *Discourse Formation in Comparative Education*. New York, NY: Peter Lang.

——— (2004). Multiple internationalities: the emergence of a world level ideology and the persistence of idiosyncratic world-view. In C. Charles, J. Schriewer & P. Wagner (Eds), *Transnational Intellectual Networks* (pp. 473–534). Frankfurt, Germany: Campus Verlag.

Schriewer, J. & Martinez, C. (2004) Constructions of internationality in education. In G. Steiner-Khamsi (Ed.), *Lessons from Elsewhere: The Politics of Educational Borrowing and Lending* (pp. 29–53). New York, NY: Teachers College Press.

Shanghai "*Zhengda*" Institute (2002). *Shanghai Ren* (Shanghai people). Shanghai: Shanghai Xuelin Chubanshe (Shanghai Scholars' Press).

Silin, J. (1995). *Sex, Death, and the Education of Children: Our Passion for Ignorance in the Age of AIDS*. New York, NY: Teachers College Press.

Skaggs, M. (2001). Facing the facts: Overrepresentation of culturally and linguistically diverse students in special education. *Multicultural Education 9* (2), 42–43.

Smith, R. & Wiswell, E. (1982). *The Women of Suye Mura*. Chicago, IL: University of Chicago Press.

Spindler, G. (2000). The four careers of George and Louise Spindler: 1948–2000. *Annual Review of Anthropology, 29,* xv–xxxviii.

Spindler, G. & Spindler, L. (1965). Researching the perception of cultural alternatives: The instrumental activities inventory. In M. Spiro (Ed.) *Context and Meaning in Cultural Anthropology* (pp. 312–337). New York, NY: Free Press.

—— (1987). Cultural dialogue and schooling in Schoenhausen and Roseville. *Anthropology and Education Quarterly, 19,* 3–16.

Steiner-Khamsi, G. (2000). Transferring Education, Displacing Reforms. In J. Schriewer (Ed.), *Discourse Formation in Comparative Education* (pp.155–186). New York, NY: Peter Lang.

—— (2004). *The Global Politics of Educational Borrowing and Lending*. New York, NY: Teachers College Press.

Su, Z. (1995). A critical examination of John Dewey's influence on Chinese education. *American Journal of Education, 103* (3), 302–325.

Takayama, K. (2007). A nation at risk crosses the Pacific: Transnational borrowing of the U.S. crisis discourse in the debate on education reform in Japan. *Comparative Education Review, 51* (4), 423–446.

Tang, S. 2005. On the development and reform of Chinese country preschool education. *Studies on Preschool Education (xueqian jiaoyu yanjiu), 6,* 38–40.

Tobin, J. (1989). Visual anthropology and multivocal ethnography: A dialogical approach to Japanese preschool class size. *Dialectical Anthropology 13,* 173–178.

—— (1992). A Dialogical solution to the problem of field site typicality. *City and Society, 6* (1), 46–57.

—— (1995). The irony of self-expression. *American Journal of Education, 103,* 233–258.

—— (1997). *Making a Place for Pleasure in Early Childhood Education*. New Haven, CT: Yale University Press.

—— (1999). Method and Meaning in Comparative Classroom Ethnography. In R. Alexander (Ed.), *Learning from Comparing: New Directions in Comparative Educational Research* (pp. 113–134). Oxford, UK: Oxford University Press.

—— (2005). Quality in early childhood education: An anthropologist's perspective. *Early Education & Development, 16* (4), 421–434.

—— (2008). An anthropologist's reflections on defining quality in education research. *International Journal of Research & Method in Education*, *30* (3), 325–338.

Tobin, J. & Davidson, D. (1991). Multivocal ethnographies of schools: Empowering vs. textualizing children and teachers. *International Journal of Qualitative Educational Research, 3*, 271–283.

Tobin, J & Hsueh, Y. (2007). The Poetics and Pleasures of Video Ethnography of Education. In R. Goldman (Ed.), *Video Research in the Learning Sciences* (pp. 77–92). New York, N.Y.: Erlbaum.

Tobin, J., Wu, D. & Davidson, D. (1989). *Preschool in Three Cultures: Japan, China, and the United States*. New Haven, CT: Yale University Press.

USDOE (2002). Executive summary (No Child Left Behind). http://www .ed.gov/nclb/overview/intro/execsumm.html.

Valdéz, G. (1996). *Con Respeto*. New York, NY: Teachers College Press.

Walsh, D. J. (1991). Extending the discourse on developmental appropriateness: A developmental perspective. *Early Education and Development, 2* (2) 109–119.

———— (2002). The development of self in Japanese preschools: Negotiating space. In L. Bresler & A. Ardichvili (Eds.), *Research in International Education: Experience, Theory, and Practice* (pp. 213–246). New York, N.Y.: Peter Lang.

———— (2003). Dimensions of Japanese early schooling: Review of Susan Holloway's *Contested Childhoods: Diversity and Change in Japanese Preschools. Contemporary Psychology, 48* (5), 690–692.

———— (2004). Frog boy and the American monkey. In L. Bresler (Ed.), *Knowing Bodies, Feeling Minds* (pp. 97–109). Amsterdam: Kluwer.

Wang, X. (2002). The post-Communist personality: The spectre of China's capitalist market reforms. *China Journal, 47*, 1–17.

White, B. (1985). *The First Three Years of Life*. New York, NY: Fireside.

White, M. (1987). *The Japanese Educational Challenge*. New York, NY: Free Press.

———— (1990) Review of *Preschool in Three Cultures: Japan, China, and the United States* by J. Tobin, David Y. H. Wu & Dana H. Davidson. *American Journal of Sociology, 95* (5), 1335–1336.

White House (1997). *White House Conference on Early Childhood Development and Learning*. http://clinton3.nara.gov/WH/New/ECDC.

———— (2001). *Good Start, Grow Smart: The Bush Administration's Early Childhood Initiative*. http://www.whitehouse.gov/infocus/earlychildhood/ toc.html.

Whiting, B. & Edwards, C. (1988). *Children of Different Worlds*. Cambridge, MA: Harvard University Press.

Wollons, R. (2000). The Missionary kindergarten in Japan. In R. Wollons (Ed.), *Kindergartens and Cultures: The Global Diffusion of an Idea*. New Haven, CT: Yale University Press.

Xu, D. (1992). *A Comparison of the Educational Ideas and Practices of John Dewey and Mao Zedong in China: Is School Society or Society School?* Lewiston, NY: Edwin Mellen Press.

Yu, D. (2005). You'er jiaoyu shiye fazhan xianzhuang ji xiangguan jianyi (An analysis of the current state of early childhood education and related suggestions). *Studies on Preschool Education (Xueqian Jiaoyu Yanjiu)* 11 (27–29).

Yu, S. & Hannum, E. (2006). Poverty, health, and schooling in rural China. In G. Postiglione (Ed.), *Education and Social Change in China* (pp. 53–74). Armonk, NY: M.E. Sharpe.

Zheng, Z. (1988). A Chinese view of the educational ideas of John Dewey. *Interchange, 19* (3–4), 85–91.

Zhou, N. and Xie, Y. (2004). The impact of rural preschool environment on children's lifestyle. *Early Childhood Education 7–8*, 38–39.

Zhu, J. & Zhang, J. (2008). Contemporary trends and developments in early childhood education in China. *Early Years, 28* (2), 173–182.

Index

Abecedarian Project, 209–10
academic pressure: China, 39–40, 85; Japan, 130; US, 167, 186–89. *See also* No Child Left Behind
Adair, Jennifer, 217
Adams, Jennifer, 81
African-Americans, 207, 218–19
Aguinaldo, Chris, 222–23
Akita, Kiyomi, xii, 144, 146–47
Alexander, Robin, 5
amae (dependence), 107–8
Amanti, Cathy, 217
Anderson-Levitt, Kathryn, 4, 5–6, 19, 247
Angel Plan (Japan), 142, 152
art. *See under* curriculum
Artiles, Alfredo, 207
Asch, Patsy and Tim, 5
Ayres, A. Jean. 35

Bailey, Chelsea, 190
Bakhtin, Mikhail, 7, 49, 117
Begley, Sharon, 211
Ben-Ari, Eyal, 113, 117–18, 238
Bennett, John, 214
bentuhua (nativization), 90, 244. *See also under* globalization
bilingual education, 170–71, 197, 202–3, 216–18
birth rate: impact on preschools in Japan, 3, 115, 140, 141–42, 148–51, 228; the one-child policy in China, 32, 37–38, 226–27
Bjork, Christopher, 153, 230
Bloch, Mimi, 183
boarding programs, 23, 31–34, 92
body, the: bathing, 118; disciplining of in China, 52–53; disembodiment in US pre-schools, 198–202; in Japanese preschools and culture, 116–19; privacy and modesty, 46–51; talk about bodily functions in

Japan, 117, 126; toilets, 23, 25–27, 44–50, 57, 114–16, 162. *See also* exercise
Boocock, Sarane, 127
borrowing. *See* globalization
bourgeoisification (*embourgeoisement*), 51, 118–19. *See also* modernization
Bradekamp, Sue, 183, 184
brain research, 3, 199, 210–12
Breur, John, 211–12
Bruner, Jerome, 19, 69, 192, 243
Buddhism, 78, 96, 145, 148
buildings and materials: at Alhambra, 170, 176–77; architecture of Madoka, 11, 122–23, 128, 146; at Daguan, 22–23, 24–25, 48; "hardware" vs. "software" distinction in China, 31, 40–41, 53–54, 78–79, 92; at Komatsudani, 96–97, 119
bullying, 107–10
Bush, George W., 178–79, 184–85, 205, 229. *See also* No Child Left Behind
business of preschool, the: in China, 34, 36–37, 82, 91–94; the Hawaiian economy's slump and, 167–68; in Japan, 119–20, 147–51, 227–28, 243; in the US, 177–78, 192, 202–10, 214, 222–23. *See also* economic change
Business Roundtable, the (US), 209–10
Butler, Judith, 190

Cao, Nengxiu, xii, 89–90
capitalism: China's transition from socialism to, 76; choice in the US curriculum, 196, 225; classroom commercialism, 3, 73, 86, 231; fostering entrepreneurial charac-ter in children, 36, 38, 87–88, 225–27, 229–30, 234; market competition among preschools, 34, 50–51, 92–94, 146, 150–51, 228, 234, 239; privatization of preschools, 33–34, 91–93. *See also* economic change

care and rearing of children: attachment
theory, 208; Chinese socialist views of,
31, 33; and Japanese parenting, 141–42;
premodern, 1, 2, 114–16, 241; in the US,
191–92, 208–14, 245. *See also* nurturance
Caudill, William, 6–7
Chard, Sylvia, 165
Charlesworth, Rosalind, 184
Che, Yi, 82
Chen Heqin, 42
child-centered pedagogy: and children's
choice, 128, 193–95, 245; in China, 35,
41–42, 45, 64–69, 71–72, 88, 225, 232;
economic change and, 225–27, 229; in
Japan, 11, 122, 126, 128–31, 145–46, 195,
230; in the US, 193–97, 231, 232. *See also*
constructivism
Children's Defense Fund, 205, 208
children's rights, 41–42, 226, 227
China Welfare Institute (China Defense
League), 42
chiteki hattatsu (intellectual development),
130–31
Chugani, Harry, 211
Clark, Scott, 118
class and cultural differences: among
Chinese preschools, 33–34, 36, 81–82,
85, 92; in Japanese preschools, 119, 122,
140–43; in the US, 168, 187, 191–92, 205,
215–21, 233
classroom management. *See* misbehavior,
dealing with
Clifford, James, 7
Clinton, Hillary, 210
Clinton, William, 210, 229
collectivism: attitudes toward in the US,
183, 196–97; and democratic values,
66; in group calisthenetics, 51–53; vs.
individualism, 44, 53, 196; in large group
activities and discussions in China,
71–72, 78, 80; single children and, 37–38;
social-mindedness (*shūdan shugi*) and
group-living skills (*shakkai seikatsu*) in Japan as forms of, 111, 120, 129, 240, 242–43;
in toileting and bathing, 45–51. *See also*
individualism
commercialism. *See* capitalism
Committee on Integrating the Science of
Early Childhood Development, 212
communism and socialism, 24, 26, 31, 74–78,

226–27, 235–36. *See also* Cultural Revolution, the
Confucianism: classical texts, 89, 93; critique
and self-improvement in, 68; Doctrine
of the Mean, 77–78; exemplars, value of,
78, 94; Neo-Confucianism, 89, 244; traditional values of, 78, 227, 236, 244
Connor, Linda, 5
constructivism: in China, 35, 53–54, 66, 70,
83, 88, 92, 236, 251; Japanese teachers scaffolding children's development, 109, 111,
123, 130–31, 240; in the US, 188, 195, 197,
207, 217, 230, 240
Copple, Carol, 184
critique (as a pedagogical strategy), 66–69,
90, 244
cultural preservation, preschools' role in,
1, 3, 232; in China, 49, 69, 88–89, 91, 244;
in Japan, 113–14, 119, 122, 229; in the US,
217, 221
Cultural Revolution, the, 42, 68, 77–78,
287, 235
curriculum: art, 27–29, 175; block play,
29, 42–44; calendar, 171–72, 183, 221;
dramatic play, 62–64, 69–73, 165, 173, 231;
enrichment classes, 30, 33, 85–86, 92; in
Japan, 127, 141, 150; mathematics, 55–56;
music, 28–29, 99, 105, 160, 175; oral expression, 68–69, 124, 131, 138–39, 197–98;
origami, 99–100, 197; pee lesson, 103, 108,
114–15, 131; physical education, 27–28,
36–37, 51–53, 57, 100, 101; reading, 102, 125,
163, 170–71, 172–73, 178–83, 219; science,
80, 160, 162–63, 189, 214–15; scrapbooking, 164–66; socio-dramatic play, 60–64,
69–73; storytelling, 12–13, 28, 58–60,
65–69; writing, 57, 125, 126, 162–67,
170–73, 178, 182–83. *See also* exercise

D'Andrade, Roy, 19–20
DAP (Developmentally Appropriate Practice). *See* NAEYC
Davidson, Dana, ix–x, 8, 20, 35, 43, 109, 112,
138, 243, 247
Delpit, Lisa, 218
democracy: in child-centered curricula, 66;
choice as exercise of, 195–96; Confucian
values and, 89; Deweyian notion of, 68,
236; individualism and, 52, 66
Deng Xiaoping, 32, 75–76, 225–26

social-mindedness (*shūdan shugi*), 240, 243. *See also* collectivism

Song Qingling, 42

special education, 171, 174, 176, 202–8. *See also* preschool types and classifications: targeted programs in the US

Spindler, George and Louise, 5, 6–7

spoiling of children, 37–39, 151, 215, 226–27

Steiner-Khamsi, Gita, 4, 84, 232, 234, 235–36

Strauss, Claudia, 19–20

student-teacher ratios and class-size: in China, 27, 33–35, 71–72, 84–85, 238; in Japan, 120, 122–23, 129–30, 138, 238, 239, 240, 241, 242–43; in the US, 160, 177, 244–45

Su Guimin, xii, 86

Su Zhixin, 235

Takayama, Keita, 131, 153, 230

Tao Xingzhi, 42

Taro Gomi, 117

tate-wari kyōiku (mixed-aged education). *See* mixed-age play

teachers: career trajectories of, in Japan, 112–13, 121, 133–34, 143–48, 153–54, 228; gender issues of, 116, 158, 200–201, 245; implicit cultural practices of, 19–20, 87, 130, 147, 239–44; preparation and training of, 25–26, 82, 85–86, 145–48, 154 239–40; *praxis* of, 19; professionalism of, 2, 24–26, 33, 82, 190–91, 230

tōban (class monitors), 103, 124

Tobin, Joseph, ix, 35, 43, 109, 112, 138, 140, 198, 201, 208, 217, 234, 243, 247

toilets: in China, 23, 25–27, 44–50, 57; pee lesson in Japan, 114–16; in US preschools, 162, 201. *See also* body, the; exercise

Tsuneyoshi, Ryoko, 153, 230

Universal PreKindergarten Movement (UPK), 12, 205, 213, 244

urban-rural differences: in China, 23, 32, 77, 81–82, 85–86; in Japan, 119, 127, 146, 151

USDOE (United States Department of Education), 199

Valdéz, Guadalupe, 217

video. *See* method issues

virtuosity, 4

Vygotsky, Lev, 84, 109, 188, 236. *See also* constructivism

wabi-sabi (melancholic longing), 140

Walsh, Daniel, 8, 116, 118, 127, 183, 196, 238

Wang, Meiyan, 81,

Wang Xiaoying, 227

Weber, Max, 112

Weikart, David, 239

White, Burton, 212

White, Merry, 95, 238

White House, the, 198, 210, 230,

Whiting, Bea, 11

Williams, Raymond, 90

Wiswell, Ella, 118–19

Wollons, Roberta, 141

world systems theory, 3–4. *See also* globalization

Wu, David, ix–x, 8, 35, 43, 109, 112, 138, 243

Xie, Yafang, 81

yangsbeng (arts of life cultivation), 52

yōchien, defined, xi–xii, 9

yomitoru. See under emotions

you'eryuan, defined, xi–xii

Yu, Shengchao, 82

yutori (room to grow) curriculum, the, 130–31

Zhang, Jie, 39, 42, 68, 81, 82, 91, 227, 234

Zhang, Qicheng, 24, 52, 244

Zheng, Deshan, 235

Zhou Nianli, 81

Zhu Jiaxiong, 39, 42, 65, 68, 81, 82, 90–91, 227, 234, 236–37

Zigler, Edward, 215